W9-CCI-990

THE WORLD ATLAS OF
COFFEE

THE WORLD ATLAS OF
COFFEE

FROM BEANS TO BREWING – COFFEES
EXPLORED, EXPLAINED AND ENJOYED

JAMES HOFFMANN

FIREFLY BOOKS

A FIREFLY BOOK

Published by Firefly Books Ltd. 2014

Third Printing, 2015

Publisher Cataloging-in-Publication Data (U.S.)

Hoffmann, James.
            World atlas of coffee : from beans to brewing, coffees explored, explained and enjoyed / James Hoffmann ; Denise Bates, editor.
[288] pages : col. photos., maps ; cm.
Includes index.
Summary: " This ultimate guide to coffee contains comprehensive details on the coffees of more than 35 countries, from Bolivia to Zambia. Also covers harvesting, processing, roasting and brewing methods, including the best ways of making great coffee at home. Detailed maps locate key growing areas and chart crucial trends worldwide." — Provided by publisher.
ISBN-13: 978-1-77085-470-3
1. Coffee. I. Bates, Denise. II. Title.
 633.73 dc 23 SB269.H6445 2014

Library and Archives Canada Cataloguing in Publication

Hoffmann, James (Coffee expert), author
      World atlas of coffee : from beans to brewing —
coffees explored, explained and enjoyed / James Hoffmann.
Includes index.
ISBN 978-1-77085-470-3 (bound)
        1. Coffee. I. Title. II. Title: Coffee.
TX415.H63 2014   641.3'373   C2014-901248-9

Published in the United States by
Firefly Books (U.S.) Inc.
P.O. Box 1338, Ellicott Station
Buffalo, New York 14205

Published in Canada by
Firefly Books Ltd.
50 Staples Avenue, Unit 1
Richmond Hill, Ontario L4B 0A7

Printed in China

Developed and produced by Mitchell Beazley, an imprint of Octopus Publishing Group Limited, Endeavour House, 189 Shaftesbury Avenue, London WC2H 8JY

Publisher Denise Bates; **Project Editor** Alex Stetter; **Copy Editor** Joanna Smith; **Executive Art Editor** Juliette Norsworthy; **Designer** Lizzie Ballantyne; **Illustrator** Grace Helmer; **Picture Research Manager** Giulia Hetherington; **Picture Researcher** Jennifer Veall; **Production Controller** Allison Gonzalves; **Cartography** Heritage Editorial; **Digital mapping** Encompass Graphics Ltd, www.encompass-graphics.co.uk

CONTENTS

INTRODUCTION

Coffee has never been better than it is today. Producers know more than ever before about growing coffee and have access to more varieties and specialist growing techniques. Coffee roasters have never before been so likely to appreciate the importance of using freshly harvested coffee, and their understanding of the roasting process continues to improve. There are now more and more cafés selling really good coffee, using the best equipment and training their staff more effectively. Many industries claim a golden age in the past, but I firmly believe coffee has yet to peak in quality, so this is an exciting time.

Consumers are now starting to engage with their coffee, prompting the coffee industry to change so that it is better able to tell the stories of where coffee is from, how it tastes and perhaps why it tastes that way. Coffee has been a staple in our lives for hundreds of years, but never before has there been this kind of interest.

The coffee industry is enormous and has grown around the world. Today 125 million people depend on coffee production for their livelihood, and it is consumed in every part of the globe. Coffee is entwined with both the economic and cultural histories of so many countries yet very few coffee drinkers have, in the past, scratched the surface to see what is underneath. 'I had no idea it was so interesting!' is a common response to those who take a look. I hope this book further encourages them.

The coffee industry can be separated into two distinct areas: commodity and speciality. In this book we will primarily be dealing with speciality coffees. These are coffees that are defined by their quality and by how good they taste. Their origin is important, as this will often determine their taste. Commodity coffee is the term used to describe coffees that are not traded on their quality, but are considered simply to be 'coffee'. Where they are grown doesn't matter much, nor when they were harvested or how they were processed. Commodity coffee has defined the way that much of the world thinks about coffee – a generic product from somewhere tropical; an efficient, if bitter, way to get caffeine into the bloodstream and to clear the fog from the brain in the morning. The idea that one might drink coffee for pleasure, to delight in its complexity of flavour, still has relatively little penetration into global culture. There are many differences between the production and international trade of speciality coffees and commodity coffees as they are quite different products.

This book is an opportunity to open the door, to reveal something of this vast industry. There hasn't yet been a book that has offered the depth of information, including maps of producing countries, that this one does and as such I'm very excited to share it with people. I hope it will encourage them to explore more of the coffees produced around the world, and to find new ways to enjoy the coffees they buy.

It is not easy to buy a bag of coffee beans that you will really, really enjoy without first having all the necessary information. There are no guarantees of flavour in coffee, one of the reasons that the speciality industry has struggled to reach a wider audience. Many factors can have a dramatic impact on how your cup of coffee will taste, from the freshness of the beans, to the way they were roasted, to when they were harvested, to the quality of water used to make the brew – and these are a fraction of the possible influencing factors. But don't be overwhelmed: this book will guide you through much of what you need to know.

During the 19th century, coffee houses in India became popular and often raucous meeting places for English gentlemen to socialize, do business, discuss the news and to gossip.

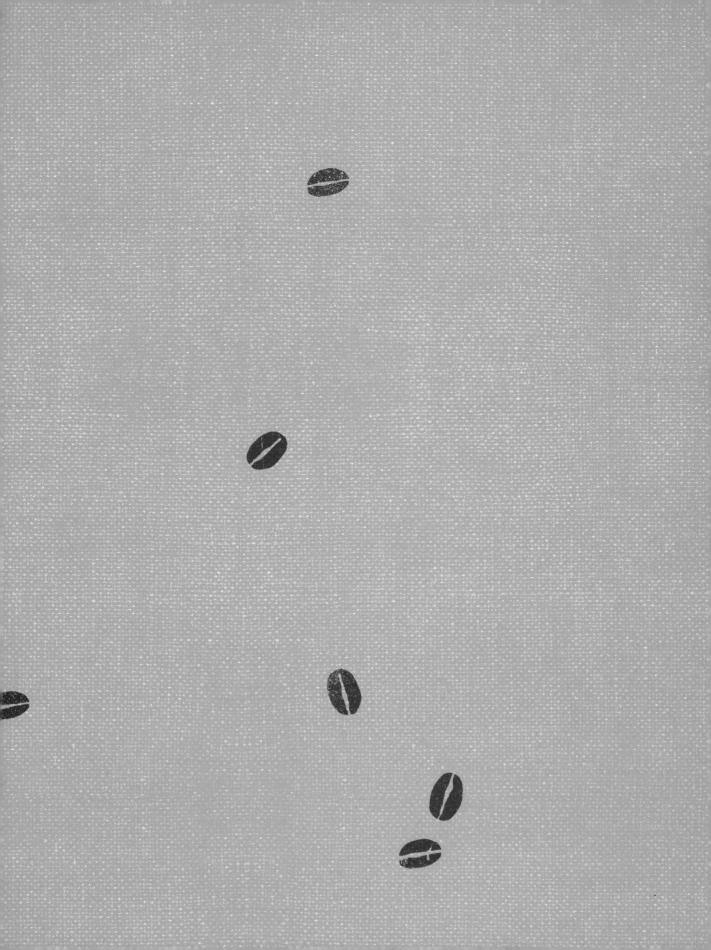

PART ONE: INTRODUCTION TO COFFEE

ARABICA AND ROBUSTA

When talking about coffee, people are usually referring to the fruit from one particular species of tree: *Coffea arabica*. Arabica makes up most of the coffee produced each year, and it is grown in dozens of countries between the Tropic of Capricorn and the Tropic of Cancer. It isn't the only species of coffee, however. In fact, over 120 different species have been identified to date but only one other is grown in any quantity and this is *Coffea canephora*, a plant we commonly refer to as Robusta.

Robusta is actually something of a brand name given to the species, chosen to highlight its attributes. It was discovered in the Belgian Congo (what is now Zaire) in the late-19th century and its commercial potential was clear. It was able to grow and fruit at lower altitudes than the existing Arabica plants, in higher temperatures, and was more resistant to disease. These attributes are what still drive much of the production of Robusta today, and because of the way it is grown it is substantially cheaper to produce. There is an inevitable downside, however: it doesn't taste very good.

Some people will make a rather specious argument that a really well-produced Robusta coffee can taste better than a poor Arabica coffee and this may be true, but it does nothing to convince us that Robusta actually tastes good. It is generally difficult to ascribe particular tastes to coffees, but I think it would be fair to say that Robusta has a woody, burnt-rubber quality in the cup. It usually has very little acidity, but will have a heavy body and mouthfeel (see page 65). There are, of course, grades of quality within Robusta, and it is possible to produce higher-quality Robustas. It has been a staple of the Italian espresso culture for many years, but currently most of the Robusta produced around the world ends up in large manufacturing plants destined to become the pariah of our industry: instant soluble coffee.

For the soluble coffee industry, price is far more important than flavour, and the global reliance on coffee as a fast-food product means that Robusta makes up around 40 per cent of the world's coffee produced each year. This percentage is somewhat variable, driven by fluctuations in price and demand. For example, an increase in the global price of coffee may result in more Robusta production, as large multinational coffee companies may need to find cheaper alternatives to Arabica. Interestingly, in the past when roasters have substituted Robusta coffees for Arabica in big commercial blends, there has been a downward trend in coffee consumption. This might be related to flavour, or it might be related to the fact that Robusta has about twice the caffeine content of Arabica. Either way, when big brands cut corners, consumers notice – or at least change their coffee-drinking habits.

THE GENETICS OF COFFEE

The coffee industry treated Robusta like an ugly sister to Arabica until a rather interesting genetic discovery was made. Once scientists began sequencing the genes, it became clear that the two species are not cousins or siblings. Instead it appears that Robusta is, in fact, a parent of Arabica. Most likely somewhere in southern Sudan, Robusta crossed with another species called *Coffea euginoides* and produced Arabica. This new species spread and really began to flourish in Ethiopia, long considered the birthplace of coffee.

Opposite: Taken from a 19th-century book of medical botany, this handcoloured copperplate engraving by James Sowerby illustrates the white flower, bean and leaf of *Coffea arabica*.

70.

Coffea arabica

Published by Phillips & Fardon, Feb.y 1.st 1807.

Currently 129 species of Coffea have been identified, mostly through the work of Kew Gardens in London, though most look very different to the plants and beans we are familiar with. Many of these species are indigenous to Madagascar, though others grow in parts of southern Asia, even as far south as Australia. None of these species has any commercial attention at the moment, but scientists are beginning to show more interest in them because of a concern facing the coffee industry: the lack of genetic diversity of the plants currently in cultivation.

The way that coffee has spread around the world means we have a global crop with a common ancestry. There is little variation in the genetic make-up of coffee plants, and this exposes global coffee production to massive risk. A disease that can attack one plant can likely attack them all, something the wine industry suffered with *Phylloxera*, an aphid that devastated huge swathes of grape vines across Europe in the 1860s and 1870s.

THE COFFEE TREE

This section deals only with the most interesting of the coffee species, *Coffea arabica*. At first glance, all Arabica trees look similar: a thin trunk with numerous branches coming off it, supporting foliage and fruit. However, if you look closer there are many differences between trees, determined by the variety of Arabica being grown. Different varieties yield different amounts of fruit, in different colours, and some carry the fruit in clusters, while others have fruit evenly spaced down the branch.

There are also big differences between the leaves of plants of different varieties, but more importantly between the cup characteristics when the seeds of these varieties are harvested and brewed. Different varieties have different qualities of flavour, and may also have different mouthfeels (see page 65). It is always important to remember that for the bulk of coffee producers, flavour is not the main reason they have selected a certain variety to grow. The yield of the tree and its resistance to disease are usually of great value to those who depend on growing coffee for their livelihood. That is not to say that all producers choose their varieties this way, but one should bear in mind the impact of these choices on the profitability and income of the producer.

FROM SEED TO TREE

Most established coffee farms have a nursery in which to raise seedlings before planting them out on the farm for production. The coffee beans are first planted in rich soil, and will soon germinate. The bean itself is then lifted out of the ground by the developing shoot, and at this stage they are often called 'soldiers'. They look strangely like a roasted coffee bean has been attached to the top of a

Left: Most of the 129 species of *Coffea* are indigenous to Madagascar but plantations around the world, such as this one in Queensland, Australia, mean that it is now a global crop.

thin green stem. Not long after this, the bean bursts open to reveal the first leaves. Coffee plants grow quickly and after 6–12 months they can be moved from the nursery into production.

Coffee growing requires the investment of not only money, but also time. A coffee farmer will usually have to wait three years for a newly planted tree to fruit properly.

PESTS AND DISEASES

The coffee tree is susceptible to a variety of pests and diseases. Two of the most common are coffee leaf rust and the coffee berry borer.

COFFEE LEAF RUST

Known as *roya* in many countries, this is a fungus (*Hemileia vastatrix*) that causes orange lesions on the leaves. It impairs photosynthesis, then causes the leaves to drop and eventually can kill the tree. It was first documented in East Africa in 1861, although it was not not studied until it began to affect plants in Sri Lanka in 1869 where it pretty much destroyed the coffee plantations over the following ten years. It spread to Brazil in 1970, perhaps brought over from Africa with a shipment of cacao seeds, and quickly spread into Central America.

It is now found in every coffee-producing country in the world and the higher temperatures brought about through climate change are exacerbating the situation. In 2013 several Central American countries declared a state of emergency due to the damage caused by rust.

COFFEE BERRY BORER

Also known widely as *broca*, this is a small beetle (*Hypothenemus hampei*) that lays its eggs inside coffee cherries. The hatching young eat the cherries, thereby reducing the quantity and quality of the crop. The beetle is native to Africa, although it is now the most harmful pest to coffee crops across the world. Research is being done into different methods of control, including chemical pesticides, traps and biological controls.

Top left: Germinated coffee shoots, known as 'soldiers', are the first stage of coffee plant growth.

Centre and left: 'Soldiers' soon burst open to reveal green leaves. Within 6 to 12 months the plants are fully established and can be moved from the nursery, ready for planting.

Above: Once or twice a year, the strongly scented blossoms of coffee appear after a long period of rainfall. Because the Arabica is self-pollinating, its flowers will always yield fruit.

Making the decision to begin growing coffee is a serious one, and this also means that if a producer abandons coffee it will be difficult to encourage him to return to the crop in the future.

BLOSSOM AND FRUIT

Most coffee trees have one main harvest per year, though the trees in some countries have a second harvest, which is usually smaller and often of a slightly lower quality. The cycle is first triggered by a prolonged period of rainfall. This causes the trees to bloom, producing lots of white blossom flowers with a strong scent that is reminiscent of jasmine.

Insects such as bees pollinate the flowers, although Arabica is able to self pollinate, meaning that unless they are knocked off the tree by adverse weather, the flowers will always yield fruit.

It takes up to nine months until the fruits are ready to harvest. Unfortunately, coffee cherries do not ripen uniformly. The coffee producer has a difficult choice between harvesting all the fruits from each tree at the same time and having a certain quantity of unripe or overripe coffee cherries in the harvest, or paying pickers to do multiple passes of the same trees so each cherry is harvested when it is perfectly ripe.

Coffee seedlings growing in Chinchiná, Colombia. Plants will be raised here for five months before being sold to plantations. After another three years of growth, the trees will begin to fruit properly.

THE COFFEE FRUIT

Coffee is a part of our everyday lives, yet how many of us outside the coffee-producing countries have ever seen, or would even recognize, a coffee cherry?

The size of the fruit varies between varieties of coffee, but on the whole they are the size of a small grape. Unlike grapes, most of the volume of the fruit is provided by the central seeds, although there is a thin layer of fruit flesh under the skin.

All cherries start out green and develop deeper colours as the fruit matures. The skin is usually a deep red when ripe, though some trees have yellow fruit, and occasionally a cross between a yellow-fruiting tree and a red-fruiting tree will yield orange fruit. While fruit colour isn't thought to influence yield, yellow-fruiting trees have often been avoided as it is harder to determine when the fruit is ripe. Red fruit starts green, goes through a yellow stage and then turns red. This makes ripeness much easier to identify when coffee is being picked by hand.

Ripeness is tied to the quantity of sugar in the fruit, which is vitally important when trying to grow delicious coffee. Generally speaking, the more sugar in the fruit

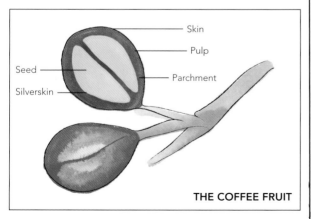

Seed
Silverskin

Skin
Pulp
Parchment

THE COFFEE FRUIT

Above: Coffee seeds are extracted from their silverskin and parchment to reveal the bean we grind and brew.

Opposite: The Hacienda de Guayabal coffee plantation, Colombia.

SWEET FRUITS

The flesh of the coffee fruit is surprisingly delicious when ripe, a pleasing honeydew melon sweetness, with a little refreshing acidity. The fruits are sometimes squeezed to make a drink, but even when ripe they are not particularly juicy, and you have to work to separate the flesh from the seeds.

the better. However, different producers harvest their cherries at different stages of ripeness. Some believe that a mixture of cherries at different stages of ripeness can add complexity to a coffee, though all the cherries should be properly ripe, and none of them overripe as they eventually develop an unpleasant flavour.

THE SEED

The seed, or coffee bean, is made up of several layers, most of which will be removed during processing, leaving behind the bean we grind and brew. The seed has a protective outer layer, called the parchment, then a thinner layer wrapped around it, called the silverskin.

Most coffee cherries contain two seeds, which face each other inside the berry, becoming flattened along one side as they develop. Occasionally, only one seed inside a berry will germinate and grow and these are known as peaberries. Instead of having a flattened surface on one side, these seeds are rounded and make up around five per cent of the crop. These peaberries are usually separated from the rest of the crop and some people believe that they have particularly desirable qualities or that they roast in a different way to the flattened beans.

COFFEE VARIETIES

The first coffee trees to be cultivated originated in Ethiopia, and this same variety, Typica, is still widely grown today. Many other varieties now exist, some natural mutations and others the result of cross-breeding. Some varieties have explicit taste characteristics of their own, while others take on their characteristics from the terroir in which they are grown, the way they are cultivated and the way they are processed after harvest.

Few coffee consumers are aware that there are different varieties of the Arabica coffee tree, mainly because much of the world's coffee always has been, and still is, traded by origin. A particular lot may come from many farms and, by the time of export, no one knows which varieties the contributing producers had grown, only which part of the world it was grown in. This is starting to change, but we still know relatively little about how much impact the variety of the tree can have on the taste of the cup of coffee.

Please note that the descriptions of the most common varieties below will not include any specific notes on taste, unless there is something definite and distinct. So many factors influence cup quality and, coupled with the lack of organized research on the way this can be influenced by variety, it would be misleading to make any bold claims in these pages.

TYPICA

This is considered the original variety from which all other varieties have mutated or been genetically selected. The Dutch were the first to spread coffee around the world for commercial production and this was the variety they took with them. The fruit is usually red and Typica is capable of producing excellent cup quality, though with a relatively small yield compared to other varieties. It is still grown extensively in many different parts of the world and, as a result, is known by several different names including criollo, sumatra and arabigo.

BOURBON

This was a natural mutation of Typica, which occurred on the island of Réunion (at the time called Bourbon). The yield is higher than that of Typica, and many in the speciality industry believe that it has a distinctive sweetness, making it prized and desirable. There are various variations in the colour of the fruit: red, yellow and occasionally orange. This variety was grown very widely in the past but in many producing countries it was replaced by higher-yielding varieties. This was at a time when the market had not yet matured sufficiently to reward a high enough price to compensate for the lower yields it produces compared to newer varieties.

VARIETIES AND VARIETALS

There is often some confusion over the terms 'variety' and 'varietal'. Varieties are genetically distinct variations of a single species, in this case *Coffea arabica*, that may show different characteristics in the tree structure, leaves or fruit. 'Cultivar' is another acceptable term to use here, as this is just a truncation of 'cultivated variety'.

'Varietal' should be used when referring to a specific instance of a variety. When referring to the production of one farm, for example, it would be correct to say that it was one hundred per cent Bourbon varietal.

MUNDO NOVO

A natural hybrid of Typica and Bourbon, this variety was named after the place in Brazil where it was discovered in the 1940s. It is grown for its relatively high yield, strength and disease resistance, and also for its success at altitudes of around 1,000–1,200m (3,300–3,900 feet) which are common in Brazil.

CATURRA

This is a mutation of Bourbon, discovered in Brazil in 1937. Its yields are relatively high, though it has the capacity for overbearing, where the tree produces more fruit than it can sustain and succumbs to die-back. However, good farm management can avoid this situation. This variety has been especially popular in Colombia and Central America, though it is still fairly common in Brazil. Cup quality is considered good, and while quality increases with altitude, yield decreases. There are both red and yellow variations and it is a low-growing variety, often referred to as dwarf or semi-dwarf, popular because they are easier to pick by hand.

CATUAI

This is a hybrid between Caturra and Mundo Novo created by the Instituto Agronomico do Campinas in Brazil in the 1950s and 1960s. It was selected as it combined the dwarf characteristics of Caturra with the yield and strength of Mundo Novo. Like Caturra, there are red and yellow varieties.

MARAGOGYPE

One of the more easily recognized varieties, Maragogype is a mutation of Typica, first discovered in Brazil. It is notable, and often considered desirable, due to the

Bourbon

Caturra

Geisha/Gesha

unusually large size of its beans. The tree also has exceptionally large leaves but a relatively low yield. This coffee is often referred to as 'Elephant' or 'Elephant Bean' coffee due to its size. The fruits usually ripen red.

SL-28

A now prized variety, SL-28 was created in Kenya by Scott Laboratories in the 1930s, selected from a drought-resistant variety from Tanzania. The fruits are red when ripe and the beans are notably larger than average. This variety is considered to be capable of producing a cup with a distinct fruit flavour, often described as blackcurrant. It is quite susceptible to coffee leaf rust, and performs better at higher altitudes.

SL-34

This variety was selected from French Mission Bourbon, a variety brought back to Africa from Bourbon (Réunion) and first appearing in Tanzania and then in Kenya. It is also capable of distinct fruit flavours but is generally considered to be inferior to SL-28 in cup quality. It is also susceptible to coffee leaf rust, and the fruits ripen red.

GEISHA OR GESHA

There is some debate over the correct name for this variety, though 'Geisha' is more commonly used. Gesha is a town in western Ethiopia and, while the variety was brought to Panama from Costa Rica, it is believed to be Ethiopian in origin. The variety is considered to produce exceptionally aromatic/floral cups, and the demand for it has driven up prices in recent years.

It has gained prominence and popularity dramatically since 2004 when one Panamanian farm, Hacienda La Esmeralda, entered a competition with a Geisha lot. The coffee proved so unusual and distinct that it attracted an incredibly high bid of $21/lb at auction. This record bid was beaten in 2006 and 2007, reaching $130/lb – nearly one hundred times more than a commodity-grade coffee. This has since encouraged many producers in Central and South America to plant this variety.

PACAS

Pacas is a natural mutation of Bourbon, discovered in El Salvador in 1949 by the Pacas family. It has red fruits and its low-growing habit makes picking easy. Its cup quality is considered similar to Bourbon, and is therefore desirable.

Pacamara

VILLA SARCHI

Named after the town in Costa Rica where it was discovered, this is another natural mutation of Bourbon that, like Pacas, exhibits dwarfism. It is currently being bred to produce very high yields, and it is capable of excellent cup quality. The fruits ripen red.

PACAMARA

This is a cross between the Pacas and Maragogype varieties, created in El Salvador in 1958. Like Maragogype, it has extremely large leaves, fruit and coffee beans. It also has distinct cup characteristics that can be positively described. It can taste like chocolate and fruit, but it also has the capacity for unpleasantly herbal, onion-like cups. The fruits ripen red.

KENT

Named after a planter who worked on a selection programme in India in the 1920s, this variety was developed for its resistance to coffee leaf rust, though it can be destroyed by new strains of the disease.

S795

Also developed in India, this is a cross between Kent and S288, an older selection resistant to coffee leaf rust. It is widely planted in India and Indonesia, although it is now considered to have lost much of its resistance.

WILD ARABICA VARIETIES

Most of the above varieties are genetically extremely similar, as they all stem from one variety, Typica. Many of the coffee trees grown in Ethiopia, however, are not selected cultivars, but are indigenous heirloom varieties that probably result from cross-breeding between different species as well as different varieties. Little work has been done so far to catalogue or explore the genetic diversity and cup quality of these wild varieties.

HARVESTING COFFEE

Careful harvesting of coffee cherries is fundamentally important to the quality of the resulting cup of coffee. Unsurprisingly, coffee beans harvested from fruit at peak ripeness generally taste the best. Many experts see the harvest as the point at which the quality of the coffee peaks, and every stage thereafter is about preserving quality rather than improving it.

The greatest challenge in harvesting high-quality coffee is perhaps the topography of the land on which the coffee is growing. Great coffee requires altitude and many coffee farms are located on steep slopes in mountainous areas. Simply navigating between the trees can be difficult, if not downright dangerous. This isn't true of every coffee farm, however.

MACHINE HARVESTING

Brazil has large areas of flat land at high altitude where coffee proliferates. The estates in these areas drive large machines down the neat rows of coffee trees to harvest the cherries. These machines essentially shake the trees until the fruit comes loose. There are numerous downsides to machine harvesting, the biggest being the issue of collecting fruit before it is necessarily ripe. The cherries on the branch of a coffee tree ripen at different rates, so each branch has both ripe and unripe cherries together. The machines do not differentiate and pick all the cherries at once. This means they must be sorted after harvest to separate the ripe from the unripe, and to discard the twigs and leaves that also get shaken off the tree. The cost of the coffee's production will be lower than any other harvesting method, but at the expense of the quality of the harvest as a whole.

Left: Arabica coffee is harvested by machine in Cabo Verde, Brazil. This method of collecting fruit is efficient, but the harvest must later be sorted to select only ripe cherries.

STRIP PICKING

A great deal of coffee is still harvested by hand as machines simply cannot operate in hilly areas. One of the faster methods of hand-picking is to strip all the cherries off a branch together with one deft movement. Like machine harvesting, this is a quick but imprecise way to pick the cherries. It doesn't require expensive equipment or flat land, but still results in a mixed bag of ripe and unripe cherries that must be sorted later.

HAND-PICKING

For high-quality coffee, hand-picking remains the most effective way of harvesting. Pickers select only the cherries that are ready for harvest, leaving the unripe fruit on the tree to be picked later. This is hard labour and producers face the challenge of incentivizing their pickers to harvest only the ripe fruit. Pickers are paid by the weight of the fruit they pick, which encourages them to pick unripe fruit to make up additional weight. Quality-conscious producers have to work carefully with their picking teams to make sure they are also paid for uniform ripeness.

Below: Cherries can be sorted in a flotation tank. Ripe cherries sink to the bottom of the tank and are pumped out for processing while unripe fruit floats to the top and is treated separately.

FALLEN FRUIT

Coffee growers collect any fruit that naturally falls off the trees – ripe or not. This is usually collected separately and will become part of the lower quality lots that even the best farms in the world inevitably produce. Leaving fallen fruit on the ground under the trees can cause problems, as they tend to attract pests such as coffee berry borer (see page 16).

THE PROBLEMS OF LABOUR

The cost of hand-picking coffee is proving a growing challenge and contributes a large part of the production costs. This is one of the primary reasons that coffees produced in developed economies – such as Kona coffees produced in Hawaii – are so expensive. In rapidly developing countries, people simply don't want to pick coffee for a living. Coffee farms in Central America often employ itinerant pickers who travel from country to country, as different regions harvest at slightly different times. Currently, many of these workers are from Nicaragua as it is the weakest economy in the region. Finding people to harvest coffee is likely to continue to be a challenge, and in fact at one stage Puerto Rico was using its prisoners to harvest coffee.

SORTING THE BEANS

After picking, the cherries are often sorted using a variety of different methods to prevent unripe or overripe coffee from joining the bulk of the lot. In parts of the world with relatively low labour costs, and little money available for investment in equipment, this is done by hand.

In more developed countries, the cherries are often sorted using a flotation tank. The cherries are poured into a large tank of water, where the ripe fruit sinks to the bottom. They are pumped from there into the main processing section. Unripe fruit floats to the top and is skimmed off to be processed separately.

Opposite, top: Where labour costs are low, cherries are picked by hand to maximize the harvest of ripe fruit.
Opposite, bottom: A worker in El Salvador sorts hand-picked fruit.

PROCESSING

How a coffee is processed after harvest can have a dramatic effect on the resulting cup, so it has become an increasingly important part of how it is described and sold. It would be a mistake to believe that coffee producers have flavour in mind when they choose their processing methods. A very small percentage do, but for most producers the goal is to ensure the processing causes the least possible incidence of 'defect' and causes no drop in the quality, and thus the monetary value, of the coffee.

After harvest, the coffee cherries are taken to a wet mill to separate the beans from the flesh and dry the beans so they are safe for storage. Coffee beans start with a moisture content of around 60 per cent, and should be dried to around 11–12 per cent to ensure they do not rot while waiting to be sold and shipped. A wet mill can be anything from a small collection of equipment on an individual farm, to a very large industrialized facility for processing enormous amounts of coffee.

The wet mill processes coffee from the cherry stage to the parchment stage, when the bean is dry but still covered with its layer of parchment or pergamino. Most believe that the coffee is pretty well protected by this outer layer, and that it does not really begin to degrade until the coffee is hulled to remove the parchment at the last possible moment before the coffee ships.

The term 'wet milling' is slightly misleading as some producers use very little, if any, water in the processing methods they use. It does, however, make the distinction between this initial processing and the later stage when the hulling and grading takes place, known as 'dry milling' (see page 37).

There is no doubt that processing can have a massive impact on the cup quality of the coffee, and there is a growing trend for skilled producers to manipulate the process in order to yield specific qualities in the cup.

However, these producers are very rare on the global production scale.

The goal of processing for most is to make the coffee as profitable as possible and this is taken into account when a producer chooses which processing method to use. Some processes require more time, investment or natural resources than others, and so it is an important decision for any coffee producer.

Opposite: Cherry harvests are processed at a wet mill, where beans are separated from the parchment and then dried, ready for storage and shipping.

DEFINING 'DEFECT'

The term 'defect' is used quite specifically in coffee. It is used to describe individual beans that have developed problems that result in bad flavours. Some defects can be spotted by taking a look at the raw coffee, while others only come to light when the coffee is tasted.

A mild defect might be a bean that has been damaged by insects, and this is easy to spot. A more serious problem is a phenolic coffee, where the coffee has a very harsh, metallic, paint-stripper flavour, mixed with notes of sulphur (it is as bad as it sounds). The cause of this defect isn't well understood yet. Bad processing can also cause defects, including giving the coffee a fermented flavour and an unpleasantly dirty, almost boozy quality. It can also add a taste reminiscent of barnyards and rotten fruit.

THE NATURAL PROCESS

Also known as the dry process, this is the oldest method of processing coffee. After harvest, the coffee cherries are spread out in a thin layer to dry in the sun. Some producers spread them out on brick patios, others use special raised drying tables, which allow a better airflow around the cherry, resulting in more even drying. The cherries must be turned regularly to avoid mould, fermentation or rotting taking place. Once the coffee is properly dry, the outer husk of skin and dried fruit are removed mechanically, and the raw coffee is then stored before export.

The natural process itself adds certain flavours to the coffee, sometimes positive but often quite unpleasant. However, if there is no access to water this may be the only process open to the producer and is therefore common in places like Ethiopia, and also parts of Brazil. Worldwide, the dry method is generally deemed only suitable for very low-quality or unripe coffee, and the bulk of coffee produced this way is processed as cheaply as possible as it usually ends up in the domestic market and has very little value. It seems counterintuitive that a producer would invest in the drying tables necessary for the little return on offer. However, there are those who choose this method to process high-quality coffee, and they often find the process to be more expensive due to the additional labour involved in the attentive, careful drying of the cherries.

This process remains quite traditional in places, and there is certainly demand for the cup qualities that a carefully processed lot can have. The process will often add fruit flavours to the coffee, regardless of variety and terroir. These are usually described as hints of blueberry, strawberry or tropical fruit, but sometimes with negative terms like barnyard, wild, ferment and manure.

High-quality naturals polarize those who work in coffee. Many see value in coffees that taste spectacularly fruity, and believe they are extremely useful for showcasing the possibilities of flavour that coffee has to offer. Others find the wild flavours unpleasant, or have concerns about buyers encouraging producers to process more of their coffee through the natural process. With such an unpredictable process, a high-quality lot could be damaged irreparably and significantly reduce the producer's income.

THE WASHED PROCESS

The goal of the washed process is to remove all of the sticky flesh from the coffee seed before it is dried. This greatly reduces the chance of something going wrong during drying, so the coffee is likely to be worth more. However, this particular process is much more expensive than the others.

After picking, the coffee cherry has its outer skin and most of the fruit flesh stripped off using a machine called a depulper. The coffee is then moved to a clean tank or trough of water where the remainder of the flesh is removed by fermentation.

The fruit flesh contains a lot of pectin and it is firmly attached to the seed but the fermentation breaks down the remaining flesh enough for it to be washed away. Different producers use different amounts of water during the fermentation stage, and there are some environmental concerns about this method, partly due to the eventual fate of the waste water, which can be toxic.

The amount of time that fermentation takes depends on several factors including the altitude and ambient temperature. The hotter it is, the faster this process will occur. If the coffee is left too long to ferment then negative flavours can creep in. There are many different methods for checking whether the process is finished.

Above: Dry processing is the oldest method with which to treat picked cherries. They are dried in the sun and turned regularly to prevent fermentation, mould and rot.

Left: A depulper machine is used to strip flesh off coffee cherries. They are then moved to a clean tank where the remaining flesh is removed through fermentation.

THE NATURAL/DRY PROCESS

Unripe cherries removed: Picked cherries are sorted by hand to get rid of green berries from the harvest.

Drying: Ripe cherries are laid out in the sunshine and manually raked through to allow even air circulation.

THE PULPED/NATURAL PROCESS

Unripe cherries removed: The harvest is placed in a flotation tank where ripe berries sink to the bottom and are removed. Unripe berries float to the top.

Pulping: Coffee is mechanically depulped to strip off all of the skin and most of the fruit flesh.

Drying: Stripped fruit is laid out on patios or drying beds where they dry quickly, increasing sweetness and body.

THE WASHED PROCESS

Unripe cherries removed: The harvest is placed in a flotation tank where ripe berries sink to the bottom and are removed. Unripe berries float to the top.

Pulping: Once picked, the outer skin and fruit flesh are stripped off coffee cherries by a mechanical depulper.

Fermentation: Coffee is placed in a clean trough of water where any remaining flesh is removed from the bean through a process of fermentation.

Resting: Coffee is traditionally rested for 30–60 days to improve the way beans age before they are shipped.

Hulling: Beans are mechanically hulled to remove the protective layer of parchment.

Grading: Once hulled, green beans are examined and graded for colour and size. Any defective beans are rejected.

Export: Beans are bagged into sturdy jute bags of 60 or 69kg (132 or 152lb), ready for shipping.

Washing: Once fermentation is complete, the coffee is washed to remove leftover debris.

Drying: Coffee is spread on patios or drying tables and turned regularly to allow slow, even drying of the beans.

Some producers rub the coffee as it will squeak if the fruit flesh has broken down, leaving the seed completely smooth. Others put a stick into the tank and if it stands up, supported by the slightly gelatinous water full of pectin, then the process is done.

After fermentation, the coffee is washed to remove the leftover debris, then it is ready to be dried. This is usually done in the sun by spreading out the coffee on brick patios or raised drying tables. In the same way as the natural method described above, the coffee must be turned regularly with large rakes to ensure slow and even drying.

Where there is a lack of sunshine or excess humidity, some producers use mechanical dryers to dry the beans down to a moisture content of around 11–12 per cent. In terms of cup quality, mechanical drying is often considered inferior to sun drying, and it seems that even drying in the sun on a patio may be too fast to achieve the best possible quality (see box on page 33). While many producers of high-quality coffee choose the wet process in an effort to reduce defect, it can also have an impact on the cup quality. Compared to other processes, wet-processed coffees tend to present a higher level of acidity, increased complexity and what is described as a cleaner cup. 'Cleanliness' is an important term used in coffee to indicate the absence of any negative flavours, such as off tastes or unusual harshness and astringency.

HYBRID PROCESSES

THE PULPED NATURAL PROCESS

Mainly used in Brazil, this process is the result of experiments run by a coffee-processing equipment manufacturer called Pinhalense. The idea was to produce coffees with high cup quality using less water than that used in the washed process.

After picking, the coffee is mechanically depulped, stripping all of the skin and much of the fruit flesh from the beans. From here it goes straight out to dry on patios or drying beds. With less flesh surrounding the beans

Below: Hulled coffee is sorted by hand to grade bean size and colour, and remove any defects. This process is time-consuming but creates coffee of a much higher quality.

there is a decreased risk of defect, yet there is still enough sugar in the surrounding fruit to see a noticeable increase in sweetness and body in the coffee. This process still requires careful drying after depulping.

THE HONEY (MIEL) PROCESS

This process is very similar to the pulped natural process but used in a number of Central American countries, including Costa Rica and El Salvador. The coffee is mechanically depulped, but the method uses even less water than the pulped natural process. The depulping machines can usually be controlled to leave a specific percentage of the flesh on the beans. The resulting coffee is then referred to as one hundred per cent honey or twenty per cent honey, for example. The name *miel* is the Spanish term for the fruit mucilage, meaning 'honey'.

With larger quantities of flesh being left on the beans, there is a higher risk of fermentation and defect when the coffee is dried.

THE SEMI-WASHED/WET-HULLED PROCESS

This process is common in Indonesia, where it is known as *giling basah*. After picking, the coffee is depulped and then briefly dried. Instead of drying the coffee to a moisture content of 11–12 per cent as the other processes do, in the semi-washed process the coffee is only dried to 30–35 per cent. It is then hulled, stripping off the parchment and exposing the green coffee beans beneath. The naked beans are then dried again until they are dry enough to be stored without the risk of rotting. This second drying gives the beans a distinctive deep swamp-green colour.

The semi-washed process is the one exception to the practice of keeping the parchment on the beans until just before shipping. It is considered by many to result in a form of defect, but the market has come to associate the flavours with coffees from Indonesia and therefore does not demand an end to the practice. Semi-washed coffees have lower acidity and more body than other coffees, and the process also creates a number of different flavours such as wood, earthy, mustiness, spice, tobacco and leather. There is strong disagreement within the industry over whether or not this is desirable. Many feel that these flavours dominate the flavour of the coffee (in the same way the natural process does), and we rarely get to find out how coffees from Indonesia really taste. However,

there are some Indonesian coffees that are processed by the wet method, and they are worth looking out for. It should be clear on the packaging as they should be described as 'washed' or 'fully washed'.

HULLING AND SHIPPING

When they leave the wet mill, the beans are still enclosed in their layer of parchment (unless they have been processed by the semi-washed method). Now the moisture content is low enough for the coffee to be stored without risk of rotting. Traditionally, coffee is intentionally stored at this stage *in reposo* (at rest) for thirty to sixty days.

The traditional practice of holding the coffee *in reposo* has not been fully researched, although anecdotal evidence suggests that if this step is missed then the coffee can taste green and unpleasant until it has aged further. There is also evidence that this stage influences how well the coffee will age once shipped, probably linked to the moisture content within the coffee.

At the end of this period the coffee is sold and then hulled to remove the parchment. Up until this point the parchment has provided a protective layer, but it also adds weight and bulk to the coffee so it is removed to make shipping less expensive.

The hulling is done mechanically in a dry mill (as opposed to a wet mill where the coffee was processed to remove the flesh and dry the beans). Dry mills also usually have equipment to grade and sort the coffee. Once hulled, the green coffee beans can be passed through a machine that examines the colour and rejects any coffee with obvious defects. The coffee can be sorted by bean size using large shaking sieves with varying hole sizes, and finally it is graded by hand.

This time-consuming process is performed at a large table with a central conveyor, or sometimes on large patios, usually by women rather than men. They pick through their allocation of coffee and remove all the defects they can, sometimes within a given time frame controlled by an automated conveyor. This is a slow process, adding significant cost to the coffee, but also massively increasing its quality. It is undeniably a difficult, monotonous job and it is right that high-quality coffees cost more, so that the people who do this difficult work can be better paid.

Workers sew up 60-kg (132-lb) jute bags near Yirgacheffe, a coffee-growing community in south-central Ethiopia. Their popular product is exported around the world.

BAGGING

The coffee is now ready for bagging, either into 60kg (132lb) or 69kg (152lb) jute bags, depending on the country of origin. In some cases the bags are lined with a protective material, such as a multilayer polyethylene, to make them resistant to moisture, or the coffee can be vacuum-packed and shipped in cardboard boxes.

Jute has long remained the material of choice because it is cheap, accessible and has little environmental impact. However, as the speciality coffee industry is increasingly concerned with the condition of coffee during shipping and in ongoing storage, new materials are being explored.

SHIPPING

Coffee is generally transported from its country of origin in shipping containers. These hold up to three hundred bags of coffee, although low-quality coffees are sometimes just tipped into a giant lining covering the walls of the container, as the waiting roaster will process the entire container on the day it arrives. The containers are emptied out like dump trucks into a receiving station at the roasting facility.

Transporting coffee in container ships has a relatively low impact on the environment (certainly compared to other aspects of the coffee industry), and it is also relatively cheap. The downside is that the coffee can be exposed to both heat and moisture that may damage its quality. Shipping is also a complicated process, with bureaucracy in many countries causing roasters huge amounts of stress as containers of coffee sit for weeks or even months in hot, humid ports waiting for their paperwork. As air freight remains both an environmentally unfriendly and financially unsustainable alternative, many in the speciality coffee industry remain frustrated by this aspect of the business.

SIZING AND GRADING

Coffee has, in many countries, been graded by size longer than it has been graded by quality. In fact the two things are still considered related, although technically they are not. Different countries will use different terminology around their grading (see box).

Grading is generally done with sieves, numbered to indicate the size of the perforations. Traditionally the even numbers (such as 14, 16 and 18) were used for Arabica, while odd numbers were used for Robusta. Once the coffee is hulled it is mechanically shaken through layers of sieves to separate out the different grades.

Peaberry (PB) is a grade based on the smallest whole beans (not the broken pieces though). Peaberries occur when a coffee berry has just one seed inside rather than two. They are considered to have a greater intensity of flavour, although this may not be universally true. It is always an interesting experience to compare the flavour of the the peaberry selection of a coffee against that of the larger beans.

While larger beans aren't necessarily better, the advantage of having a relatively small size range is that roasting the coffee is easier, and the resultant roast is likely to be more uniform. This is because coffee beans of different sizes also have different densities. During roasting, the smaller coffee beans, or the less dense ones, will roast much faster than the larger, or denser beans. This will mean that at least a portion of the coffee in a mixed batch will not have reached the ideal roast level.

COMMON SIZE GRADES

These are the most common sizing grades used in the following coffee-producing areas.

COLOMBIA

Supremo and Excelso are very common grades. Excelso is screen sizes 14–16, and is smaller than Supremo which is sizes 16–18 (or above). Colombia pioneered how it sold its coffee, and uses grades like this to emphasize its quality (see page 188).

CENTRAL AMERICA

Here the larger sizes are traditionally referred to as Superior (again, emphasizing quality through size). Peaberries are known as *caracol*.

AFRICA

The largest screen size is generally considered AA, then AB and then A. Coffee-producing countries such as Kenya have a strong focus on quality relating to size grading and AA lots tend to sell for higher prices in their internal auction system.

PEABERRIES

The result of only one seed forming inside the coffee fruit

AB GRADE

Considered good quality based on size, but of less value than AA grade

AA GRADE

The largest and most valuable beans from a particular lot of coffee

PULPED NATURAL PROCESS

A little fruit flesh is still stuck to beans, giving a slight orange colour

FULLY WASHED

These fully washed beans appear cleaner than the other two processes

NATURAL/DRY PROCESS

Typically a very orange/ brown colour compared with other green coffee due to the processing

PACAMARA/MARAGOGYPE

Unusually large in size and often considered desirable as a result

HOW COFFEE IS TRADED

It is often quoted that coffee is the second-most traded commodity in the world. It is not and, whether based on frequency or monetary value, is not even in the top five. Nonetheless, how coffee is traded has become a focus for ethical trade organizations. The relationship between the buyer and the producer is often seen as the First World exploiting the Third World. However, while there are undoubtedly those who wish to exploit the system, they are in the minority.

T he price paid for coffee is generally quoted in US dollars per pound in weight ($/lb). There is something of a global price for coffee, often referred to as the C-price. This is the price for commodity coffee (see page 7) being traded on the New York Stock Exchange. Coffee production is often discussed in bags. A bag usually weighs 60kg (132lb) if it comes from Africa, Indonesia or Brazil, or 69kg (152lb) if it comes from Central America. While bags may be the units of purchase, on the macro scale coffee is usually traded by the shipping container, which contains around three hundred bags.

Contrary to popular belief, a rather small percentage of coffee is actually traded on the New York Stock Exchange, but the C-price does provide a sort of global minimum price for coffee, the minimum a producer would be willing to accept for his coffee. Prices for particular lots of coffee often have a differential added to the C-price, a kind of premium. Certain countries have, historically, been able to get higher differentials for their coffee, including Costa Rica and Colombia, although this type of trading is still mostly focused on commodity grade, rather than speciality coffee.

The problem with basing everything on the C-price is that this price is somewhat fluid. Usually prices are determined by supply and demand, and to some extent

this is true of the C-price. As global demand increased at the end of the 2000s, the market saw an increase in price and coffee supply began to look scarce. This produced one of the highest spikes in the price of coffee, reaching above $3.00/lb in 2010. This price wasn't simply about supply and demand, however, it was also influenced by other factors, not least the influx of cash into the industry

from traders and hedge funds who saw an opportunity to make money. This produced a volatile market, the like of which had never really been seen before. From that spike, prices steadily declined again to levels that can be considered unsustainable for profit.

The C-price for coffee does not reflect the cost of production, and as such producers may end up in a

Above: Coffee bags being loaded on to ships at the port of Santos, Brazil, in 1937. Nowadays coffee is usually transported in shipping containers, which hold around three hundred bags each.

position where they lose money growing coffee. There have been a number of reactions to this problem and the most successful has been the Fair Trade movement, although there are many other sustainable coffee certification schemes, including those of the Organic Trade Association and the Rainforest Alliance (see box below).

FAIR TRADE

There remains some confusion about exactly how Fair Trade works, although it has undoubtedly become a successful tool to help those who wish to purchase coffee with a clear conscience. Many people presume that the promises of Fair Trade are far wider reaching than they actually are, and that any coffee could (in theory) be certified as Fair Trade. This is not the case. And to make matters worse, it is easy for detractors to allege that the farmer is not getting the premium because of the complex nature of financial transactions within the coffee industry.

Fair Trade guarantees to pay a base price that it considers sustainable, or a \$0.05/lb premium above the C-price if the market rises above Fair Trade's base price. Fair Trade's model is designed only to work with cooperatives of coffee growers, and as such cannot certify single estates that produce coffee. Critics complain about a lack of traceability or true guarantee that the money definitely goes to the producers, and isn't diverted through corruption. Others criticize the model for providing no incentive to farmers to increase the quality of their coffee. This has encouraged many in the speciality coffee industry to change the way they source their coffee, moving away from the commodity model, where coffee is bought at a price determined by global supply and demand and little regard is given to its provenance or quality.

THE SPECIALITY COFFEE INDUSTRY

A number of different terms are used to describe the various ways in which speciality roasters are buying their coffee and their relationships with the growers.

CERTIFICATION/ VERIFICATION	ORGANIC	FAIR TRADE CERTIFIED	RAINFOREST ALLIANCE
MISSION	Create a verified sustainable agriculture system that produces food in harmony with nature, supports biodiversity and enhances soil health.	Support a better life for farming families in the developing world through fair prices, direct trade, community development and environmental stewardship.	Integrate biodiversity conservation, community development, workers' rights and productive agricultural pratices to ensure comprehensive sustainable farm management.
HISTORY AND DEVELOPMENT	Can be traced back to 19th-century practices formulated in England, India and the United States. First certification in 1967. Developed into internationally recognized system with production throughout the world.	Began as Max Havelaar in the Netherlands in the 1970s. Now the German-based Fairtrade Labelling Organizations International (FLO) collaborates with more than twenty national branches throughout the world.	Begun in 1992 by Rainforest Alliance and a coalition of Latin American NGOs, the Sustainable Agriculture Network (SAN). First coffee farm certification in 1996. The Rainforest Alliance CertifiedTM programme requires that farms meet comprehensive standards covering all aspects of production, the protection of the environment, and the rights and welfare of farm families and their local communities.

Relationship Coffee is used to describe an ongoing relationship between producer and roaster. There is usually a dialogue and collaboration to work towards better quality coffee and more sustainable pricing. For this arrangement to have the desired positive impact, the roaster would have to be buying the coffee in sufficient quantity.

Direct Trade is a term that has arisen more recently, where roasters wish to communicate that they bought the coffee directly from the producer, rather than from an importer, an exporter or another third party. The problem with this message is that it plays down the important role of importers and exporters in the coffee industry, potentially unfairly portraying them as middlemen simply taking a slice of the producer's earnings. To be viable, this model also requires the roaster to buy enough coffee to make an impact.

Fairly Traded may refer to a purchase where there has been good transparency and traceability and high prices have been paid. There is no certification to validate the ethics of the purchase, but those involved are generally trying to do good with their trading. Third parties may be involved but are considered to have added value. This isn't a very commonly used term, except in situations where a customer asks if a particular coffee is Fair Trade.

The idea behind all these buying models is for roasters to try to buy more traceably, to remove unnecessary middlemen from the supply chain, and to pay prices that incentivize the production of higher quality coffee. However, these terms and ideas are not without their critics. Without third-party certification it can be difficult to ascertain whether or not a roaster is actually buying the way they say they are. Some roasters may buy coffees that have been kept traceable by importers and brokers, and claim this as a direct trade or relationship coffee.

There are no guarantees of a long-term relationship for the producers either, with some coffee buyers simply chasing the best lots of coffee they can each year. However, at least they are paying handsomely for it. This type of approach makes long-term investment in quality difficult and it should also be noted that some middlemen provide a valuable service, especially to those who are working on a smaller scale. The logistics of moving coffee around the world require a level of specialization and skill that many small roasters simply do not have.

ADVICE TO CONSUMERS

When buying coffee, it is difficult for consumers to ascertain how ethically sourced a particular coffee really is. Some speciality roasters have now developed buying programmes certified by third parties, but most have not. It is fairly safe to presume that if the coffee has been kept traceable, has the producer's name(s) on it, or at least the name of the farm, cooperative or factory, then a better price has been paid. The level of transparency you should expect will vary country by country, and is covered in more detail in each of the sections on the producing countries. If you find a roaster whose coffee you like, you should be able to ask them for more information about how they source it. Most are more than happy to share this information, and are often extremely proud of the work they do.

AUCTION COFFEES

There has been a slow and steady increase in coffees that are sold through internet auction. The typical format for this involves holding a competition in a producing country wherein farmers can submit small lots of their best coffee. These are graded and ranked by juries of coffee tasters, usually a local jury for the first round and then an international cadre of coffee buyers will fly in for the final round of tasting. The very best coffees are sold at auction and generally achieve very high prices, especially the winning lot. Most auctions display the price paid for the coffee online, allowing full traceability behind the whole process.

This idea has also been embraced by a small number of coffee-producing estates that have managed to build up a brand based on the quality of their coffee. Once they have sufficient interest from international buyers they can make an auction work. This idea was pioneered by a farm in Panama called Hacienda La Esmeralda, a farm that had previously set records for the huge prices paid for its competition-winning coffees (see pages 238–40).

Harvested coffee cherries are sorted and cleaned to remove unripe and overripe fruit as well as leaves, soil and twigs. This is often done by hand, using a sieve to winnow away unwanted materials.

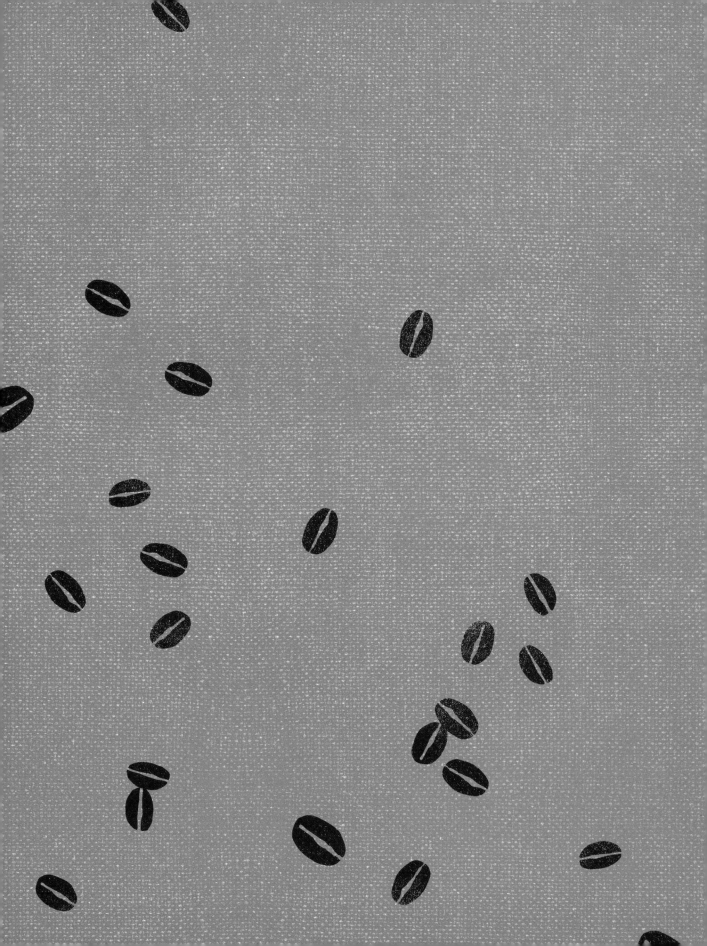

PART TWO: FROM BEAN TO CUP

COFFEE ROASTING

Roasting is one of the most fascinating aspects of the coffee industry. It takes the green coffee seed, which has almost no flavour beyond a quite unpleasant vegetal taste, and transforms it into an incredibly aromatic, astonishingly complex coffee bean. The smell of freshly roasted coffee is evocative, intoxicating and all-round delicious. This section deals with roasting on a commercial scale; see pages 116–17 for information about home roasting.

A huge amount of research has gone into the commercial roasting of relatively low-quality coffee, most of it to do with the efficiency of the process and the methods used in producing instant soluble coffee. As these coffees aren't particularly interesting or flavoursome, very little work has been done on the development of sweetness, or the retention of flavours unique to a particular coffee's terroir or variety.

Speciality roasters around the world are, by and large, self trained and many have learned their trade through careful trial and error. Each roasting company has its own style and aesthetic, or roast philosophy. They may well understand how to replicate what they enjoy drinking, but they do not sufficiently understand the whole process to manipulate it to produce a variety of different roast styles. That is not to say that delicious and well-roasted coffee is rare: it can be found in almost every country in the world. If anything, it suggests that the future is bright for quality coffee roasting, as there is still a lot to explore and develop that can only lead to better roasting techniques.

FAST OR SLOW, LIGHT OR DARK?

To simplify matters, it can be said that the roast of a coffee is a product of the final colour of the coffee bean (light or dark), and the time it took to get to that colour (fast or slow). To simply describe a coffee as a light roast is not enough, as the roast could have been relatively fast or it could have been quite slow. The flavour will be quite different between the fast and the slow, even though the bean may look the same.

A whole host of different chemical reactions occur during roasting, and several of them reduce the weight of the coffee, not least of course the evaporation of moisture. Slow roasting (14–20 minutes) will result in a greater loss of weight (about 16–18 per cent) than faster roasting, which can be achieved in as little as ninety seconds. Slow roasting will also achieve a better, if more expensive cup of coffee.

The roasting process can be controlled to determine three key aspects of how the coffee will taste: acidity, sweetness and bitterness. It is generally agreed that the longer a coffee is roasted, the less acidity it will have in the end. Conversely, bitterness will slowly increase the longer a coffee is roasted, and will definitely increase the darker a coffee is roasted.

Sweetness is presented as a bell curve, peaking in between the highs of acidity and bitterness. A good roaster can manipulate where a coffee may be sweetest in relation to its roast degree, producing either a very sweet, yet also quite acidic coffee, or a very sweet, but more muted cup by using a different roast profile. However, adjusting a roast profile can never improve a poor-quality coffee.

Opposite: The roasting process affects acidity, sweetness and bitterness of bean flavours. Roasters seek to balance these three aspects through carefully controlled use of heat and timing.

THE STAGES OF ROASTING

There are a number of key stages during roasting, and the speed at which a particular coffee passes through each of these stages is described as its roast profile. Many coffee roasters track their roast profiles carefully so they can replicate them to within very tight boundaries of temperature and time.

STAGE 1:
DRYING

Raw coffee contains 7–11 per cent water by weight, spread evenly through the dense structure of the bean. Coffee won't turn brown in the presence of water, and in fact this is true of browning reactions when cooking anything.

After the coffee is loaded into a roaster, it takes some time for the beans to absorb sufficient heat to start evaporating the water and the drying process therefore requires a large amount of heat and energy. The coffee barely changes in look or smell for these first few minutes of roasting.

STAGE 2:
YELLOWING

Once the water has been driven out of the beans, the first browning reactions can begin. At this stage, the coffee beans are still very dense and have an aroma of basmati rice, and a little breadiness. Soon the beans start to expand and their thin papery skins, the chaff, flakes off. The chaff is separated from the roasting beans by the air flowing through the roaster and is collected and safely removed to prevent the risk of fire.

These first two roasting stages are very important: if the coffee is not properly dried then it will not roast evenly during the next stages and while the outside of each bean is well roasted the inside will essentially be undercooked. This coffee will taste unpleasant, with a combination of bitterness from the outside, and a sour and grassy flavour coming from the underdeveloped inside. Slowing the roasting process after this will not fix the problem as different parts of the coffee will always be progressing at different rates.

STAGE 3:
FIRST CRACK

Once the browning reactions begin to gather speed there is a build-up of gases (mostly carbon dioxide) and water vapour inside the bean. Once the pressure gets too great, the bean will break open, making a popping noise and nearly doubling in volume. From this point onwards, the familiar coffee flavours develop, and the roaster can choose to end the roast at any point.

A roaster will see a decrease in the rate at which the coffee is increasing in temperature at this point, despite the fact that they may be adding a similar amount of heat. Failure to add enough heat can stall the roast and 'bake' the coffee, resulting in poor cup quality.

STAGE 4:
ROAST DEVELOPMENT

After the first crack stage, the beans will be much smoother on the surface but not entirely so. This stage of the roast determines the end colour of the beans and the roast degree. Here the roaster can determine the balance of acidity and bitterness in the end product as the acids in the beans are rapidly degrading while the level of bitterness is increasing as the roast continues.

STAGE 5:
SECOND CRACK

At this point the beans begin to crack again, but with a quieter and snappier sound. Once you reach second crack, the oils will be driven to the surface of the coffee bean. Much of the acidity will have been lost and a new kind of flavour is developing, often referred to as the generic 'roast' flavour. This flavour doesn't depend on the kind of coffee used as it is a result of essentially charring or burning the coffee, rather than working with its intrinsic flavours.

Progressing a roast past the second crack usually results in the beans catching fire which is extremely dangerous, especially with large commercial roasting machines.

There are terms used in coffee roasting such as 'French Roast' or 'Italian Roast'. Both of these terms are used to indicate very dark roasts, typically high in body and bitterness but with many of the characteristics of the raw coffees lost. While many enjoy coffees roasted in this manner, these kinds of roasts are not suitable for exploring the flavours and characteristics of high-quality coffees from different origins.

RAW COFFEE

10–12 per cent moisture, no coffee flavour yet and very dense/hard.

BEFORE FIRST CRACK

The coffee is now browning, but there is a lot of harsh acidity/plant-like flavour in the coffee

DRYING

Water is starting to evaporate, but no flavours/ aromas developed yet.

FIRST CRACK

The coffee starts to pop and expand in size due to the build up of gas pressure inside the bean.

YELLOWING

The coffee has started to roast. This stage often smells like basmati rice.

DEVELOPMENT

The coffee now smells/ tastes like coffee but may need more time to develop sweetness and ideal flavours.

YELLOWING

Most of the water has now been removed and the coffee is starting to brown slightly.

DEVELOPMENT

The beans are increasingly smooth on the outside, and the aromas are increasingly pleasant.

YELLOWING

Despite starting to look brown, the aromas at this stage are more like bread than coffee.

DEVELOPED

Where a coffee achieves ideal development is often down to the opinion of a roaster. For many, this is sufficiently developed, while others may wish to roast the coffee for longer.

Bouchardon inv.

Caffé Caffé

Gravé à l'eau-forte par C. S. et terminé au burin par Et. Fessard.

ETUDES
Prises dans le bas Peuple
ou
les Cris de Paris
Cinquieme suite
1746.
Avec Priv. du Roy
Envir. chez Fessard, rue de la Harpe vis à vis la rue serpente

SUGARS IN COFFEE

Many people talk about sweetness when describing a coffee and it is important to understand what happens to the naturally occurring sugars during roasting.

Green coffee can contain reasonable quantities of simple sugars. Not all sugars are necessarily sweet to the taste, though simple sugars usually are. Sugars are quite reactive at roasting temperatures and, once the water has evaporated out of the bean, the sugars can begin to react to the heat in different ways. Some go through caramelization reactions, creating the caramel notes found in certain coffees. It should be noted, however, that the sugars that react this way become less sweet, and will eventually start to add bitterness. Other sugars react with the proteins in the coffee in what are known as Maillard reactions. This is an umbrella term covering the browning reactions seen in roasting a piece of meat in the oven, for example, but also when roasting cocoa or coffee.

By the time coffee has finished the first crack stage, there are few or no simple sugars left. They will all have been involved in various reactions resulting in a huge number of aromatic compounds.

ACIDS IN COFFEE

Green coffee contains many different types of acids, some of which are pleasant to taste and some that are not. Of particular importance to the roaster are the chlorogenic acids (CGAs). One of the key goals of roasting is to try to react these unpleasant acids away without creating negative flavours, or driving off the desirable aromatic components of the coffee. Some other acids are stable throughout the roasting process, such as quinic acid, which can add a pleasing, clean finish to a coffee.

AROMATIC COMPOUNDS IN COFFEE

Most of the aromatics in a good cup of coffee are created during roasting through one of three groups of processes: Maillard reactions, caramelization and Strecker degradation, another type of chemical reaction involving amino acids. These are all brought about by the heat

Opposite: Coffee vendors have plied their aromatic trade for centuries, as depicted in this 18th-century engraving of a Parisian street hawker by Anne Claude Comte de Caylus.

during roasting and can result in the creation of over eight hundred different volatile aromatic compounds that flavour the cup of coffee. Although more aromatic compounds have been recorded in coffee than in wine, an individual coffee will only have a selection of these different volatiles. That said, the smell of freshly roasted coffee is so complex that all attempts to manufacture a realistic, synthetic version of this smell have failed.

ROAST PROFILE

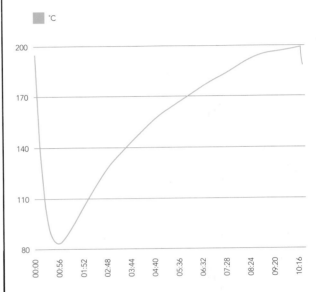

Above: Roasters track the temperature of the coffee beans during roasting: by changing how quickly a roast progresses at different times, the roaster can alter the flavour of the final coffee.

QUENCHING

After roasting, the coffee must be cooled quickly to prevent over roasting or the development of negative (or 'baked') flavours. In small-batch roasting this is often achieved using a cooling tray, which rapidly draws air through the coffee to cool it down. With large batches of coffee, air alone is not effective enough: a mist of water is sprayed on to the coffee, and as it evaporates and turns to steam, it draws heat out of the beans. Done correctly, this has no negative effect on cup quality, but the coffee will age a little quicker. Unfortunately, however, many companies add more water than necessary to increase the weight of the beans and add monetary value to the batch. This is both unethical and bad for cup quality.

Coffee tends to be roasted close to where it will be consumed, as green coffee is more stable than roasted beans – coffee is at its best when used within a month of roasting. Roasting methods vary, but the two most commonly used types of machines are drum roasters and hot-air or fluid-bed roasters.

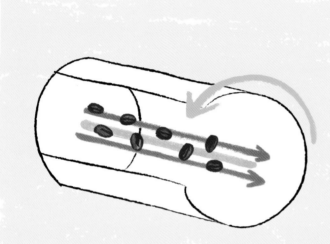

DRUM ROASTERS

Invented around the beginning of the 20th century, drum roasters are popular with craft roasters, as they are able to roast at slower speeds. A metal drum rotates above a flame, moving the coffee beans constantly during the process to aid even roasting.

The roaster can control the gas flame, and therefore the heat being applied to the drum, and can also control the flow of air through the drum, which dictates how quickly the heat is transferred to the coffee.

Drum roasters come in a range of different sizes, the largest being able to roast up to around 500kg (1,100lb) per batch.

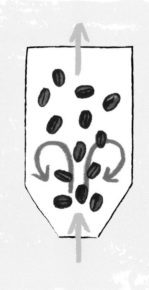

FLUID-BED ROASTERS

Invented by Michael Sivetz in the 1970s, fluid-bed roasters tumble and heat the beans by pumping jets of hot air through the machine. Roast times are significantly shorter than in a drum roaster so the beans tend to swell a little more as a result. The higher volume of air conducts heat more quickly into the coffee, which means that this roasting process is faster than drum roasting.

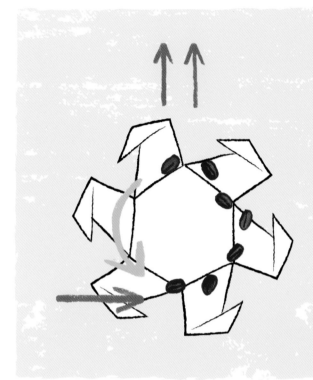

TANGENTIAL ROASTERS

Built by a company called Probat, tangential roasters are similar to large drum roasters but they have internal shovels to mix the coffee evenly during heating, which allows a bigger batch to be roasted effectively. The capacity isn't much larger than a very large drum roaster, but this type is able to achieve faster roasting speeds.

CENTRIFUGAL ROASTERS

Centrifugal roasters allow very large quantities of coffee to be roasted incredibly quickly. The coffee is placed inside a large inverted cone, which spins to draw the coffee beans up the walls as they are heated. The beans are then flung back down into the middle of the cone to repeat their journey. Roast times can be as low ninety seconds using machines like this.

Roasting at very high speeds minimizes weight loss and increases the amount of coffee that can be extracted from the beans, which is important when making instant soluble coffee. Roasting at these speeds is not designed to produce the best possible cup.

Cafés serving Italian-style coffee were a novelty in 1950s London. With coffee enjoying a resurgence of popularity in recent years, interest in coffee shops and how to make the perfect brew has increased again.

BUYING AND STORING COFFEE

There is no foolproof way to ensure you get great coffee every time you buy a bag. However, there are a few points to remember, starting from when you are choosing where to shop to how you store the coffee you have bought, which will increase your chances of ending up with a very good cup of coffee.

Most people buy their coffee in a supermarket but there are many reasons to avoid this practice, not least because of the freshness of the coffee on offer (see page 62). However, perhaps the best reason to avoid buying coffee from a supermarket is because of the sheer pleasure to be found in buying from a specialist shop. Small shops offer the opportunity to build a relationship with someone passionate and knowledgeable about coffee. It helps when choosing if you can get some advice and even try a coffee before you buy. Dealing with someone directly means you have a better chance of buying a coffee you'll really enjoy, especially if you let them know what you enjoyed previously.

STRENGTH GUIDES

You'll often see a strength guide on the side of a bag of coffee, especially those on offer in supermarkets. These have nothing to do with strength, which is really about how much coffee you use to brew a cup, but more to do with the level of bitterness you can expect to find in that particular coffee. This is usually determined by the roast level of the coffee – light-roasted coffees usually have lower strength ratings and dark-roasted coffees have higher strength ratings. I would avoid coffees that come with a strength rating because, more often than not (and

there are exceptions), the quality and flavour of the coffee have not been the primary concern of the producer.

TRACEABILITY

There are thousands of different coffee roasters, and hundreds of thousands of different roasts of coffee from different farms. Not all of them can be good, and variations in price and the way they are marketed can make buying fairly confusing. This book aims to explain where coffee comes from, and how and why its origin can affect its flavour. The best advice I can give is to buy as traceable a coffee as possible.

In many cases it is possible to find a coffee from one specific farm, or one cooperative. However, that level of traceability is not possible in every coffee-producing country in the world. Each of the sections on the different countries offers an idea of how traceable the coffees from

Above: The best cup of coffee begins with a well-chosen bean. Choose freshly roasted beans from a specialist shop; they should also be able to advise you about the coffee's origins.

that country can be. Much of Latin America is able to produce coffees that are traceable down to a particular small farm because most of the coffee there is grown on small private estates. In other countries small-scale land ownership by farmers is unusual, or the trade regulations of a country may interfere with the export process, making traceability difficult.

To keep a batch of coffee traceable throughout the entire supply chain adds cost, and this investment can only be returned if the coffee is sold for a higher price. This means it is only worth keeping high-quality coffees traceable, as doing so with low-quality lots would make them uncompetitive in the market place. In an industry plagued by ethical concerns, and dogged by an image of exploitation of the Third World, knowing exactly where

a coffee comes from is a powerful piece of information. As communication technology, especially around social media, spreads and develops we're likely to see increased interaction between those who produce the coffee and those who ultimately drink it.

GOLDEN RULES FOR FRESH COFFEE

Everyone agrees fresh-roasted coffee is better, so I would make the following recommendations:

1. Buy coffee that has a clear roast date on the packaging
2. Try to buy within two weeks of roasting
3. Buy only enough coffee for a couple of weeks at a time
4. Buy whole beans and grind them yourself at home.

STORING COFFEE AT HOME

Once the staling process begins, there is very little that can be done to prevent it continuing. As long as you are buying fresh coffee and using it relatively quickly the impact on your cup of coffee should be minor. However, there are ways to store coffee at home that will keep it in the best possible condition.

1   **Keep the coffee airtight** If the bag can be resealed, then make sure it is kept that way. If the bag can't be completely resealed, transfer the coffee to an airtight container, such as a plastic tub with a lid or one designed specifically for storing coffee.

2   **Keep the coffee in a dark place** Light rapidly accelerates the staling of coffee, especially sunlight. If you keep your coffee in a clear container, place it inside a cardboard box.

3   **Don't put it in the refrigerator** This is a common practice, but it does not extend the life of coffee, and you can get cross-contamination of aromas if you have something particularly fragrant in the refrigerator with the coffee.

4   **Keep it dry** If you can't keep it in an airtight container, then at least avoid placing it in a humid environment.

If you need to store some coffee for a long period of time, place it in the freezer to slow down the staling process. It is important to package it in an airtight container first. When you want to use the coffee, defrost it thoroughly first, but be sure only to defrost the amount you are planning to use straight away.

Above: Beans last longest when stored in an airtight container, in a dry, dark place.

FRESHNESS

Over the years most people have been conditioned not to think of coffee as being a fresh food product. For some it is because instant coffee is what they associate with coffee and that doesn't really ever go stale. Coffee sold in supermarkets will often have a best-before date that is 12–24 months after the date it was roasted. This is because coffee is considered shelf stable and it is safe to consume two years after roasting, but it will taste pretty terrible at that point. It is more convenient for all involved if coffee isn't treated like a fresh product, with the exception of the ultimate consumer.

The speciality coffee industry has failed to make a real impact because there is no strong agreement on how quickly coffee goes stale, and at what point it will have passed its best-before date.

I would recommend buying coffee that clearly shows the date of roasting on the label. Many coffee roasters now suggest that the coffee is used within a month of roasting and I would follow this advice. The coffee is at its most vibrant during the first few weeks and after this an increasingly unpleasant stale flavour begins to develop. Many specialist shops stock bags of coffee that were recently roasted and delivered, and buying online direct from the roaster usually ensures your coffee is delivered to your home within a few days of roasting.

STALING

When coffee goes stale there are two main changes occurring. The first is the slow but steady loss of aromatic compounds, the compounds that give coffee its flavour and smell. As they are volatile, these compounds slowly leach from the coffee so the older it is the less interesting it will taste.

The second change is the staling caused by oxygen and moisture. This type of staling creates new flavours, often relatively unpleasant ones. As the coffee changes it will develop a generic stale taste, and much of its original character will be lost. Stale coffees tend to taste flat, woody and vaguely of cardboard.

The darker the coffee has been roasted, the faster it will go stale. This is because the roasting process makes the coffee bean more porous, so it is easier for oxygen and moisture to penetrate and start the staling reactions.

'RESTING' COFFEE

To further confuse the issue, it is quite common to see recommendations for 'resting' the coffee before brewing it. When coffee is roasted the chemical reactions that cause the beans to brown produce large volumes of carbon dioxide. Much of this gas remains trapped inside the beans, and slowly leaches out over time. The coffee will de-gas quite quickly in the first few days and then the rate will slow. Adding hot water to coffee will cause the gas to be released very quickly, which is why bubbles often form when coffee is brewing.

Espresso is a brew method that takes place under a great deal of pressure, and when there is a lot of carbon dioxide in the coffee it makes the brewing process a little more difficult and can prevent the proper extraction of flavour. Many coffee shops let the coffee de-gas for anything from five to twenty days before using it to help increase their consistency when brewing. At home, I would recommend leaving a gap of at least three to four days between roasting and brewing, but waiting too long may mean that the coffee starts to stale by the time you finish the bag. With filter-coffee brewing this is not as important, but I do think coffees taste better after two to three days than immediately after roasting.

PACKAGING COFFEE

Coffee roasters have three main choices for packaging their coffee. They will make this decision based not only on the preservation of the coffee, but also on the environmental impact, cost and look of the packaging.

UNSEALED CRAFT PACKAGING

The coffee is packed into craft paper bags with a simple greaseproof lining to prevent any leaching of the oil from the coffee. While the bag may be rolled up at the point of sale, the coffee is still exposed to oxygen and will stale quickly. Many roasters who use this kind of packaging will emphasize the importance of freshness, often suggesting the coffee be used within seven to ten days. When they retail the coffee they must be sure that the coffee on the shelves is as fresh as possible, though this can lead to some undesirable wastage. This type of packaging is sometimes recyclable and is generally considered to have the least impact on the environment.

VALVE

Above: Triple-ply foil bags are common in the speciality coffee industry as they reduce staling until the package is opened.

SEALED FOIL PACKAGING

Triple-ply foil bags are sealed as soon as the coffee is packed to prevent fresh air getting in, but have a valve to allow the carbon dioxide to escape. Coffee will become stale slower inside these bags, but once opened the rate of staling will increase. While packaging like this is not currently recyclable, many speciality roasters choose this option as they consider it the best compromise in terms of cost, environmental impact and freshness.

GAS-FLUSHED SEALED FOIL PACKAGING

This is the same as the above, with one crucial difference. During the sealing process, a machine flushes the bag of coffee with an inert gas such as nitrogen to expel any oxygen from the bag, as oxygen causes staling to occur. This type of packaging slows staling down the most, although once the bag is opened the staling process will start. Despite this being the most effective way to package coffee, it is not widely used due to the additional costs of equipment, process time and the inert gas.

TASTING AND DESCRIBING COFFEE

Coffee drinking is often tied into a ritual, a specific part of our day. We might drink a cup of coffee first thing in the morning, or as a break from work. Our attention is usually focused on the people we are with, or the newspaper we are reading over breakfast. Few people really concentrate on tasting the coffee they drink, but when they start to notice it, their appreciation increases rapidly.

The process of tasting happens in two different places – in our mouths and in our noses – and it is helpful to think about these two parts of the process separately when learning to taste and talk about a coffee. The first part of the process occurs on the tongue and it is here we detect the relatively basic tastes of acidity, sweetness, bitterness, saltiness and savouriness. When reading the description of a coffee, we might be attracted to the flavours described, such as chocolate, berries or caramel. These flavours are actually detected the same way as smells – not in the mouth but by the olfactory bulb in the nasal cavity.

For most people these two separate experiences are completely intertwined, and the separation of taste and smell is extremely difficult. It gets easier if you try to focus on one particular aspect at a time, rather than taking the extremely complex taste experience in one go.

PROFESSIONAL TASTERS

Before it reaches the final consumer, a coffee will have been tasted a number of different times along its journey through the coffee industry. Each time it is tasted, the

As coffee tasters work, they may record their notes on a score sheet. Different processes require different score sheets but in almost all cases the following attributes are being assessed:

SWEETNESS

How much sweetness does the coffee have? This is a very desirable trait in coffee, and generally the more the better.

ACIDITY

How acidic is the coffee? And how pleasant is this acidity? If there is a lot of unpleasant acidity, the coffee will be described as sour. A lot of pleasing acidity, however, gives the coffee a crispness or juiciness.

For many people learning to taste coffee, acidity is a difficult attribute. They may not have expected coffee to have much acidity, and certainly would not have considered this a positive quality in the past. Apples can be a great example of positive acidity: in an apple, high acidity can be wonderful, adding a refreshing quality.

Coffee professionals tend to develop a preference for high acidity in coffees, much as beer aficionados may develop a preference for very hoppy beers. This can result in a difference of opinion between industry and consumer. In the case of coffee, unusual flavours – such as fruit notes – are determined by the density of the coffee. Generally, denser coffees are also more acidic, so coffee tasters learn to associate high acidity with quality and interesting flavours.

MOUTHFEEL

Does the coffee have a light, delicate, tea-like mouthfeel or is it more of a rich, creamy, heavy cup? Again, more is not necessarily better. Low-quality coffees often have quite a heavy mouthfeel, coupled with low acidity, but are not always pleasant to drink.

BALANCE

This is one of the most difficult aspects of a coffee to assess. A myriad of tastes and flavours occur in a mouthful of great coffee but are they harmonious? Is it like a well-mixed piece of music, or is one element too loud? Does one aspect dominate the cup?

FLAVOUR

This is not just about describing the different flavours and aromas of a particular coffee, but also about how pleasant the taster finds them. Many new tasters find this the most frustrating aspect of coffee tasting. Each of the coffees they taste are clearly different but the language to describe them remains elusive.

Opposite: Each brew is affected by the origin, preparation and roasting of the beans, which create its distinct flavour.

Below: A professional coffee taster will often use a score sheet similar to the one below to rate the different properties of a brew.

NAME _____ # _____ DATE _____ Rnd 1 2 3 Sn 1 2 3 4 5 TLB# _____ Country _____

	ROAST	AROMA	DEFECTS	CLEAN CUP	SWEET	ACIDITY	MOUTH FEEL	FLAVOUR	AFTER TASTE	BALANCE	OVERALL	TOTAL
	COLOUR	DRY CRUST BREAK	# x i x 4 = score	0 4 6 7 8	0 4 6 7 8	0 4 6 7 8	0 4 6 7 8	0 4 6 7 8	0 4 6 7 8	0 4 6 7 8	0 4 6 7 8	(+36)
		3 3 3 / 2 2 2 / 1 1 1										
1.												
2.												
3.												
4.												
5.												

taster might be looking for something different. It might first be tasted early on to detect any presence of defect. It will then be tasted by a roaster as part of the purchasing process, or by a jury ranking coffees for an auction of the best lots from a particular place. It will be tasted by the roaster again as part of their quality control to make sure that the roasting process was done correctly and then it may be tasted by a café owner selecting the range they wish to stock. Finally it will be tasted, and hopefully enjoyed, by the consumer.

The coffee industry uses a pretty standardized practice called 'cupping' to taste coffee. The idea behind cupping is to avoid any impact on flavour from the brewing process, and to treat all coffees being tasted as equally as possible. For that reason, a very simple brewing process is used, as bad brewing can easily change the flavour of a coffee quite dramatically.

A fixed amount of coffee is weighed for each bowl. It is ground at a fixed setting and then a specific amount of water, just off the boil, is added. For example, for 12g (1/2 oz) of coffee, 200ml (7fl oz) of water might be added. The coffee is then left to steep for four minutes.

To end the brewing process, the layer of floating grounds on top of the bowl, called the crust, is stirred. This causes almost all of the coffee grounds to fall to the bottom of the bowl where they stop extracting. Any grounds and foam that remain on top can be skimmed off and the coffee is ready to taste.

Once the coffee has cooled to a safe temperature, tasting begins. Coffee tasters use a spoon to get a small sample of coffee, which they then aggressively slurp from the spoon. This slurping process aerates the coffee and sprays it across the palate. It is not essential to tasting, but does make tasting a little easier.

HOW TO TASTE AT HOME

How does a professional coffee taster develop his skills so rapidly compared to a consumer? It isn't through the use of cupping bowls or spoons. Neither is it by using score sheets, or having large amounts of data about where the coffee is from. It is through regular opportunities for comparative tasting. Where the coffee taster gains a quiet advantage is by going through a process of focused, conscious tasting and this can also be done at home very easily.

1   Buy two very different coffees. It is a good idea to ask your local coffee roaster or speciality shop for guidance. The comparative part of tasting is vitally important. If you taste just one coffee at a time you have nothing to compare it with and you are basing your judgements on your memories of previous coffees, which are likely to be patchy, flawed and inaccurate.

2   Buy two small French presses (see page 76), as small as you can get, and brew two small cups of coffee. You could obviously do this with bigger presses and bigger cups, but this way will prevent excess waste or drinking too much coffee.

3   Let the coffee cool a little bit. It is much easier to discern flavours in warm rather than hot coffee.

4   Start to taste them alternately. Take a couple of sips of one coffee before moving on to the other. Start to think about how the coffees taste compared to each other. Without a point of reference, this is incredibly difficult.

5   Focus on textures first, thinking about the mouthfeel of the two coffees. Does one feel heavier than the other? Is one sweeter than the other? Does one have a cleaner acidity than the other? Don't read the labels as you taste, instead note down a handful of words about each coffee.

6   Don't worry about flavours. Flavours are the most intimidating part of tasting, as well as the most frustrating. Roasters use flavours not only to describe particular notes – such as 'nutty' or 'floral' – but also to convey a wide range of sensations. For example, describing a coffee as having 'ripe apple' notes also communicates expectations of sweetness and acidity. If you do identify individual flavours, note them down. If not, then don't worry. Any words or phrases that describe what you are tasting qualify as being useful, whether they are random words or specific flavours.

7   When you have finished, compare what you have written down with the roaster's description on the packet. Can you see now what they are trying to communicate about the coffee? Often on reading the label your frustration will be relieved as you find the word to describe what you tasted. It can suddenly seem so obvious and this is part of building a coffee-specific vocabulary of flavours. Describing coffee gets easier and easier, though this is something even industry veterans still work on.

Below: The skill of coffee tasting can be developed by comparative tasting. Choose and prepare a brew of two different coffees, then try comparing texture, taste, acidity and flavour.

GRINDING COFFEE

The smell of freshly ground coffee is evocative, heady and indescribable, and in some ways it is worth paying for a coffee grinder for this alone. However, grinding your own beans at home will also make an enormous difference to the quality of your cup, compared to buying pre-ground coffee.

Above: A burr grinder will cut beans into evenly sized pieces and can be adjusted to various grind sizes. They are an ideal investment for making a great brew at home.

The aim of grinding the beans before brewing is to expose enough surface area to extract enough of the flavour locked inside the beans to make a good cup of coffee. If you brewed whole beans you'd end up with a very weak brew. The finer the beans are ground, the more surface area is exposed and, in theory, the faster the coffee could be brewed because the water has more access to it. This is important when considering how finely the coffee should be ground for different brew methods. The fact that the size of the coffee grounds changes the speed at which the coffee brews also makes it very important that we try to make all the pieces the same size when grinding coffee. Finally, grinding the coffee exposes more of it to the air, which means that the coffee will go stale more quickly (see page 62), so it should ideally only be ground just before brewing.

There are two main types of coffee grinder available for domestic use:

THE (WHIRLY) BLADE GRINDER

These are common and inexpensive electric grinders. They have a metal blade attached to a motor that spins and smashes the coffee to pieces. The biggest problem is that this smashing action produces some very fine powder and some very large pieces. When you brew coffee ground like this, the tiny pieces will quickly add a bitter flavour to the brew, while the larger pieces will add an unpleasant sourness. This uneven brew won't be very enjoyable.

THE BURR GRINDER

These are increasingly common and available as electric or manual models. They have two cutting discs, called burrs, facing each other and you can adjust the distance between them to change the size of the grounds of coffee produced. Because the coffee grounds can't escape until they have been cut down to the size of the gap between the burrs, the resulting grounds are very even in size. Burr grinders produce even pieces and an adjustable range of sizes, so they are ideal for brewing great coffee.

Burr grinders are more expensive than blade grinders but the manual models are relatively cheap and easy to use. If you enjoy coffee, it will prove to be an invaluable investment, especially if you are brewing espresso. However, because grind size is so important in espresso – variations of a few hundredths of a millimetre make a difference – it is important to buy a burr grinder designed for espresso with a good motor capable of grinding the beans very fine. Some grinders can grind for both filter coffee and for espresso, but most do one or the other.

Above: Beans ground in a blade grinder (left) will be of a more uneven size and make a less palatable brew than those milled from a burr grinder (right), which has two cutting discs.

Different manufacturers use different materials to make the burrs, such as steel or ceramic. Over time, the cutting teeth on the burrs will start to dull and the machine will start to mill the coffee rather than cutt it cleanly, producing a lot of tiny pieces that make the coffee taste flat and bitter. Follow the manufacturer's recommendations for how often to change the burrs – new burrs are a small but worthwhile investment in your coffee-brewing setup.

Many people who enjoy coffee as a hobby like to upgrade their equipment from time to time. I would strongly recommend investing in a better grinder first. More expensive grinders have better motors and cutting burrs capable of a more uniform grind size. You will make a better cup of coffee with a high-end grinder and a small domestic espresso machine than with a cheap grinder and a top-of-the-range commercial espresso machine.

DENSITY AND GRIND SIZE

Unfortunately not all coffees should be treated equally in the grinder. Darker roasts are more brittle in the grinder, and you may need to grind a little coarser.

Equally, if the coffee is from a much higher altitude than you typically drink – for example, you've been drinking a delicious coffee from Brazil, and then you switch to a coffee from Kenya – you may need to go finer in your grinder for the high-grown coffee. Once you've made the switch a few times you can make a well-educated guess when changing coffees, and prevent too many bad brews.

GRIND SIZE

Communicating grind size is not easy. Terms such as 'coarse', 'medium' and 'fine' aren't particularly helpful because they are relative. There is no common setting among grinder manufacturers either, so setting one grinder to a numerical setting of '5', for example, won't replicate the grind of another grinder set to the same setting, even if it is the same model.

Below are some different expressions of grind size, with the accompanying photographs shown at life size. This should get you close to the perfect grind, then with a little experimentation each morning you should be able to achieve a much more delicious cup of coffee very quickly.

VERY FINE FINE MEDIUM COARSE

WATER FOR BREWING

The role of water in the brewing process is absolutely crucial in creating a great cup of coffee. At first glance the recommendations below may seem somewhat excessive, but making a little effort with water will bring enormous returns.

If you live in a hard water area, try buying a small bottle of mineral water to brew a single cup of coffee. Brew another coffee straight afterwards in exactly the same way, but using regular tap water instead. From seasoned coffee taster to interested novice, every person who has ever compared the two has been shocked at the difference in quality.

THE ROLE OF WATER

Water is a vital ingredient in a cup of coffee as it makes up around 90 per cent by volume of an espresso and 98.5 per cent of a cup of filter coffee. If the water doesn't taste good to start with, neither will the cup of coffee in the end. And if you can taste the chlorine, the resulting cup of coffee will be terrible. In many cases a simple water filter jug that contains active carbon (such as a Brita filter) will do a good job of removing negative tastes, but it still might not produce the perfect water for brewing coffee.

Water acts as a solvent, doing the work of extracting the flavours in the coffee during the brewing process. This is where the quality of the water plays a major role, as the hardness and the mineral content can significantly affect how the coffee brews.

HARDNESS

Water hardness is a measure of how much limescale (calcium carbonate) is dissolved in the water, and this is determined by the bedrock in the local area. Heating water causes the limescale to come out of solution and accumulate over time as a chalky white build up. Those who live in hard water areas struggle with the frustrations of limescale affecting kettles, showers and washing machines.

The hardness strongly influences the way the hot water and the ground coffee interact. Harder water seems to change the rate at which the solubles in the coffee go into solution, essentially changing the way the coffee brews at a chemical level. To make broad statement: it seems a small amount of hardness is desirable, but anything from moderate to hard water does a poor job of brewing coffee, producing a cup lacking in nuance, sweetness and complexity. Also, on a practical level, having soft water is very important if you are using any sort of coffee machine that heats water, such as an espresso machine or a filter coffee machine. Limescale build up will quickly cause a machine to malfunction, and many manufacturers will consider the use of hard water to have invalidated the warranty.

Right: The quality of water used to brew your coffee will affect the taste. Mineral water is ideal but filtered water will also improve the flavour of your coffee.

MINERAL CONTENT

Aside from a good flavour and just a little hardness, there isn't too much else we really want in the water, but a relatively low mineral content is desirable. Manufacturers of mineral water are required to list the mineral content on the bottle and it is usually described as the total dissolved solids (TDS), or the 'dry residue at 180°C' (365°F).

THE PERFECT WATER

The Specialty Coffee Association of America (SCAA) publishes suggested guidelines for the perfect water for coffee brewing. The table below offers a summary.

If you want to understand the quality of your domestic water supply, contact your water supply company or look on its website, as most are obliged to publish data on the content of their water. If you can't find this information, buy a water-testing kit from a pet shop (sold to test the water in fish tanks), which will give you accurate readings of the key elements.

CHOOSING A WATER

All this information may seem a little overwhelming and complex, but it can be summarized as follows:

- If you live in a soft to moderately hard water area, use tap water but filter it first to improve the taste.
- If you live in a moderate to very hard water area, bottled water is the current best option for brewing coffee. Choose a bottled water close to the above targets; own-brand supermarket waters tend to be lower in mineral content compared to the big brand waters. While it is not ideal to recommend bottled water, if you really wish to get the best out of your coffee, you must use a water suitable for brewing.

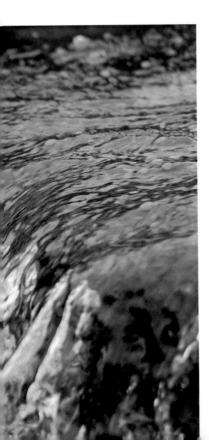

GUIDELINES FOR THE PERFECT WATER FOR COFFEE BREWING

	Target	Acceptable Range
Odour	Clean, fresh, odour-free	
Colour	Clear	
Total Chlorine	0mg/l	0mg/l
Total Dissolved Solids (TDS) at 180°C (365°F)	150mg/l	75–250mg/l
Calcium Hardness	4 grains or 68mg/l	1–5 grains or 17–85mg/l
Total Alkalinity	40mg/l	At or near 40mg/l
pH	7.0	6.5–7.5
Sodium	10mg/l	At or near 10mg/l

BREWING BASICS

A key moment in the journey from crop to cup is the process of brewing. All the hard work up until this point, all the potential and deliciousness locked within the coffee can be lost by bad brewing. It is upsetting how easy it is to brew coffee badly, but understanding the basic principles can lead to better results and make the process more enjoyable.

A coffee bean is composed mostly of cellulose – it is very similar to wood. Cellulose cannot be dissolved in water, so this is what makes up most of the spent grounds we throw away after brewing a cup of coffee. Broadly speaking, everything else that makes up the coffee bean can be dissolved in water and can end up in the cup, but not everything that we can get from the coffee tastes good.

From the 1960s, there has been ongoing research into measuring how much of the coffee we actually want to extract for the resulting cup to taste good. If you don't take enough from the grounds then the cup of coffee will not only be weak, but it will often also be sour and astringent. This is called 'underextraction'. And if we take too much from the grounds then the cup of coffee will taste bitter, harsh and ashy. This is what we call 'overextraction'.

It is possible to calculate whether we have extracted as much as we want from the coffee. In the past this was done relatively simply: the grounds were weighed before brewing, then after brewing the spent grounds were placed in a low oven until they were completely dry. When they were weighed again, the difference in weight would indicate how much of the coffee had been extracted during the brewing process. Now a combination of a specialized refractometer and smartphone software allows us quickly to calculate how much has been extracted from the grounds. Generally it is agreed that a good cup of coffee contains 18–22 per

cent by weight of the ground coffee used to brew it. The exact numbers are not important to most people at home, but understanding how to adjust different parameters to improve the cup is useful.

STRENGTH

This is an important term when talking about a cup of coffee, but one that has been quite widely misused. The term is commonly used on bags of coffee sold in the supermarket, and in this instance is completely inappropriate. What they are trying to communicate here is how dark the roast of the coffee is, and how intense the bitterness will be.

The word 'strength' when used to describe a cup of coffee should be used in the same way it is used to describe alcoholic drinks. A beer that is four per cent strength means that four per cent of what you drink is alcohol. In the same way, a strong cup of coffee has a higher percentage of dissolved ground coffee in the hot water than a weak cup. When it comes to strength there is no right and wrong – there is only individual preference.

There are two ways to control strength and the first and most common way is by varying the ratio of coffee to water. The more coffee used to brew a cup, the stronger the resulting cup is likely to be. When talking about brewing, we tend to describe the strength by the number of grams of coffee per litre of water, for example 60g/l. To brew a cup of coffee of this strength, you would first decide how much coffee you want to brew, for example 500ml. You would then use the ratio to calculate how much coffee to use, in this case 30g.

The preferred ratio of coffee to water varies around the world from around 40g/l up to nearly 100g/l in Brazil and Scandinavia. Generally people find a ratio that they enjoy and they stick to it for most brew methods. I would recommend 60g/l as a starting point. Changing the coffee to water ratio is how most people at home change the strength of their brews, but it is not always the best way.

The other way to change strength is to change the level of extraction. As we steep coffee in a French press, the water is slowly taking more and more out of the coffee, and the resulting drink is getting stronger and stronger as it brews. The challenge is to control the level of extraction so we take enough from the grounds that it tastes good, before we start to extract bitter and unpleasant flavours. Many people don't think about changing the level of extraction when they get a poor cup of coffee, but an error of extraction can certainly lead to a disappointing cup.

EXACT MEASUREMENTS

Small changes in how coffee is brewed can have a big impact on taste. One of the biggest variables is how much water you use (see page 73), and being consistent

is one of the most important aspects of brewing. It is a good idea to put the coffee brewer on scales so you can measure exactly how much boiling water you are adding. Remember than 1ml of water weighs 1g. This will give you a lot more control and massively improve the quality and consistency of your brews. A set of simple digital scales is not expensive and many people already have one in the kitchen. While it seems a little obsessive at first, once you start brewing this way you will never want to go back.

MILK, CREAM AND SUGAR

Most people who are interested in coffee are aware that milk and sugar are considered somewhat taboo by those who work in the industry. Many people consider this a form of snobbery, and it is something of contentious point between coffee professionals and consumers.

What is often forgotten by the professionals is that most coffee served in the world requires something to help make it more drinkable. Cheap commodity coffee that has been poorly roasted or badly brewed is often incredibly bitter and lacks any sweetness. Milk, and even more so cream, does a great job of blocking some of the bitterness, and sugar makes it more palatable. Many people get accustomed to the taste of milk and sugar in coffee and will then add them to an interesting cup of coffee brewed with care. This may cause frustration for the barista, professional roaster or a person simply passionate about great coffee.

Excellent coffee should have its own sweetness, and instead of suppressing bitterness the milk will obscure the flavour characteristics of the coffee, hiding the work of the producer and the expression of terroir that the coffee has. I would always recommend trying a coffee before adding anything to it. If it is not sufficiently palatable as black coffee, then add milk or sugar so you enjoy the cup. However, exploring this wonderful world is extremely difficult drinking anything other than black coffee, and the investment of time and effort learning to appreciate it this way will be extremely rewarding.

Left: A set of digital scales is a worthwhile investment for anyone interested in making consistently good coffee.

Opposite: Excellent coffee should have its own sweetness, and while everyone has personal preferences when it comes to milk and sugar, it is good to try a coffee first before adding anything to it.

THE FRENCH PRESS

The French press, also known as a cafetière or coffee plunger, is probably the most underrated method of brewing coffee. It is cheap, easy, repeatable and just about everyone has one at home.

Considering its name, it seems somewhat surprising to discover that the most familiar version of the French press was invented and patented by an Italian called Attilio Calimani in 1929. However, a very similar brewer had been patented first by two Frenchmen, Mayer and Delforge, in 1852.

A French press is an infusion brewer. With most methods of brewing coffee, the water passes through the grounds. Here the water and coffee steep together, which helps produce a more uniform extraction.

The other relatively unique aspect of the French press is the way that it filters the grounds from the brewing liquid: by using a metal mesh. Due to the relatively large holes in the mesh, more of the non-soluble material from the coffee gets into the cup. The advantage of this is you get a little of the coffee oil and some tiny suspended pieces of coffee in the cup, which gives the resulting brew a bigger, richer body and texture. The disadvantage is what puts many people off of the French press: the sludge. At the bottom of the cup you will often find a reasonable quantity of silty particles of coffee that (if accidentally drunk) are quite unpleasant and sandy in the mouth.

The brewing method opposite is designed to achieve a great brew with the minimum amount of sludge. It requires a little more work and patience but you will be rewarded with a great cup of coffee that will give you easy access to all the unique flavours and characteristics of the bean.

Right: Brewing coffee in a French press results in a drink of uniform extraction. The metal mesh allows for small particles to flavour the water, creating a rich body and texture.

THE FRENCH PRESS METHOD

Ratio: 75g/l. I recommend a slightly higher ratio of coffee to water when using an infusion brewer if you want to produce a brew with a strength similar to a pour-over brewer.

Grind: Medium/caster (superfine) sugar (see page 69). Many people grind their beans very coarsely when brewing in a French press, but I don't think this is necessary unless your grinder produces a lot of very fine pieces and your brews quickly turn bitter.

1 Grind the coffee just before you start brewing. Be sure to weigh the coffee first.

2 Boil a kettle of fresh water with a low mineral content, suitable for brewing coffee.

3 Put the ground coffee in the French press and place it on the scales. **A**

4 Pour in the correct amount of water, weighing as you pour so you achieve the ratio of 75g/l. Pour relatively quickly and try to get all the coffee wet.

5 Leave the coffee to steep for four minutes. During this time the coffee will float to the top to form a crust-like layer.

6 After four minutes, take a large spoon and stir the crust at the top. This will cause most of the coffee to fall to the bottom of the brewer.

7 A little foam and some floating grounds will remain on the top. Use the spoon to scoop them off and discard them. **B**

8 Wait another five minutes. The coffee would be too hot to drink anyway, and leaving it in the brewer allows more and more of the coffee and fine particles to sink to the bottom.

9 Place the mesh plunger in the top of the beaker, but do not plunge. Plunging will create turbulence, which will stir up all the silty coffee at the bottom of the pot.

10 Pour the coffee slowly through the mesh into the cup(s). Until you get close to the bottom, this liquid will have very little silt in it. If you can resist pouring out the very last bit you will end up with a delicious, flavourful brew of coffee that has very little silt. **C**

11 Allow the coffee to cool in the cup(s) a little, then enjoy.

Many people recommend pouring out the entire pot once the brew is done, to prevent the grounds continuing to steep and start to overextract. If you follow the instructions above the coffee should not continue to brew or add negative flavours, so this is not necessary.

POUR-OVER OR FILTER BREWERS

The term 'pour-over' is used to describe a host of different brew methods. The common factor is that they brew by percolation, which means that the water passes through a bed of coffee, extracting flavour along the way. Usually there is some sort of material to filter the grounds from the resulting drink, and it can be anything from paper to cloth to a fine metal mesh.

Simple cup-top filter brewers have probably been used since coffee brewing began but the innovations on the theme came relatively late. Only cloth filters were used originally; the invention of the paper filter is credited to a German entrepreneur, Melitta Bentz, in 1908. Now controlled by her grandchildren, the Melitta Group still sells filter papers, coffee and coffee machines today.

The invention of paper filters encouraged the move away from the electric percolator, a terrible brewer which recirculated hot water through the grounds, brewing an incredibly bitter cup. The final death knell for the percolator was the next major innovation in drip-coffee brewing, the electric coffee machine. The invention can be credited to another German company called Wigomat. Variations on the electric filter coffee machine are still incredibly popular today, though not all produce good coffee (see page 83).

Currently there is a huge range of different brewers, brands and devices on offer, all designed to do this same job and each with its own advantages and idiosyncrasies. The good news is that the principle behind this method of brewing is universal and the technique is easily adapted to different brewers.

THE KEY PRINCIPLES

When coffee is brewed in this way, three variables affect the resulting cup of coffee. Unfortunately they are not independent of each other, which is why precise measurement of both coffee and water is so useful, especially if you are bleary eyed when making the coffee first thing in the morning.

1   **The grind of the coffee** The finer the coffee, the more is extracted from it as the water passes through. This is because there is a greater surface area, and because

POURING KETTLES

When using the pour-over method to brew coffee, the rate at which you add the water plays a role in the brewing process. Pouring slowly and carefully from a standard kettle is difficult to do, and recently there has been a dramatic rise in coffee bars using special pouring kettles. These are usually placed on the stove, but electric models are available. The common factor is that the spout is very narrow, so they issue a very slow, steady stream of water on to the coffee.

Despite their popularity in the industry, I am not convinced they are a truly worthwhile expense for the home-brewer. They do make pouring easier, but if not used properly the water can drop in temperature and prevent the coffee from brewing as well as it could. They could be viewed as an overly serious and complicated gadget when, in truth, we just want to pour water slowly over the coffee. However, if we pour at different rates on different days (something that is very easy to do) then we will get different-tasting coffee from one day to the next, which is not a good scenario.

water flows through finer coffee more slowly so there will be more contact time.

2 **The contact time** This is not only how quickly the water flows through the coffee, but also how long it takes us to add the water. We can extend the brew time by adding the water very slowly to increase the extraction of the coffee.

3 **The amount of coffee** The more coffee there is, the longer the water will take to flow through and the longer the contact time.

To replicate a good brew, these three variables must be kept as consistent as possible. If, for example, someone reduces the amount of coffee by accident, they might assume that the reason the coffee did not brew long enough was due to the grind being wrong. If we do not pay attention, it is very easy to get confused and start to make bad coffee.

THE BLOOM

This is the common practice of adding just a little water to the coffee at the start of the brew, usually just enough to get all the coffee wet. When you add the hot water, the grounds start to release the trapped carbon dioxide and the bed of coffee will swell like dough rising. It is typical to wait 30 seconds before starting to add the rest of the brew water.

Despite the widespread nature of this practice, there isn't a lot of science to justify it. It might be that releasing some of the carbon dioxide helps make the coffee easier to extract, and some studies seem to support this. I think it also adds a pleasant moment in the morning coffee ritual as watching the grounds bloom is a little mesmerizing.

Above: When making pour-over coffee, it is common practice to add just a little water at first to allow the coffee to swell, or bloom.

Above: The strength of a pour-over coffee will depend on the grind size, and the timing and speed of the water flowing through it.

Ratio: 60g/l. I recommend this as a starting point for all pour-over and filter coffee methods, but be sure to experiment to find your preference.

Grind: Medium/caster (superfine) sugar (see page 69) would be suitable for brewing around 30g coffee to 500g water. You will need to grind the beans more finely if you are brewing a single cup, and more coarsely if you want to brew more.

1 Grind the coffee just before you start brewing. Be sure to weigh the coffee first.

2 Boil a kettle of fresh water with a low mineral content, suitable for brewing coffee.

3 While the kettle is boiling, place the paper filter in the brewer and rinse briefly under the hot tap. This helps to reduce any taste the paper might impart to the coffee, and also warms up the brewing device.

4 Add the coffee to the brewer, place the brewer on top of the cup or jug and place on the scales. **A**

5 Wait ten seconds once the kettle has boiled if you are pouring straight from it. If you are using a pouring kettle, decant the water into it immediately.

6 Using the scales as a guide, pour a little water on to the coffee, about twice as much as the coffee by weight. Don't worry about being too accurate, just make sure you add enough to wet the coffee. I like to pick the cone up and give it a little swirl to make sure all the coffee is wet. Careful stirring with a spoon is another option. Wait thirty seconds before starting to pour the rest of the water. **B**

7 Slowly pour the remainder of the water on to the coffee, weighing as you go to get an accurate amount and taking into account the water already added. Try to pour directly on the coffee and not the walls of the brewer as water may pass through without really extracting the coffee. **C**

8 Once you have added all the necessary water, and the surface of the liquid is 2–3cm (about 1in) below the top of the cone, give it a gentle swirl again. This stops any coffee from sticking to the walls of the brewer. **D**

9 Let it drip through until the bed of coffee looks dry. It should be relatively flat at the base of the brewer. **E**

10 Discard the coffee and paper, remove the brewer from the cup and enjoy the coffee.

If you are not happy with the resulting cup of coffee, think about what you want to change. I would recommend using the grind to change the flavour of the coffee. If the coffee is bitter it may be overextracted so you should try your next brew using a slightly coarser grind. If it is weak, sour or astringent, try grinding the coffee more finely for the next brew. Very quickly you will know the best grind settings for the coffees you enjoy.

DIFFERENT KINDS OF FILTERS

There are three main types of filters used in pour-over and filter coffee brewing. Each affects the resulting brew by straining out different things from the liquid that you eventually drink.

PAPER

Paper filters are the most common type of filter and they produce the cleanest cup of coffee. They strain out all of the suspended material, as well as any oils that may have ended up in the brew. The resulting cup is a fairly clear liquid, often with a reddish hue. I always recommend bleached white papers over unbleached brown papers as the brown papers tend to impart an unpleasant papery taste to the coffee.

CLOTH

Cloth has been used to filter coffee for a very long time. When used well, it can produce a distinctive and very enjoyable cup. Like paper, it strains out all of the suspended pieces of coffee but it does allow some of the oil to come through. The resulting cup is very clean, but has a richer, fuller mouthfeel.

The problem with cloth is that it is designed to be reused and must be cleaned and well maintained. After use, you should immediately rinse it as well as possible, then dry it quickly. If you leave the cloth to dry slowly it will develop unpleasant flavours, similar to the smell of forgotten laundry that has been left in the machine too long. If you use the cloth regularly, keep it stored wet in a glass of water in the refrigerator. If you plan to store a cloth for a long time, put it wet into a ziplock bag and freeze it. Repeatedly freezing and thawing it will cause the cloth to degrade a little quicker, however, and should be avoided.

The cloth shouldn't be allowed to get too stained and should be cleaned regularly. For cleaning I would recommend a product called Cafiza, made by Urnex. While this is marketed as an espresso machine cleaner, the original formula was developed to clean the cloths used in very large filter brewers back before paper was popular. The product is organic and non-toxic. Dissolve a small amount in hot water and soak the cloth in it, then rinse thoroughly and store.

METAL

CLOTH

PAPER

THE ELECTRIC FILTER MACHINE METHOD

The big advantage of an electric coffee machine is that it takes away a lot of the guesswork and adds plenty of repeatability. We still have to be consistent in how much coffee we use, and how much cold water we put into the machine, but aside from that we can trust the brewer to do its job.

However, most domestic filter coffee machines, especially cheaper models, tend to make pretty bad coffee. This is primarily because they are not capable of heating the water up to the correct temperature. If you're shopping for a new one, make sure it has been certified to reach suitable temperatures. Organizations such as the Specialty Coffee Association of America or the European Coffee Brewing Centre certify machines, and I would strongly recommend a machine endorsed by one of these organizations.

I would also avoid buying a machine with any sort of hot plate. Keeping a jug of coffee on a hot plate very quickly 'cooks' the coffee, producing some very unpleasant flavours. Choose instead a machine that stores the coffee in a thermal carafe.

THE ELECTRIC FILTER MACHINE METHOD

Ratio: 60g/l. I recommend this as a starting point for all pour-over and filter coffee methods, but be sure to experiment to find your preference.

Grind: Medium/caster (superfine) sugar (see page 69), if making between 500ml and 1l of coffee. You will need to grind the beans more coarsely if brewing large volumes, as many machines can brew up to 1l at a time, if not more.

1 Grind the coffee just before you start brewing. Be sure to weigh the coffee first.

2 Put the filter paper in the brewing basket, then rinse under the hot tap.

3 Place the brewing basket in the machine, then add fresh water with a low mineral content, suitable for brewing coffee.

4 Switch on the machine and, as the brew starts, keep an eye on it. If some of the coffee is not getting wet, give it a quick stir with a spoon.

5 Allow the brew to finish.

6 Discard the paper and grounds.

7 Enjoy your coffee.

As in the pour-over cone method, adjusting the grind size is a better way to change the flavour than adjusting the amount of coffee you add if you are not happy with your cup.

THE AEROPRESS

The Aeropress is a rather unusual coffee maker, but I have yet to meet someone who has one and does not love using it. It was invented in 2005 by Alan Adler, the inventor of the Aerobie throwing ring – hence its name. It is a cheap, durable and very portable brewer that many coffee professionals take with them when they travel around the world. In addition, this brewer is very easy to clean.

The interesting thing about the Aeropress is that it combines two different brewing methods. Initially the water and coffee steep together, as they would in a French press. However, to complete the brew, a piston is used to push the water through the grounds and then through a paper filter – a little like an espresso machine and a little like a filter coffee maker.

Compared with other brewers, the number of different recipes and techniques that can be used with the Aeropress is enormous. There is even a competition each year for the best technique, which started in Norway but has ended up growing into an international event dubbed the World Aeropress Championships. Each year the organizers publish the top three methods from the competition on their website (www.worldaeropresschampionship.com), which should give you an idea of how variable these machines can be.

I would, however, argue against any claims that the Aeropress can be used to produce espresso or anything like it. It can make small, strong cups of coffee, but a person pushing down on a plunger simply cannot replicate the very high pressures used in an espresso machine.

The two main methods of using this machine are described below.

RATIO AND GRIND SIZE

The relationship between grind size, brew time and the amount of brewing water used is incredibly important here. For best results with an Aeropress, you should first decide what kind of cup of coffee you want to drink.

- If you want to brew something short and strong, I suggest starting with a ratio of 100g/l. If you want to brew a little quicker then you will need to grind relatively fine. You can use a coarser grind if you choose but you will need to extend the brewing time for best results.
- If you want something closer to a regular cup of coffee, I suggest using a ratio of 75g/l. This is the same ratio as that recommended for the French press because this is also an immersion brewing method. Again, you can match your brewing time to your grind size.

Left: The Aeropress is like a hand-operated cross between an espresso machine and a filter coffee maker: a piston is used to push water through the grounds and then through a paper filter.

This method will allow you to brew slightly more coffee than the inverted method described below. It is also a little less fussy and there is less potential for mess in the kitchen.

Because there are so many factors at play, it is tempting to adjust many variables at once. Pushing harder will speed up the brew but also extract a little more from the coffee; extending the steep time will also extract more, as will grinding the coffee on a finer setting. However, it is always best to change only one thing at a time, and more experimentation simply means more opportunities to drink interesting cups of coffee.

1 Grind the coffee just before you start brewing. Be sure to weigh the coffee first.

2 Put a filter paper into the filter holder and lock into the body of the brewer.

3 Run some hot water through to heat the brewer and rinse the paper.

4 Place a mug on your digital scales, put the main part of the brewer on top and add the coffee. **A**

5 Boil a kettle of fresh water with a low mineral content, suitable for brewing coffee.

6 Wait ten to twenty seconds after the kettle has boiled, turn on the scales, then add the desired amount of water to the Aeropress (for example, for 15g of coffee I would add 200ml (200g) of water). Start a timer. **B**

7 Give the coffee a quick stir, then put the piston part of the Aeropress in place. Make sure it seals, but don't push down yet. This creates a vacuum above the coffee, preventing the liquid from dripping out of the bottom of the brewer before you want it to. **C**

8 After a period of brewing (I recommend starting with one minute)

take the mug and brewer off the scales and slowly push down the plunger until all the liquid has been expelled. **D**

9 Pull the piston back a few centimetres (1in) to stop the brewer from dripping when you discard the spent coffee. Remove the filter holder and, holding the brewer over the waste bin, push the plunger out to get rid of the grounds. Tap out any loose bits, then immediately rinse and clean the bottom of the piston and brewer. **E**

10 Enjoy your coffee.

I want to describe this method because it is so popular, but also because it often goes wrong. I recommend starting with – and generally using – the traditional method, but if you want to experiment, here is how to do it safely.

The idea behind this alternative method is to invert the device, so that it is impossible for the brewing liquid to escape during the infusion phase. You will have to flip over the brewer full of coffee on to a cup before you push the plunger and this is where things go wrong – vessels full of hot liquid should be flipped with caution. It is also important to note that this method will not allow you to brew as much coffee: the maximum brew is probably 200ml of water.

1 Grind the coffee just before you start brewing. Be sure to weigh the coffee first.

2 Put a filter paper into the filter holder and lock into the body of the brewer.

3 Run some hot water through to heat the brewer and rinse the paper.

4 Insert the piston about 2cm (¾in) into the brewer, turn the device upside down and place it on the digital scales. Add the coffee. **A**

5 Boil a kettle of fresh water with a low mineral content, suitable for brewing coffee.

6 Wait ten to twenty seconds after the kettle has boiled, turn on the scales, then add the desired amount of hot water to the Aeropress. **B**

7 Start a timer and give the coffee a quick stir. Steep for one minute.

8 While the coffee is steeping, remove the brewer from the scales. Put the filter holder containing the paper on to the brewer. If you have rinsed the paper it should stick when turned upside down.

9 Slowly pull the top part of the brewer down on to the piston until the liquid is nearly touching the filter. This will make the piston much more stable and less likely to pop off during the flip. **C**

10 At the end of the steep, place a mug upside down on top of the brewer and, with one hand on each, carefully flip them over. **D, E**

11 Slowly push down the plunger until all the liquid has been expelled into the mug. **F**

12 Empty and rinse the brewer as on page 86.

13 Enjoy your coffee.

STOVE-TOP MOKA POT

Most homes have a moka pot in use or at least buried in a cupboard. In many ways I struggle to explain its popularity, as it is not the most user-friendly device in the world and it is not easy to produce delicious coffee with one. It tends to produce very strong, very bitter coffee but it is sufficiently palatable to espresso drinkers that just about every household in Italy uses one religiously.

The patent for the moka pot belongs to Alfonso Bialetti, who invented it in 1933. The Bialetti company continues to produce very popular brewers today. Moka pots are often still made from aluminium (about which there was a false scare story some years ago), although it is possible, and more desirable, to buy a stainless-steel model.

The method below is a little different to the way most people use their moka pot, but the advice may help even those who are already happy with the coffee they produce from it. My biggest issue with this type of coffee maker is that the brewing water reaches temperatures so high that you start to extract very bitter compounds from the coffee. Some people treasure the bitterness of a moka pot brew, others utterly hate the device because of it. The technique below has helped people find a new respect for their long-forgotten brewer and enjoy their coffee a different way.

However, because of the high coffee to water ratio, and because the brew time is quite fast, it is still difficult to make light-roasted, dense or particularly acidic and juicy coffees taste good using this brewing method. I would recommend using a light espresso roast, or perhaps a coffee that is grown at lower altitudes. I would steer away from dark roasts because of the propensity of this method to produce a bitter cup.

Left: To get the best results from your stove-top moka pot, choose a light espresso roast or coffee grown at lower altitudes. This will avoid making an overly bitter brew.

Ratio: 200g/l. In most cases, you do not really have much control over the ratio. You simply fill up the ground coffee holder and then fill the unit with water until it reaches just below the overpressure valve, so there is little room for manoeuvre.

Grind: Quite fine/salt (see page 69). I do not recommend using an espresso/very fine grind, a somewhat controversial stance. I prefer a slightly coarser grind than most people would choose because I prefer to minimize the bitterness in the resulting cup.

1 Grind the coffee just before you start brewing, and fill the basket so it is even and level. Do not compress the coffee.

2 Boil a kettle of fresh water with a low mineral content, suitable for brewing coffee. The advantage of starting with hot water is that the pot is on the heat for less time and the ground coffee doesn't get as hot, which helps reduce the bitterness.

3 Fill the bottom section of the brewer with hot water to just below the small valve. Do not cover the valve with water; it is a safety valve which prevents too much pressure from building up. **A**

4 Put the coffee basket in place. Make sure the circular rubber gasket is completely clean, then carefully assemble the brewer. If this does not seal properly, the brewer will not work properly. **B**

5 Put the pot on a low to medium heat, leaving the lid up. When the water starts to boil in the lower chamber, the pressure created by the steam pushes the water through the tube that feeds it to the coffee. The faster and harder you boil the water, the more pressure you will create and the faster the brew process will be – you don't want to go too quickly. **C**

6 Coffee should slowly start to appear in the top chamber. Listen carefully: when you hear a gurgling sound, it is time to turn off the heat and stop brewing. This sound indicates that most of the water has been pushed up already and that steam is now starting to come through the coffee, which will make the brew more bitter.

7 To stop the brew, run the base of the brewer under cold running water. This drop in temperature will cause the steam to condense and the pressure to disappear. **D**

8 Enjoy your coffee.

Make sure the brewer has cooled down to a safe temperature before taking it apart for cleaning. It must be completely dry before you put it way. Avoid storing it locked fully into position, as this will cause the rubber seal to age more quickly.

THE VACUUM POT

The vacuum coffee pot, also now known as the syphon brewer, is a very old and exceedingly entertaining way to make coffee. It is, however, also extremely annoying in many respects and sufficiently frustrating that many people relegate their brewer to a cupboard or a shelf as a display piece.

Vacuum coffee pots first appeared in Germany in the 1830s. A patent was issued for one in 1838 to a French woman, Jeanne Richard. The design has not really changed a great deal since its conception. The brewer has two chambers, the lower of which is filled with water and heated to boiling point. The upper chamber, which contains the coffee grounds, is then placed on top, creating a seal and allowing steam to build up in the lower chamber. This trapped steam pushes the water from the bottom chamber up through a tube and a filter into the upper chamber. The water is, at this point, just below boiling point and suitable for making coffee. The brew is left to steep for the desired amount of time; it is important to keep heating the lower chamber while the coffee steeps.

To finish the brew, the vacuum pot is removed from the heat source. As the steam cools, it condenses back into water and creates a vacuum, which sucks the coffee from the upper chamber back through the filter into the bottom chamber. The grounds remain trapped and separate in the upper section and the coffee can be poured from the bottom carafe. The whole process is a pleasing application of physics, and is often likened to a classroom experiment. Unfortunately, it is sufficiently difficult to get right that most people try a couple of times and then give up, which is a shame.

ADDITIONAL TOOLS

An independent heat source is required for this brewing method. Some vacuum coffee pots are designed to sit directly on a kitchen stove, others come with their own alcohol-burning candle. These candles are best replaced with a very small, butane camping stove. In Japan and in some specialist coffee shops, the preferred heat source is a halogen lamp placed under the brewer. This is not the most efficient source of heat but it does look fantastic.

Some people use small bamboo paddles to stir the coffee but these do nothing special and a spoon works equally well. While I cannot deny there is pleasure in acquiring and using a special set of tools for a ritual, I won't claim they make any difference to the coffee.

THE FILTER

Most traditional vacuum pots use a cloth filter, which is wrapped around a metal disc. It is important to keep this cloth clean. After every use, clean the cloth as thoroughly as possible under a hot tap. If it is not going to be used for a few days, clean it with a suitable detergent. For more information about cleaning and storing cloth filters, see page 82). There are alternatives to cloth, such as paper or metal, but these often need special adapters.

Left: Vacuum coffee pots are an elaborate way to make coffee by immersion. Steam rises from the lower chamber and steeps the coffee grounds held above, then condenses the brew into the lower carafe.

THE VACUUM POT METHOD

Ratio: 75g/l. Some people prefer to use a little more coffee than this for syphon brewing, especially in Japan where this method is commonly used.

Grind: Medium/caster sugar (see page 69). Because this is an immersion method, you can match your brew time to the grind size. I would caution against going too fine as you can stall the draw-down process to end the brewing. A very coarse grind will mean a very long brew time at higher temperatures, which can make the brew rather bitter.

1 Grind the coffee just before you start brewing. Be sure to weigh the coffee first.

2 Boil a kettle of fresh water with a low mineral content, suitable for brewing coffee.

3 Fit the filter into the upper chamber, making sure it is completely flush.

4 Place the bottom chamber on your digital scales and pour in your calculated amount of hot water, following your desired ratio.

5 Transfer the lower chamber to your heat source (a small butane burner, an alcohol burner or a halogen lamp, as shown here) using the handle to move it.

6 Place the upper chamber on top, but do not seal it yet. If you put the seal on too soon, the expanding gases will push the water up into the top chamber before it is the right temperature, making your coffee taste bad.

7 When the water starts to boil, seal the top chamber on top of the lower chamber. If you are using a controllable heat source, reduce the heat to low at this point. The boiling water will now start pushing up into the top chamber. Look directly down on the filter to make sure it is centred: if it isn't, you will see lots of bubbles flowing from one side. Use your paddle or a spoon to push the filter carefully into place so it is correctly positioned.

8 Initially the bubbling in the top chamber will be quite aggressive, with large bubbles. Once the bubbles become smaller, you are ready to brew. Add the coffee to the water and stir it in until it is all completely wet, then start a timer. **A**

9 A crust will form on top. After thirty seconds, give it a gentle stir to knock the floating coffee back into the brew. **B**

10 After another thirty seconds, turn off the heat source. Once the coffee begins to be drawn down into the lower chamber, stir it gently once clockwise and then once anticlockwise to prevent it sticking to the walls of the brewer, but if you stir too much you will get a large dome of coffee at the end of the brew, which suggests uneven extraction.

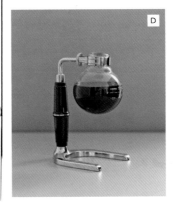

11 Allow the coffee to draw down completely. A slightly domed bed of grounds will be left in the top chamber. Pour the coffee into a coffee pot, as the retained heat from the carafe can give the coffee a cooked taste. **C**

12 Let the coffee cool. This brewing method produces an incredibly hot cup of coffee. **D**

Coffee was first discovered in ninth-century Ethiopia, and the Tomoca coffee shop in Addis Ababa is the oldest surviving café in the country. The later influence of Italian rule is seen in the sleek espresso machines.

ESPRESSO

Over the last fifty years, espresso has come to be considered by many to be the 'best' way to drink coffee. This is not true, since no brew method can be inherently better than any others, but espresso is now the most popular coffee drink consumed out of the home, and many cafés charge more for an espresso than for a filter coffee.

Undeniably espresso has been the driver of coffee retail, whether it is part of the Italian-style coffee culture now widely popular, or the Americanized, fast-food version we see in chain coffee shops across the globe.

Making espresso is both incredibly frustrating and also very rewarding. I must offer a word of caution here: don't invest in an espresso machine at home unless you want a new hobby. The fantasy of whipping up a couple of delicious cappuccinos to drink on a lazy Sunday morning while reading the paper is a very long way away from the work involved in preparing the drinks (and cleaning up afterwards). If you just want the drinks and not the work, then do what I do and pop out to a local café where someone else can deal with it all. However, I accept that, for many of us, great coffee is not available locally and this is a good reason to master the art of espresso brewing at home.

THE INVENTION OF ESPRESSO

As we have already seen, when you brew coffee, the grind size is very important. The finer you grind the beans, the easier it will be to extract the coffee, and the less water you require to do so. This means you can produce a stronger cup of coffee. The problem starts when you try to grind the beans so fine that gravity alone cannot push the water through the bed of coffee. This puts a limit on how strong a cup of coffee you can produce.

This problem has been recognized for a very long time, and the first solution used the pressure of trapped steam to push water through the coffee. Initially this early espresso machine was simply used by cafés to make regular strength coffee much quicker, hence the name. However, the pressure you can generate from steam

alone, without endangering lives, is actually relatively low so various other methods such as air pressure or mains water pressure were tried.

The big breakthrough came with Achille Gaggia's invention. This used a large lever, pulled by the operator, to compress a spring. When the spring was released, the pressure forced the very hot water through the coffee. The sudden jump in pressure was dramatic, and allowed the use of a much finer grind of coffee to produce a much smaller, stronger, but well extracted cup.

CREMA

For most coffee drinkers, one of the key features of espresso is not just the strength of the cup but also the layer of dense foam that tops the drink. *Crema* is simply Italian for cream and it is the natural head of foam that forms on top of the coffee, much like a head appears on a pint of beer.

The reason this happens is that when water is under very high pressure it is able to dissolve more carbon dioxide, the gas present in coffee that was produced during the roasting process. When the brewed liquid gets back to normal atmospheric pressure on its way to the cup, the liquid can no longer hold on to all of the gas so it comes out of solution as innumerable tiny bubbles. These bubbles become trapped in the coffee liquid and appear as a stable foam.

For a long time crema was considered important, but in fact it can only tell you two things. Firstly, whether the coffee is relatively fresh – the longer ago it was roasted, the less carbon dioxide it will contain so the less foam it will produce. And secondly, whether the cup of espresso is strong or weak. The darker in colour the foam, the stronger the liquid will be. This is because crema is just a foam of the liquid, lighter in colour because of the way the bubbles refract light, so the colour of the coffee determines the colour of the crema. For this reason, coffee that has been roasted darker will also produce a darker crema. The crema cannot tell you if the raw coffee is good, or has been well roasted, or if the equipment used to make the espresso is clean – all key factors in a delicious cup of coffee.

Right: Patented in 1905, this La Pavoni two-group Ideale model was the first machine of its kind to be marketed. It introduced espresso-style coffee to Europe and, later, to the rest of the world.

THE BASIC TECHNIQUE

To brew espresso, the ground coffee is placed in a small metal basket held in a handle. The basket has tiny holes that allow the liquid to pass through but prevent any of the pieces of ground coffee, with the exception of the tiniest particles, from making it into the cup.

The coffee in the basket is compressed (tamped) so it is flat. The handle containing the coffee is locked into the espresso machine and the pump then activated. The machine pumps near-boiling water from the reservoir in the machine through the coffee; the liquid then drips into the waiting cup below. With some machines the operator decides when to switch off the pump to finish brewing, either gauging the end of the brew by eye or by weighing the coffee as it

Above: A great barista produces the desired amount of coffee in a certain time frame. Even when using a machine as sleek as this 1956 La San Marco, the first thing to check is that the grind of coffee is right.

comes out to make sure the desired amount of water has been used. Other machines dispense a specific amount of water and then stop automatically.

Great espresso is about recipe, and good coffee roasters will supply you with plenty of information about how to brew their coffee to get great results. A good recipe is about accurate measurements and should include the following:

- The weight of ground coffee to use in grams (g).
- The amount of liquid you should produce from that coffee, ideally expressed in grams or at least expressed in volume (ml).

- How long the brewing process should take.
- How hot the water should be for brewing.

Rather than just give a basic guide, I want to offer some information that will help produce genuinely excellent espresso at home, techniques that I have taught to baristas around the world for years and that I believe are key to brewing espresso as well as is currently possible.

PRESSURE AND RESISTANCE

The aim when brewing an espresso is to have the machine produce a desired amount of liquid in a certain time frame. For example, the recipe might state that we want to brew 18g of ground coffee and produce around 36g of liquid in 27–29 seconds. To achieve this, what we need to control is how quickly the water flows through the ground coffee.

The speed at which the water flows through the coffee determines how much flavour is extracted. If the water passes through too slowly, we take too much out of the coffee and it will be overextracted with a bitter, ashy and very harsh taste. If the water flows through too quickly, we don't extract enough from the coffee and it will taste very sour, astringent and weak.

The way we control the flow of water through coffee is by changing how easy it is for the water to pass through. This can be achieved by varying two factors: the amount of coffee we use (the more you put in the basket, the longer it takes for the water to pass through), and the size of the coffee particles.

The finer we grind the coffee, the better the pieces fit together and the more difficult it is for the water to pass between them. If you took two jars and filled one with sand and one with the same weight of pebbles, water would flow through the pebbles much faster than through the sand. In the same way, the coarser we grind coffee the faster the machine can push the water through it.

The problem many people experience, and one that brings frustration to thousands of baristas around the world every day, is that when the flow rate is wrong and the coffee doesn't taste good, it is not immediately obvious if the grind was incorrect or if the coffee dose was wrong. For this reason, in the home environment, I recommend measuring the coffee wherever possible. It will reduce mistakes, frustration and waste. If you have used the correct weight of coffee, you will know that it is the grind size that needs to be changed.

Espresso is probably the most intolerant method of preparation of any food or drink in the world. This is not an understatement. A few seconds outside of the target brew time, a gram of ground coffee too little in the basket, a few grams too little liquid in the cup – all of these will have a dramatic effect on the taste of the coffee and may be the difference between a delightful cup and pouring the results of your hard work down the sink.

My recommendation is to keep as many things as possible constant, and only alter one variable at a time if you can. If you get a disappointing cup of coffee, try altering the grind size first, because if this is wrong, trying to fix something else won't deliver you the results you want, either.

TAMPING

Tamping is the term used for the compression of the ground coffee before brewing. We do this because ground coffee is fluffy, and if we put uncompressed coffee into the machine the high-pressure water would find the air pockets between the coffee grounds and pass through quickly, skipping much of the coffee. When water does not pass evenly through the coffee we call it channelling. When this happens, the resulting espresso will taste very sour and unpleasant, because the water has not evenly extracted the ground coffee.

Many people place a great deal of importance on tamping, but I do not believe it is as important as people think. The goal is simply to push the air out of the coffee bed and to make sure the bed is level and even before brewing. How hard you compress the coffee doesn't make an enormous difference to how quickly the water passes through it. Once you push all the air out, there is little or no reward for pushing any harder. The espresso machine pushes the water on to the coffee at nine bars or 130psi (pounds of force per square inch), and this is much more aggressively than a human can push down. The goal is simply to produce an even coffee bed, and do no more.

If they notice a little coffee stuck to the walls of the basket, some people will use the tamper to tap the handle to loosen them so they can be tamped down in to the coffee bed. Don't tap. If you tap the handle, you may knock the puck of coffee loose from the walls of the basket, allowing the shot to channel. Secondly, you may damage your tamper and the nice ones are beautiful objects in their own right.

My final piece of advice is to hold the tamper properly. It should be held like a flashlight, with your thumb pointing straight down. When you apply pressure to the coffee, your elbow should be directly above it and your wrist should be straight. If you imagine a screwdriver in your hand, and a screw sticking directly up out of the work bench, you should put your arm in this same position as you push down in order to protect your wrists (see page 98). Repeatedly performing this action incorrectly has given a huge number of professional baristas trouble with their wrists.

ESPRESSO METHOD

In this process we're going to make two cups of espresso. These could go into two separate cups, or into one cup as a double espresso.

1 Fill the reservoir in the espresso machine with water with a low mineral content, suitable for brewing coffee, then switch on the machine to heat the water.

2 Grind the coffee just before you start brewing. Be sure to weigh the coffee first. **A**

3 Make sure the basket is clean. Wipe it with a small dry cloth to make sure it is dry and to remove any leftover grounds once you have tapped out the puck of coffee from the last brew. The cloth will help remove the oily residue from the last brew as well.

4 If you can, place the entire brew handle (also called the portafilter) on the scales to weigh out the coffee. If this is not possible, remove the basket from the handle and place it on the scales. **B**

5 If your scales are accurate enough, weigh the ground coffee to within 0.1g of your recipe, whether it is your own recipe carefully honed over time, or the recipe given to you by the roaster. This level of accuracy may seem like overkill, but digital scales are now relatively cheap and I promise that using a set will help you make more delicious coffee more often.

6 Remove the handle from the scales and tamp the coffee flat in the basket, keeping your wrist straight, to make sure the coffee bed is even. Leaving the tamper on top of the

coffee – observing the angle of the handle will show you whether or not it is sufficiently flat. **C**

7 Weigh the cup or cups into which you are going to brew the coffee.

8 Turn on the machine to flush some water through the group head. This will help to stabilize the temperature of the brew water, as well as rinse off any coffee grounds remaining from the previous brew.

9 Carefully lock the handle into the machine and arrange the cup(s) in place to receive the coffee.

10 Get your timing device ready. If the machine doesn't have a time display showing you how long the shot has been brewing, use a simple stopwatch on your mobile phone or a kitchen timer.

11 As soon as possible, start brewing the coffee. When you start to brew, start the watch. Brew the coffee for the length of time recommended by the roaster. If you don't have a recommendation, try somewhere between 27 and 29 seconds.

12 When the desired brew time is up, stop the machine. When the handle has finished dripping (after a few seconds), return the cups to the weighing scale to check how much coffee you have made.

JUDGING THE RESULTS

Ideally, the weight should be within a few grams of the roaster's recommendations. If it is not, we can make a simple change to try next time:

• If there is too much liquid, the flow was too fast. We need to slow the water down by grinding the coffee finer.

• If there is not enough liquid, the flow was too slow. We should increase the flow rate by grinding the coffee more coarsely.

For many people this kind of precision seems a little extreme, and some prefer to use volume in the cup (gauged by eye) instead of weight. This same protocol will work, but it is not as accurate.

Once a grinder is set for a particular batch of coffee, there will be limited need to adjust it, unless your home is subject to dramatic swings in temperature during the day.

CHANGING THE GRIND

With espresso, you really need to be grinding the coffee yourself with a burr grinder that allows you to adjust the grind size easily. When you start brewing a new bag of coffee you will need to set the grinder for it. The term we use for setting a grinder in the industry is 'dialling in'.

Just about every grinder has some ground coffee left inside it after grinding. This means that if you change the grind setting, the first coffee it will push out will actually be the old grind size. A common practice is to purge the grinder by grinding a few extra grams of beans at the new size to push out the old grounds, and then to throw this coffee away. If you change the grind size but don't see a change in the brewing process, it is likely you did not purge enough coffee from the grinder.

I would always recommend making small changes when adjusting a grinder. When you get a new grinder, it is a good idea to buy some cheap (though ideally fresh) coffee to play with to make sure you understand how big an effect a small change in the grind setting has on the brewing process. Most grinders have numbers on the settings. The actual value of the numbers is meaningless, but if you want to grind finer, turn the dial to a smaller number and vice versa. Many grinders have marked

Opposite: The original home of the espresso is Caffe Florian on St Mark's Square, Venice, which has been serving coffee since 1720.

steps that you can select, sometimes whole numbers and sometimes divisions of numbers. Start by changing the setting by a single step when the grind is wrong.

BREW RATIO

There are many different styles of espresso, and people have different preferences for how long or strong they like their espresso to be. Commercially we tend to talk about the brew ratio: how much liquid should you be brewing from a fixed weight of ground coffee? My own personal preference, and recommended starting point, is to brew two parts of liquid out of one part ground coffee. For example, if I start with 18g of ground coffee, I would want my espresso to weigh 36g (2 x 18). The Italians generally prefer a smaller coffee, so if I were making a double espresso I might use 14g of ground coffee to produce 28g (2 x 14) of liquid. The ratio of coffee to water is fixed to maintain my strength preference.

If I want a stronger espresso, I can change my ratio. Instead of 1:2 I might use 1:1.5, which would mean my 18g of ground coffee produces only 27g (1.5 x 18) of liquid. This shorter espresso will be very strong, and I would have to adjust the grind finer so the brewing process takes a similar amount of time. If I just let a smaller amount of water come through at the same flow rate as before, the brew will be over faster and I will have failed to extract all of the good flavours that I want.

BREW TEMPERATURE

The coffee industry is only now recovering from an obsession with the stability of brew temperature in espresso brewing. Changing the brew temperature does have an effect on the extraction and the taste of the coffee, but I don't believe it is as important as many make it out to be. The hotter the brew water, the more effective it will be at extracting flavour. So for lighter roasts I would recommend a higher brew temperature than for darker roasts, which give up their flavours more easily.

There are claims that a change in temperature of 0.1°C (0.18°F) will change the taste of the coffee. I believe that to be nonsense. I think 1°C (1.8°F) creates the smallest change that most of us could detect, and that a slightly incorrect brew temperature is so rarely the reason I am served a poor espresso.

If you can control the temperature on your espresso machine, I would recommend a water temperature of between 90°C (194°F) and 94°C (201°F). If the espresso does not taste right, try adjusting other aspects of the recipe first. However, if there is a persistent negative taste (such as a constant sourness) try increasing the temperature, and if there is a persistent bitterness, try decreasing the temperature (after you have checked your equipment is properly clean).

BREW PRESSURE

The first espresso machines created pressure using a compressed spring to push the water through the coffee. As the spring expanded, the pressure it produced would decline, so it started with a very high pressure and ended up relatively low. When electric pumps became common, they needed to be set at a constant pressure. Some say that the setting of nine bars (130 psi) was chosen because it was the approximate average of the varying pressure created by the springs on older machines.

Luckily, this also appears to be the pressure at which we get the best flow rate. At pressures below nine bars, the coffee bed provides so much resistance that the flow rate drops. At pressures above nine bars, the coffee bed

becomes so compacted that the flow rate drops again. As long as your machine produces roughly the right pressure you should have no trouble. If the pressure is too low, your espresso may lack body and the desired creaminess. At very high pressures, there can be a strange woody bitterness to the espresso that is not enjoyable.

There is now equipment available that allows baristas to adjust the pressure of their brew water, but there is not yet enough data to make a viable case for introducing this technology to home machines.

CLEANING AND MAINTENANCE

I would estimate that 95 per cent of the commercial coffee machines in business throughout the world are not cleaned properly and this is one of the reasons people are served disappointing, bitter and unpleasant coffee every day. There is no such thing as too clean, and although it requires a little bit of work each time you finish making coffee, a clean machine will make your coffee taste consistently sweet and clean.

COFFEES ROASTED FOR ESPRESSO

Espresso is quite different from the other brewing methods, and because of the small amounts of water being used it is often a challenge to fully extract the coffee. Additionally, because the concentration is so high (the coffee being so strong), balance is very important. A coffee that may taste delicious and balanced as a weaker brew can become dominated by overpowering acidity when consumed as a stronger cup.

For that reason, many roasters change how they roast their coffee when they know it is going to be used for espresso. Though this practice is not universal, I would certainly recommend a slightly slower and slightly darker roast for espresso than I would recommend for a coffee being brewed with a filter.

However, roasters around the world disagree strongly about what the right level of roast is for espresso and there is a wide spectrum on offer from relatively light through to a much darker roast. Personally, I prefer lighter roasts because they allow the particular characteristics of the raw coffee to be appreciated. Darker roasts often carry a more generic 'roasted coffee' flavour, and also have a higher level of bitterness, which I don't enjoy. What I prefer is only really important to me, however, and everyone has their own preference.

The darker the roast of coffee, the easier it is to extract. This is because the coffee bean becomes increasingly porous and brittle as it is roasted. This means that less water is required in the brewing process to properly extract the coffee. If body and mouthfeel are important to you, then you might prefer slightly darker roasts brewed at a 1:1.5 brew ratio. If sweetness and clarity of flavour are important, I would recommend a lighter espresso roast brewed at a ratio of 1:2.

- When you finish making coffee, remove the basket from the handle and clean underneath it with soapy water on a scourer. If you don't do this, an unpleasant patina of dried coffee will accumulate there and it will smell and taste awful.
- Espresso machines dispense water through a mesh screen. If this is easily removable on your machine, take it out and clean it, and also clean the water dispersion block it sits against.

- While the dispersion screen is out, clean the rubber gasket. If coffee builds here, the basket won't make a seal against the machine and water will leak out during brewing, often dripping down the sides of the brew handle into the cup.
- Remove the brew basket from the handle and replace with the cleaning basket. This is the basket with no holes in it that will have been supplied with your machine.
- I recommend using a commercial espresso machine cleaner at the end of every session of coffee making. This will clean out any liquid coffee left inside the machine, which will turn increasingly rancid and unpleasant over time. Follow the manufacturer's instructions for how to use a cleaning powder on your machine.
- Make sure the steam wand is clean if you have used it.

Some people claim that a machine can taste too clean, and that you need to brew an espresso or two to 'season' it after cleaning to take away the metallic taste. I have never found this to be the case, and as long as your machine is properly warmed up (add at least ten to fifteen minutes on top of manufacturer's recommendation), it should make great coffee straight away.

I recommend keeping the machine switched off when not in use. Use a timer to make sure it is ready to make coffee when you want it, but turn it off when you have finished. Espresso machines use quite a lot of power and it is a waste to leave them on if they are not being used.

To keep your machine in good working order, make sure the water you use is suitable. If you use hard water, limescale will build up quickly in the machine and cause it to malfunction. Many manufacturers offer advice for descaling, as some limescale will form even in soft water areas (it will just take a lot longer). Err on the side of caution because if you let your machine scale up completely, it may be difficult to descale without help from a professional (and a bill to go with it).

Over time, the rubber gasket in the group head may need changing. When you lock in your brew handle, it should stick out at ninety degrees to the machine. If it starts to twist much further across, the rubber may be wearing and it should be replaced.

Customers congregate around baristas at London's first espresso bar, the Moka Bar at 29 Frith Street, which was established in 1953 and opened by the Italian actress Gina Lollobrigida.

STEAMING MILK

Well-steamed milk combined with well-brewed espresso is a wonderful sensory experience. Great milk foam is like liquid marshmallow: soft, moussey and undeniably enjoyable to drink. The goal is to create bubbles so small that they are almost invisible (often called 'microfoam'). Foam like this is elastic and pourable, and adds a wonderful lift to the texture of drinks like cappuccino and café latte.

It is important to use fresh milk for steaming. As it reaches its use-by date, milk tastes fine and is still safe to drink but it starts to lose its ability to create a stable foam. It will foam as normal when you steam it, but the bubbles will soon break down. If you lift the jug of foamed milk to your ear, you will hear it fizzing like a freshly poured soda as the air escapes.

When we steam milk we have two separate tasks to accomplish: we must whip in air to create the bubbles and we must heat the milk. With most steam wands it is best to tackle one task at a time, so the first thing to focus on is creating the bubbles. Then, when we have added enough air to the milk and it is the desired volume, we can focus solely on heating it to the desired temperature.

THE RIGHT TEMPERATURE

The ideal temperature for milk, when combined with coffee, is a subject of some contention between many coffee shops and their customers. Milk begins to irreversibly degrade in flavour and texture above 68°C (154°F). This is because the heat alters and denatures the proteins, creating new flavours, though not always good ones. The smell of cooked milk reminds me of eggs at best, and baby sick at worst.

A very hot cappuccino will lack the texture, flavour and sweetness of a drink made with milk that has only been heated to 60°C (140°F). It is impossible to produce good microfoam when the milk has been heated to boiling point. Unfortunately this is the nature of milk – we can either have a very hot or a very delicious drink. This is not to say that all drinks should be served lukewarm, instead that they should be enjoyed as soon as they are made.

WHOLE MILK OR SKIMMED?

It is the protein in the milk that supports the bubbles, so milk will foam well regardless of whether it is skimmed or whole. However, the fat content does play a role: it adds a wonderful texture to the drink, but also changes the way flavour is released. A cappuccino made with skimmed milk has an immediate, intense coffee flavour which does not linger. If the cappuccino is made with whole milk, the flavours will be less intense but will last longer. I always recommend using whole milk, but I also prefer relatively small milk drinks. I think a small, rich cappuccino is a delight.

A

This technique is suitable for traditional steam wands. If your machine has a range of attachments or automatic frothing functions, follow the manufacturer's instructions.

1 Start by pointing the steam wand over the drip tray or into a cloth and briefly opening the valve. This will get rid of any condensation inside the wand. This is known as purging. **A**

2 Pour cold fresh milk into a clean stainless-steel steaming pitcher. It should not be more than sixty per cent full.

3 Dip the steam wand into the milk so just the tip is submerged.

4 Open the valve to full flow and gently lower the pitcher until the wand is almost out of the milk. Listen carefully: you want to hear the slurping sound of the steam wand start to whip air into the milk. As the milk expands, lower the pitcher a little more to bring it back to the surface if you wish to add more air.

5 When you have your desired amount of foam, which should ideally happen before the milk feels warm to the touch, then submerge the steam tip again to start heating the foam – you want it to be just under the surface. Position it slightly to one side and you will see the milk start to spin and churn. The process should now be relatively quiet.

6 To test whether the milk is warm enough, place your free hand on the bottom of the jug. Continue to heat the milk until the jug becomes uncomfortable to touch. At this point the milk will be about 55°C (131°F). Remove your hand from the bottom of the jug and continue to steam for three to five seconds, depending on how hot you like your milk. **B**

7 Close the steam valve fully and put the milk pitcher down. Wipe the steam wand with a clean, damp cloth and purge the wand into the cloth to remove any leftover milk from inside the wand.

8 Don't worry if your foam contains a few large, ugly bubbles. If you let it sit for a few seconds, the milk will drain off the surface of the larger bubbles, making them very brittle. A couple of gentle taps of the steaming pitcher on the counter will usually pop them.

9 If you want to pour a combination of milk and foam into your drink, which I strongly recommend, you must make sure that they are fully combined. After the tapping, swirl the milk and foam together, much like you might swirl wine in a glass before smelling it. You can be quite aggressive, as you want to make sure that the liquid milk is fully combined with the wonderful microfoam. Swirl until the milk foam has a glossy finish, then pour it into your drink. **C**

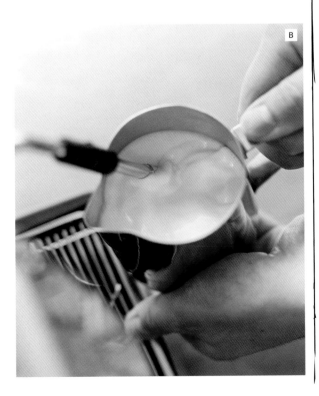

ESPRESSO EQUIPMENT

There are espresso machines to suit almost any budget, from cheap units with which you can make a start, to smarter machines that can cost as much as a small car. All of them are designed to do the same thing: heat water, then push it forwards at high pressure.

The more money you pay, the more the machines improve in build quality, control and consistency. Most of this consistency concerns how the machine heats water, and how it creates water pressure, and different types of espresso machine achieve this in different ways.

THERMOBLOCK MACHINES

The cheapest domestic espresso machines use this technology to produce espresso. There is a single unit inside the machine with an element to heat the water. Most of these machines have two settings: one to heat the water up to a suitable temperature for brewing coffee, and the other to boil water to generate steam. This means that the machine can only perform one function at a time, and I would recommend brewing coffee first, and then heating up the machine to steam milk.

Broadly speaking, these machines do not produce a very consistent water temperature, and the lack of ability to perform both brewing and steaming at once limits how many drinks the machine can practically make, which can be frustrating for the user. However, when paired with a good grinder, they can certainly produce good espresso.

Thermoblock machines usually use a vibration pump to generate pressure. These have two disadvantages: they are quite noisy, and they are rarely accurately set. The desired pressure for espresso is around nine bars (130psi). These pumps are usually set much higher and manufacturers will often proudly boast that their machine can produce fifteen bars (220psi) of pressure, as if more is somehow better.

The machines have an overpressure valve that opens above nine bars (130psi) to alleviate the excess pressure. These valves are not usually very well calibrated, and may need adjustment over time. However, I do not recommend opening up your machine as you will probably invalidate your warranty.

Below: Customers in Rome in the 1950s are served their espresso by a smartly dressed barista. Though a gleaming machine is a delight to look at, it is more important to have an excellent coffee grinder.

Thermoblock machines are undoubtedly the most popular and widespread of espresso machines, but many people who enjoy making espresso soon begin to feel constrained and start to think about an upgrade.

HEAT-EXCHANGE MACHINES

Although it is still common in commercial espresso machines, this technology is available in home machines too. The machine still has a single element, but it heats a small boiler of water to around 120°C (248°F). This generates plenty of steam, which is always available for foaming milk. However, the water in this boiler is too hot to brew coffee, so the machine pumps fresh cold water through what is called a heat exchange. This is usually some sort of tube that passes through the steam boiler. While the coffee-brewing water is kept separate from the boiler water, heat from the boiler is quickly passed to the brewing water to bring it up to the desired temperature.

These kinds of machines are often referred to as 'prosumer', as they straddle the divide between consumer prices and professional performance. The disadvantage of heat-exchange machines, certainly domestic ones, is that changes in the boiler temperature will affect the temperature of the brew water. If you want more steam, you have to increase the boiler temperature, which will also increase the brew temperature. If you want to noticeably reduce the brew temperature, your steaming performance may suffer.

Many of these machines use mechanical thermostats to control the boiler temperature and these can result in some variation. Better machines have more reliable control over the steam boiler temperature.

Heat exchange machines can be fitted with either a vibration pump (see above) or a rotary pump. Rotary pumps are used on commercial equipment and are quieter and easier to adjust, but there is not a lot of difference in performance between the different types of pump if they are set to the same pressure.

DUAL-BOILER MACHINES

The idea here is to separate the coffee brew water entirely from the water used to generate steam, and as the name suggests the machine does this by having one boiler and element for the brewing water, and then a

separate small steam boiler that heats its water up to a higher temperature for producing steam and boiling water for tea or americanos, for example.

The temperature in the coffee boiler is usually very finely tuned with digital controls, allowing easy adjustments of temperature and greater levels of stability. These machines can undeniably produce coffee as good as any commercial machine, but they often come with price tags to match.

ESPRESSO GRINDERS

A grinder suitable for use with an espresso machine will need to do two key things: it must be able to grind the coffee finely enough to make good espresso, and it must be easily adjustable to make very small changes in the grind size.

More expensive grinders tend to have better control over the grind setting, and a more powerful motor inside, which will be quieter. At the top end are the burr grinders with cutting discs inside, which produce fewer very tiny pieces of coffee that can add bitterness to the cup.

Many people who are passionate about espresso end up with a small, basic commercial grinder, rather than a top-end domestic model. However, there are good domestic machines out there. Ideally, try to find a grinder described as 'grind to order', which means that it does not have a chamber to store large quantities of ground coffee, but is instead designed to dispense the grounds straight into the basket in the brew handle.

ESPRESSO-BASED DRINKS

Whether they are long, short, milky or dark, there is a wide variety of coffee drinks that start with an espresso as their base.

ESPRESSO

There are many definitions for what makes an espresso an espresso, some extremely precise and some more general. I would define an espresso as a small, strong drink made using finely ground coffee under high water pressure. I would also add that an espresso should have crema. More precisely, I would say the ratio of the weight of ground coffee to the weight of the finished beverage is about 1:2. I would rather have an open definition and treat espresso as a broad church, than be overly prescriptive about what is right and wrong.

RISTRETTO

This translates from the Italian as 'restricted' and the idea is to produce an even smaller and stronger cup of coffee than an espresso. This is done by using less brewing water for the same amount of ground coffee. The grind of the coffee should be finer so the brew time remains long enough to extract all the desirable aromatics from the coffee.

LUNGO

The lungo, or 'long' coffee, was until recently considered deeply unfashionable in the speciality coffee world. It was usually brewed using an espresso machine but with two or three times the amount of water to the same weight of coffee to make a much longer drink. The resulting cup was much weaker and, while a longer-lasting experience for the consumer, it was considered inferior due to the lack of body and mouthfeel. In fairness, most coffee brewed this way is terrible, and tastes very bitter and ashy.

However, recently there has been a movement within the speciality coffee industry to brew lighter roasted coffees this way, resulting in a complex and balanced brew that I think can be delicious. If ever you are struggling to balance the acidity in an espresso blend, try making it into a longer drink by adding more water to the same amount of coffee. The grind will need to be made a little coarser to allow a faster flow and prevent overextraction.

MACCHIATO

This drink takes its name from the idea of 'marking' or 'staining' an espresso with some milk foam. In Italy it is not unusual to see a busy barista line up several cups of espresso on the bar for the customers. If one of the customers likes just a drop of milk in their drink, it is important to add a small dollop of milk foam as well to mark which cup it is. If you pour just a little milk into a freshly made espresso it will disappear under the crema, and you won't be able to spot it.

In the last decade or so, many quality-focused coffee shops have done something quite different with the drink. They have turned a macchiato into an espresso topped up with foamed milk. This is often done at the request of the customer, who wants a longer, weaker and sweeter drink. Sometimes, however, it is done because the barista likes to show off and pour latte art in very small cups.

To further confuse matters, Starbucks have a drink called a Caramel Macchiato. This is an entirely different drink, much closer to a caffe latte that has been 'marked' or 'stained' by caramel syrup. This has created some customer confusion, especially in North America, so it is now common to see coffee shops refer to what they offer as a 'traditional macchiato'.

CAPPUCCINO

There remain a great many myths around the cappuccino. One to get out of the way quickly is that the name has nothing to do with the hoods of monks' robes, nor the bald spot on their heads. The original name for the drink was a *kapuziner*, and it was a Viennese drink in the 19th century. It was a small brewed coffee mixed with milk or cream until it attained the same shade of brown as the Capuchin monks' robes. Essentially the name implies the strength of the drink.

Another recent myth surrounding the cappuccino is the rule of thirds. The rule of thirds is passed around to this day, and describes a traditional cappuccino as being one-third espresso, one-third milk and one-third foam. I was taught this very early on in my coffee career but this recipe has no root in tradition. I have read quite a few books about coffee and the first reference to the cappuccino rule of thirds I can find was written in the 1950s. It describes cappuccino as 'an espresso mixed with equal amounts of milk and foam.' This sentence appears almost verbatim a number of times in the book. The phrase is a little ambiguous as it could be saying that only the milk and foam are in equal quantities, or that all three ingredients are. So instead of the recipe being 1:1:1, the author could easily have meant it was 1:2:2. The 150–175ml cappuccino made with a single shot of espresso in the ratio of 1:2:2 does have a long tradition,

and is still widely served in much of Italy and the parts of Europe that haven't yet succumbed to more generous portions of coffee as fast-food retail. This drink is also, when well made, absolutely delicious.

I think a great cappuccino is the pinnacle of milk-based espresso drinks. A rich layer of dense, creamy foam combined with sweet, warming milk and the flavours of a well-brewed espresso are an absolute delight. The closer to lukewarm you can enjoy a cappuccino, the sweeter it will be, and I confess that the best ones I've drunk disappear in a few greedy mouthfuls – impossible if the drink is too warm.

CAFFE LATTE

This drink did not originate in Italy. When espresso first spread around the world, it was a bitter, intense and extraordinary coffee experience for most. For some people, the bitterness was a problem so they added hot milk to make the drink sweeter and less bitter. The caffe latte was created to satisfy the customers who wanted the coffee experience with less intensity.

Typically there is more liquid milk in a caffe latte than a cappuccino, making the coffee flavour less intense. It is also traditional to have less foam in the milk.

I am always careful to describe the drink as a caffe latte, rather than just a latte, because many people travel to Italy and if they order a latte there, they will suffer the humiliation of simply receiving a glass of milk.

FLAT WHITE

Different coffee cultures around the world have contributed different drinks, and while the argument continues over whether the flat white was invented in Australia or New Zealand, it is undeniably from Australasia and has been spread by those who have travelled to Europe and North America to open businesses there. In the UK, the name first became synonymous with the offerings of quality-focused cafés,

ONE CAPPUCCINO A DAY

There is a tradition in Italy of having just one cappuccino in the morning, then drinking only espresso for the rest of the day. I believe this is a fascinating example of culture reflecting diet. Like most southern Europeans, many Italians are lactose intolerant. However, a lactose-intolerant person can consume a small amount of milk without a problem, hence the daily cappuccino. A second or third cappuccino, however, even a small Italian one, could result in some gastric distress, so Italian culture prevents the excessive consumption of milk by making it a small cultural taboo to keep drinking cappuccino throughout the day.

LUNGO

MACCHIATO

AMERICANO

FLAT WHITE

RISTRETTO

CAPPUCCINO

CAFFE LATTE

ESPRESSO

to the point that it was adopted by the major chains and put on their menus. The drink probably had lowlier origins, however. By the 1990s it was common, almost everywhere outside Italy, for a cappuccino to come with an enormous head of dry, meringue-like foam. Sometimes this would rise up from the top of the cup like a mountain, carefully dusted with chocolate powder. Many consumers were frustrated to be sold a cup of coffee that seemed to be mostly air and began to ask for a flat, white coffee. No foam, just coffee and milk. These became sufficiently part of the culture there that when people started focusing on quality more and more, and on better milk texture and latte art, the flat white was remade as something delicious.

The best description I can offer is that a flat white is like a small, strong latte. It should have a strong coffee flavour, and is usually made with a double ristretto or a double espresso, topped up with hot milk to make a 150–175ml drink. The milk has a little foam added to it, but not very much. This makes it relatively easy to pour intricate patterns, known as latte art, into the drink.

AMERICANO

The story goes that the American soldiers stationed in Italy after World War II found the espresso too strong. They often asked for their espresso to be served with some hot water, or diluted down to the point that it resembled the coffee they were used to at home. This style of drink picked up the name 'caffe americano'.

Although it resembles a cup of filter coffee, I think the americano is somewhat inferior. However, it remains popular with café owners because it allows them to serve filter coffee-strength brews without having to buy additional equipment.

My recommendations for making an americano are simple. Pour some fresh, clean hot water into a cup, then brew a double espresso on top. If your espresso machine has a steam boiler, it should be able to deliver the hot water, although if you have not taken water from the machine for a while it may taste unpleasant.

Opposite: A promotional poster for Perles des Indes, established in 1905 by René Honoré. The largest French importer of coffee, the company roasted more than 2,000kg (4,400lb) of beans daily.

Some people claim that you should never add very hot water to an espresso, and always brew the espresso on top of the hot water. I don't think it makes a great deal of difference, I just find the resulting coffee is cleaner and looks better.

The one disadvantage of diluting espresso is that you increase the perceived bitterness slightly. For that reason, as soon as you finish brewing the americano, I would recommend scooping the crema off the top of the drink and discarding it. Crema is delightful to look at, but there are many tiny pieces of ground coffee trapped in the foam so the crema contributes additional bitterness to the drink. Removing the crema before stirring and drinking definitely improves the flavour of an americano. (I would also recommend tasting an espresso after you remove the crema – the difference in flavour is dramatic. While I actually prefer the taste of an espresso without crema, I don't want the extra work and am happy enough to enjoy it as it is. With an americano, however, I really do think the extra work is worthwhile.)

CORTADO

This is one of the few coffee-based drinks that does not have Italian origins. In fact, it comes from Spain, most likely Madrid, where it is commonly served. Traditionally the Spanish brew their espresso slightly longer, often a little weaker than the Italians. To make a cortado, about 30ml of espresso is combined with an equal quantity of steamed milk. This is traditionally served in a glass. The drink seems to have spread and has been reinterpreted in a few different ways, but this is the basic idea behind it.

HOME ROASTING

In the past, it was not uncommon for a household to buy raw coffee and roast it at home. Since World War II, however, the trend has undeniably favoured convenience. Roasting coffee at home is fun and relatively inexpensive, although it will be a considerable challenge to achieve the same quality of roasted coffee as the very best commercial roasters.

Home roasting allows you to roast smaller batches of raw coffees than you might be able to buy roasted, so you can explore a greater number of green coffees and learn as you go. Like any hobby, there will probably be terrible failures and surprise successes along the way.

HOME-ROASTING MACHINES

It is possible to roast coffee in almost anything that generates enough heat: you can put raw coffee on a baking sheet and bake it in the oven until browned, but the results will be pretty terrible. Many people start out with something a bit more sophisticated, like using a heat gun and agitating the coffee beans regularly as they roast, or a modified electric popcorn machine. Second-hand popcorn machines can be acquired cheaply and do a reasonable job of roasting coffee: they will usually roast a small batch of coffee quite quickly – in around four or five minutes – but don't do a great job of producing even results at lighter roasts. People who prefer darker, more developed roasts seem to have more success with them.

If you really want to roast coffee at home successfully, you will need a machine designed for the purpose. Start small and decide if you enjoy the ritual, the regularity of it and the overall process. Starting this way is easy and fun, and there is no regret if you decide you would rather leave this part of the process to the professionals.

There are two main types of machine available to the home roaster: hot-air roasters and drum roasters.

HOT-AIR ROASTERS

These mimic, on a much smaller scale, commercial fluid-bed roasters (see page 56). The hot air agitates and moves the beans around to produce an even roast, as well as providing the necessary heat to turn them brown. These roasters are cheaper than drum roasters and a great starting point for someone looking to dip a toe in the roasting process.

Some do a better job than others of dealing with the smoke and smells produced during roasting, but I would still recommend roasting in a well-ventilated area. However, if you roast outside and it is very cold, roasting times may be slower than you want.

DRUM ROASTERS

These are similar in design to commercial drum roasters, but they are not built with the same quality and weight of materials. The coffee is tumbled around in a drum while being heated. The drum is designed to keep the beans moving to allow even browning.

Some drum machines offer more programming functions, allowing you to create your own roast profiles. The intensity of the heat can be varied throughout the roast, and then the machine can automate the process to allow easy replication of your favourite roasts.

Left: Like any new hobby, roasting coffee beans at home will have some failures and surprise successes, but is worth trying if you want to experiment with tasting a range of green coffees.

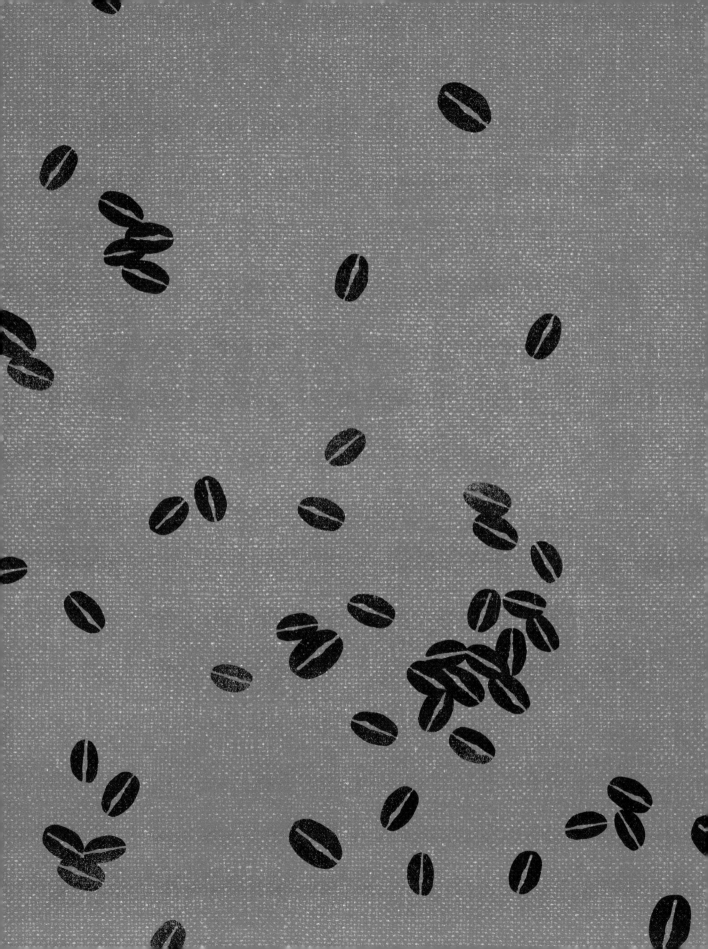

PART THREE: COFFEE ORIGINS

AFRICA

While Ethiopia is commonly recognized as the birthplace of coffee, significant coffee crops are also grown in central and eastern Africa. There are established export markets for beans from Kenya, Burundi, Malawi, Rwanda, Tanzania and Zambia. Each country has its own particular techniques and varieties, creating a diverse selection for buyers. This section discusses key coffee-growing regions within each country and highlights the typical harvest process, taste profile and traceability of beans.

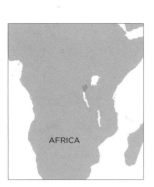

AFRICA

BURUNDI

Coffee came to Burundi in the 1920s under Belgian colonial rule, and from 1933 every peasant farmer had to cultivate at least fifty coffee trees. When Burundi gained its independence in 1962, coffee production went private. This changed in 1972, along with the political climate, but since 1991 coffee has slowly been returning to the private sector.

Coffee growing had been increasing steadily, but the civil war in 1993 caused a precipitous drop in production. Since then, efforts have been made to increase both production and the value of coffee in Burundi. Investment in the industry is seen as crucial, as Burundi's economy has been shattered by conflict. In 2011 Burundi had one of the lowest per capita incomes in the world with ninety per cent of the population relying on subsistence agriculture. Coffee and tea exports combined make up approximately ninety per cent of total foreign exchange earnings. Coffee production is recovering, but has not yet reached the levels of the early 1980s. However, there is hope for coffee in Burundi. With 650,000 families dependent on the crop, movements towards higher prices through improvement of quality can only be a good thing. However, the constant fear of political instability returning looms large.

Burundi's geography is well suited to coffee. Much of it is mountainous, providing the necessary altitudes and climates. There are no coffee estates in Burundi, instead coffee is produced by large numbers of smallholder farmers. Recently these producers have become more organized, usually centring around one of the 160 washing stations in the country. Around two-thirds of these washing stations are under state ownership, the others are privately owned. Anything from several hundred up to two thousand producers feed their coffee into each washing station.

Within each region, these stations are grouped together into SOGESTALs (Sociétés de Gestion des Stations de Lavage), which are effectively management organizations for groups of washing stations. Development of quality in recent years has been directed through these organizations, mainly through the provision of better infrastructure in their regions.

The best coffees from Burundi are fully washed and usually made up of the Bourbon variety, though other varieties are grown. In many ways there are similarities between Burundi and its neighbour Rwanda: the countries have similar altitudes and coffee varieties, and both face the challenges of being landlocked, which can hinder the rapid export necessary for the raw coffee to arrive in the consuming countries in good condition. As in Rwanda, coffees in Burundi are also susceptible to the potato defect (see page 143).

TRACEABILITY

Until recently, the coffees from all the washing stations within each SOGESTAL were blended together. This meant that coffees exported from Burundi were only traceable back to their SOGESTAL, which is effectively their region of origin.

In 2008 Burundi began to embrace the speciality coffee sector, allowing more direct and traceable purchasing. In 2011 there was a coffee quality competition in Burundi called the Prestige Cup, a precursor to the more established Cup of Excellence. The lots from individual washing stations were kept separate and ranked on quality, then they were sold at auction with their traceability intact. This means that we are likely to see more unique and interesting coffees coming out of Burundi in the future and there is great potential for quality.

TASTE PROFILE

Great coffees from Burundi can have complex berry fruit flavours, and a great juicy quality.

Population: 8,749,000

Number of 60kg (132lb) bags in 2013: 167,000

Burundi is such a small country that it doesn't really have distinct growing areas. Coffee grows right across the country, wherever there is suitable land and altitude. The country is divided into provinces, and coffee farms are clustered around the washing stations (wet mills) there.

BUBANZA

This region is in the northwest of Burundi.

Altitude: average of 1,350m (4,400ft)
Harvest: April–July
Varieties: Bourbon, Jackson, Mibrizi and some SL varieties

BUJUMBURA RURAL

Located in western Burundi.

Altitude: average of 1,400m (4,600ft)
Harvest: April–July
Varieties: Bourbon, Jackson, Mibrizi and some SL varieties

BURURI

This southwestern province contains three of Burundi's national parks.

Altitude: average of 1,550m (5,050ft)
Harvest: April–July
Varieties: Bourbon, Jackson, Mibrizi and some SL varieties

CIBITOKE

This province is in the very northwest of Burundi, close to the border with the Democratic Republic of Congo.

Altitude: average of 1,450m (4,750ft)
Harvest: April–July
Varieties: Bourbon, Jackson, Mibrizi and some SL varieties

GITEGA

This central region contains one of the two state-owned dry mills, used for the final stages of preparation and quality control before export.

Altitude: average of 1,450m (4,750ft)
Harvest: April–July
Varieties: Bourbon, Jackson, Mibrizi and some SL varieties

KARUZI

This region is slightly west of central Burundi.

Altitude: average of 1,600m (5,200ft)
Harvest: April–July
Varieties: Bourbon, Jackson, Mibrizi and some SL varieties

KAYANZA

This northern region, near the Rwandan border, has the second highest number of stations.

Altitude: average of 1,700m (5,600ft)
Harvest: April–July
Varieties: Bourbon, Jackson, Mibrizi and some SL varieties

KIRUNDO

This region is in the northernmost part of the country.

Altitude: average of 1,500m (4,900ft)
Harvest: April–July
Varieties: Bourbon, Jackson, Mibrizi and some SL varieties

MAKAMBA

One of the most southerly provinces in Burundi.

Altitude: average of 1,550m (5,050ft)
Harvest: April–July
Varieties: Bourbon, Jackson, Mibrizi and some SL varieties

MURAMVYA

A small region in the central part of the country.

Altitude: average of 1,800m (5,900ft)
Harvest: April–July
Varieties: Bourbon, Jackson, Mibrizi and some SL varieties

MUYINGA

This region borders Tanzania in the northeastern part of the country.

Altitude: average of 1,600m (5,200ft)
Harvest: April–July
Varieties: Bourbon, Jackson, Mibrizi and some SL varieties

MWARO

Another small region in the middle of the country.

Altitude: Average of 1,700m (5,600ft)
Harvest: April–July
Varieties: Bourbon, Jackson, Mibrizi and some SL varieties

NGOZI

The most concentrated region for coffee production, in the north of the country, with 25 per cent of the washing stations.

Altitude: average of 1,650m (5,400ft)
Harvest: April–July
Varieties: Bourbon, Jackson, Mibrizi and some SL varieties

RUTANA

This region is in southern Burundi, west of Mount Kiziki. It has one washing station.

Number of washing stations: 1
Altitude: average of 1,550m (5,050ft)
Harvest: April–July
Varieties: Bourbon, Jackson, Mibrizi and some SL varieties

Above: Coffee pickers bring their harvest to be washed in Kayanza, Burundi.

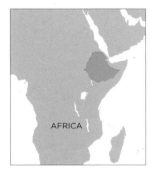

AFRICA

ETHIOPIA

Of all the coffee-producing countries, Ethiopia is perhaps the most compelling. Its fascination stems not only from the unusual, astonishing coffees it produces, but from the mystery that shrouds so much of it. The explosively floral and fruity coffees from Ethiopia have opened many a coffee professional's eyes to the diversity of flavour that coffee can have.

Ethiopia is universally referred to as the birthplace of coffee, although this should come with some caveats. It is likely *Coffea arabica* first appeared in southern Sudan, but it only flourished once it spread into Ethiopia. It was here that it was first consumed by humans, initially as a fruit rather than a beverage. Yemen was the first country to start growing coffee as a crop, but it had been harvested from the wild in Ethiopia long before.

Coffee was probably first exported from Ethiopia in the 1600s, at a time when cafés began to appear in Yemen and the Middle East. Interest from European traders was often rebuffed and it then waned as coffee plantations began to appear in Yemen, Java and ultimately the

Americas. Coffee production in Ethiopia at the time was essentially the harvest of wild coffee trees that grew in the districts of Kaffa and Buno, rather than from established plantations.

Interest returned to Ethiopian coffee in the early 1800s, when there is a record of the export of one hundred quintals of coffee from Enerea, an area of modern-day Ethiopia. In the 19th century, there were two common grades of Ethiopian coffee: Harari (cultivated around the town of Harrar) and Abyssinia (grown in the wild in the rest of the country). For this reason Harrar has a long-standing reputation for being desirable and of high quality (which it does not always earn).

The 1950s were a time of increased structure in the Ethiopian coffee industry and a new grading system was introduced. In 1957 the National Coffee Board of Ethiopia was formed. The overthrow of Emperor Haile Selassie brought change in the 1970s, however. This wasn't a peasant uprising, more a coup from the elite class tired of famine and conflict. The vacuum of power was filled by the military, which was strongly influenced by socialist ideals. Up until that point the country had been close, in some ways, to a feudal system of government. Among the new ideals was the redistribution of land, and the government quickly began to nationalize it. Some argue that this move was hugely beneficial to the population, increasing the earnings of the rural poor by up to fifty per cent. Strict Marxist rules prevented land ownership or hired labour, and this had a huge impact on the coffee

KEY

Coffee growing regions

ERITREA

N

Mekele

Rash Dashen △

Gonder

Lake Tana

DJIBOUTI

SUDAN

Bahir Dar

ETHIOPIA

Blue Nile

GHIMBII/ LEKEMPTI

Dire Dawa

ADDIS ABABA

Harrar

HARRAR

Adama

GREAT RIFT VALLEY

Gambela

JIMA

Jima

TEPPII/ BEBEKA

Awasa

SIDAMO

YIRGACHEFFE

Shebelle

SOMALIA

SOUTH SUDAN

0   miles   200

0   km   200

KENYA

Above: Ethiopia is commonly accepted as the birthplace
of coffee. This Ethiopian woman performs an age-old coffee
ceremony in Wollo, Lalibella.

industry. Large-scale farming was abandoned and
Ethiopia went back to harvesting its coffee from the wild.
The 1980s was a decade of famine, affecting eight million
people and killing one million of them.

THE MOVE TOWARDS DEMOCRACY

In 1991 the Ethiopian Peoples' Revolutionary
Democratic Front overthrew the Military Junta. This
began a process of liberalization and moved the country
towards democracy. International markets opened up for
Ethiopia, but with them came the effects of fluctuating
market prices. Coffee farmers in Ethiopia in particular
have had to cope with large, uncontrollable price swings.
This has given rise to the formation of cooperatives,
offering support to their members, such as funding,
market information and transport.

THE ETHIOPIAN COMMODITY EXCHANGE

The largest change to the trade of Ethiopian coffee
in recent years, and one of great concern to speciality
coffee buyers, was the introduction of the Ethiopian
Commodity Exchange (ECX) in 2008. The ECX was
created for various different commodities in Ethiopia
with the aim of creating an efficient trading system that
protected both sellers and buyers alike. However, the
system frustrated those who wished to buy a distinct,
traceable product rather than a commoditized one.
Coffees were delivered to the ECX warehouse where they
were allocated a numerical denomination of regional

Coffee beans are hand-graded by women at a factory in Ethiopia. The range of flavours found in Ethiopian coffee beans is broad, owing to the variable climates of different growing regions.

origin for washed coffees (from 1–10). All natural-process coffees were marked 11. The coffees were then graded for quality and assigned a number from 1–9, or labelled UG for ungraded.

This process stripped the coffee of its exact traceability before auction, but on the positive side farmers did receive payment for their coffee sooner than they had before. The system also restricted which coffees could be offered on the international market and increased the financial transparency in contracts.

Today there are increasing opportunities to work outside the constraints of the ECX model, and more and more high-quality and traceable coffees are reaching consumers abroad.

Right: Once difficult to trace, the quality and provenance of coffee is becoming more accessible. This allows consumers to make informed choices about where and how their coffee is harvested.

GROWING REGIONS

Population: 93,877,000
Number of 60kg (132lb) bags in 2013: 6,600,000

The growing regions of Ethiopia are among the most recognizable names in coffee, and are used to sell the coffee today and probably will be in the foreseeable future. The genetic potential of the indigenous and wild varieties of Arabica make the future of coffee in Ethiopia an exciting one, too.

SIDAMO

Sidamo is one of the three regions (along with Harrar and Yirgacheffe) that the Ethiopian government trademarked in 2004 to bring wider recognition to their distinctive coffees. Sidamo produces a mixture of washed and naturally processed coffees that are incredibly popular among those who enjoy a fruity and intensely aromatic cup.

The region itself was formed after Ethiopia achieved liberalization from Italy in 1942, and was named after a group of native people called the Sidama. For this reason, both 'Sidamo' and 'Sidama' can be used to describe coffees from the region. This region grows some of the highest coffee in Ethiopia.

Altitude: 1,400–2,200m (4,600–7,200ft)
Harvest: October–January
Varieties: Heirloom varieties

LIMU

While it does not have the same reputation as Sidamo and Yirgacheffe, Limu still produces some astonishing coffee. This region's producers are mostly smallholders, but there are some large government-owned plantations in the area.

Altitude: 1,400–2,200m (4,600–7,200ft)
Harvest: November–January
Varieties: Heirloom varieties

JIMA

This region, in the southwest, produces a large portion of Ethiopia's coffee. Coffees from this region have recently been a little eclipsed by those from other parts of the country but they are definitely worth investigating. The name of this region can also be written as 'Jimmah', 'Jimma' or 'Djimmah'.

Altitude: 1,400–2,000m (4,600–6,600ft)
Harvest: November–January
Varieties: Heirloom varieties

TRACEABILITY

It is possible to find Ethiopian coffees from a single estate, though they are relatively rare. Traceability is more likely to lead back to a specific cooperative. However, a coffee roaster may simply have bought a coffee that had come through the ECX and it could still be astonishing despite its lack of transparency. These coffees have so much to offer, so I would recommend finding a roaster whose coffees you already enjoy and asking them for guidance on what is excellent.

TASTE PROFILE

The flavours of Ethiopian coffees are notably diverse – from citrus, often bergamot, and florals through to candied fruit or even tropical fruit flavours. The best washed coffees can be incredibly elegant, complex and delicious and the best naturally processed ones can be wildly fruity, and enchantingly unusual.

GHIMBI/LEKEMPTI

The regions surrounding the two towns of Ghimbi and Lekempti are often combined into one, and a roaster may use one name or the other, or sometimes both. Lekempti is the capital city, but a coffee that is described by this name could actually come from Ghimbi over 100km (62 miles) away.

Altitude: 1,500–2,100m (4,900–6,900ft)
Harvest: February–April
Varieties: Heirloom varieties

HARRAR

This is one of the oldest producing regions, surrounding the small town of Harrar. Coffees from this region are quite distinctly different, and are often grown in environments requiring extra irrigation. Harrar has maintained a strong reputation for many years, although the naturally processed coffees can veer between an unclean, woody earthiness to a more explicit blueberry fruit flavour. The coffees are often so unusual that they are remembered fondly by those who work in the industry as the coffees that opened their eyes to the diversity of flavours possible within a cup.

Altitude: 1,500–2,100m (4,900–6,900ft)
Harvest: October–February
Varieties: Heirloom varieties

YIRGACHEFFE

The coffees from this region are, in many ways, truly unique. So many of the great washed coffees from Yirgacheffe are explosively aromatic, full of citrus and floral notes and have a light and elegant body, so this is undeniably one of the greatest and most interesting regions for growing coffee. The best coffees from this region fetch rightfully high premiums, and while they can remind some people more of a cup of Earl Grey tea than of a cup of coffee, they are absolutely worth seeking out. There are naturally processed coffees produced in this region too, which can also be exceptionally interesting and enjoyable.

Altitude: 1,750–2,200m (5,750–7,200ft)
Harvest: October–January
Varieties: Heirloom varieties

AFRICA

KENYA

Despite the fact that neighbouring Ethiopia is considered the home of coffee, Kenya did not start production until relatively late. The earliest documented import of coffee dates to 1893 when French missionaries brought coffee trees from Réunion. Most agree that the variety of coffee they brought was Bourbon. It yielded its first crop in 1896.

nitially coffee was produced on large estates under British colonial rule, and the resulting crop was sold in London. In 1933 the Coffee Act was passed, establishing a Kenyan Coffee Board and moving the sale of coffee back to Kenya. In 1934 the auction system was established and it is still in use today; a year later

protocols were created for the grading of coffee to help improve quality.

Not long after the Mau Mau uprising in the early 1950s, an agricultural act was passed to create family holdings that combined subsistence farming with the production of cash crops for additional income. This act was known as the Swynnerton Plan, named after an official in the Department of Agriculture. This marked the start of the transfer of coffee production from the

Below: Kenyan women carry buckets of freshly picked ripe coffee cherries to be sorted and processed.

British to the Kenyans. The effect on the production of smallholdings was significant, with total income rising from £5.2 million in 1955 to £14 million in 1964. Notably, coffee production accounted for 55 per cent of this increase.

Kenya gained independence in 1963, and now consistently produces extremely high-quality coffees from a variety of sources. The research and development in Kenya is considered excellent, and many farmers are highly educated in coffee production. The Kenyan auction system should help to reward quality-focused producers with better prices, but while buyers are paying high prices for the excellent coffees, corruption within the system may prevent those premiums filtering back to the farmers.

GRADING

Kenya uses a grading system for all of its exported coffee, regardless of whether the lot is traceable or not. As in many other countries, the grading system uses a combination of bean size and quality. The definitions clearly define size and, to some extent, they also assume quality is linked to the size of the beans. While this is often true – the AA lots often being the superior coffees – I have recently seen harvests where the AB lots appeared to be more complex and of higher quality than many of the AA lots.

E – These are the elephant beans, the very largest size, so lots tend to be relatively small.

AA – This is a more common grade for the larger screen sizes, above screen size 18 (see page 40), or 7.22mm. Typically, these fetch the highest prices.

AB – This grade is a combination of A (screen size 16, or 6.80mm) and B (screen size 15, or 6.20mm). This grade accounts for around thirty per cent of Kenya's annual production.

PB – This is the grade for peaberries, where a single bean has grown inside the coffee cherry instead of the more usual two.

C – This is the grading size below the AB category. It is unusual to see this grade in a high-quality coffee.

KEY

Coffee growing regions

TT – A smaller grade again, normally comprising the smaller beans removed from AA, AB and E grades. In density sorting, the lightest beans are usually TT grade.

T – The smallest grade, often made up of chips and broken pieces.

MH/ML – These initials stand for Mbuni Heavy and Mbuni Light. Mbuni is the name used for naturally processed coffees. These are considered low quality, often containing underripe or overripe beans, and they sell for a very low price. They account for around seven per cent of the annual production.

TRACEABILITY

Kenya's coffee is grown both on large estates, and by smallholders who feed their coffee into their local washing station. This means it is possible to get extremely traceable coffees from the single estates, but in recent years the higher-quality coffees have increasingly come from the smallholders. Typically what one might

An aerial view of a coffee plantation in Kenya. The country consistently produces beans of a very high quality, from a variety of sources that include large estates and smallholders.

Population: 44,354,000

Number of 60kg (132lb) bags in 2013: 850,000

Central Kenya produces most of the nation's coffee, and the best Kenyan coffees come from this part of the country. There is growing interest in the coffees being produced in Western Kenya, in the Kisii, Trans-Nzoia, Keiyo and Marakwet regions.

NYERI

The central region of Nyeri is home to the extinct volcano of Mount Kenya. The red soils here produce some of the best coffee in Kenya. Agriculture is hugely important to the area and coffee is one of the main crops. Cooperatives of smallholder producers are common, rather than large estates. The coffee trees in Nyeri produce two crops a year and the main crop tends to produce higher-quality lots.

Altitude: 1,200–2,300m (3,900–7,500ft)

Harvest: October–December (main crop), June–August (fly crop)

Varieties: SL-28, SL-34, Ruiru 11, Batian

MURANG'A

Around 100,000 farmers produce coffee in the Murang'a region, within the Central Province. This inland region was one of the first to be settled by missionaries, who were prevented from settling around the coast by the Portuguese. This is another region that benefits from the volcanic soil, and also has more smallholders than estates.

Altitude: 1,350–1,950m (4,400–6,400ft)

Harvest: October–December (main crop), June–August (fly crop)

Varieties: SL-28, SL-34, Ruiru 11, Batian

KIRINYAGA

The eastern neighbour of Nyeri, this county also benefits from volcanic soils. The coffee tends to be produced by smallholders and the washing stations have been producing some very high-quality lots that are well worth trying.

Altitude: 1,300–1,900m (4,300–6,200ft)

Harvest: October–December (main crop), June–August (fly crop)

Varieties: SL-28, SL-34, Ruiru 11, Batian

EMBU

Near Mount Kenya, this region is named after the town of Embu. Approximately seventy per cent of the population are small-scale farmers, and the most popular cash crops are tea and coffee. Almost all of the coffee comes from smallholders and the region is a relatively small producer.

Altitude: 1,300–1,900m (4,300–6,200ft)

Harvest: October–December (main crop), June–August (fly crop)

Varieties: SL-28, SL-34, Ruiru 11, Batian, K7

MERU

Coffee is grown on the slopes of Mount Kenya and in the Nyambene Hills, mostly by smallholders. The name refers to both the region and the Meru people who inhabit it. In the 1930s, these people were among the first Kenyans to produce coffee, as a result of the Devonshire White Paper of 1923, which asserted the importance of African interests in the country.

find is a particular lot from a washing station that will still carry a size grading (such as AA), though that lot may have come from a group of several hundred farmers. These washing stations (or factories as they are known) play a role in the quality of the final product, so these coffees are definitely worth seeking out.

TASTE PROFILE

Kenyan coffees are renowned for their bright, complex berry/fruit qualities as well as their sweetness and intense acidity.

Opposite: Women grade beans according to their size and quality at a coffee factory in Komothai, in Ruiri, Kenya.

KENYAN VARIETIES

Two particular Kenyan varieties attract great interest from the speciality coffee industry. These are named SL-28 and SL-34, and are among the forty experimental varieties produced as part of the research led by Guy Gibson at Scott Laboratories. These make up the majority of high-quality coffee from Kenya, but they are susceptible to leaf rust.

A lot of work has been done to produce rust-resistant varieties in Kenya. Ruiru 11 was the first to be considered a success by the Kenyan Coffee Board, although it was not warmly received by speciality coffee buyers. More recently, they have released a variety called Batian. There remains some scepticism towards its cup quality after the disappointment of Ruiru, although quality seems to be improving and there is more positivity around the potential of Batian to have great cup quality in the future.

Altitude: 1,300–1,950m (4,300–6,400ft)
Harvest: October–December (main crop), June–August (fly crop)
Varieties: SL-28, SL-34, Ruiru 11, Batian, K7

KIAMBU

This central region's production is dominated by large estates. However, the spread of urbanization has seen the number of estates decline as owners have found it more profitable to sell their land for development. Coffees from the region are often named for places within it, such as Thika, Ruiru and Limuru. Many of the estates are owned by multinational companies, which means that farming practices are often mechanized with an eye towards higher yields rather than quality. There are a reasonable number of smallholders in the region, too.

Altitude: 1,500–2,200m (4,900–7,200ft)
Harvest: October–December (main crop), June–August (fly crop)
Varieties: SL-28, SL-34, Ruiru 11, Batian

MACHAKOS

This is a relatively small county in the centre of the country, named after the town of Machakos. Coffee production here is a mixture of estates and smallholders.

Altitude: 1,400–1,850m (4,600–6,050ft)
Harvest: October–December (main crop), June–August (fly crop)
Varieties: SL-28, SL-34

NAKURU

This region, in the centre of the country, has some of the highest-growing coffee in Kenya. However, some trees suffer from 'dieback' at high altitudes and stop producing. The region is named after the town of Nakuru. Coffee is produced by a mixture of estates and smallholders, although production is relatively low.

Altitude: 1,850–2,200m (6,050–7,200ft)
Harvest: October–December (main crop), June–August (fly crop)
Varieties: SL-28, SL-34, Ruiru 11, Batian

KISII

This region is in the southwest of the country, not far from Lake Victoria. It is a relatively small region and most of the coffee comes from cooperatives of small producers.

Altitude: 1,450–1,800m (4,750–5,900ft)
Harvest: October–December (main crop), June–August (fly crop)
Varieties: SL-28, SL-34, Blue Mountain, K7

TRANS-NZOIA, KEIYO & MARAKWET

This relatively small area of production in Western Kenya has seen some growth in recent years. The slopes of Mount Elgon provide some altitude, and most of the coffee comes from estates. Coffee is often planted to diversify farms that once focused on maize or dairy.

Altitude: 1,500–1,900m (4,900–6,200ft)
Harvest: October–December (main crop), June–August (fly crop)
Varieties: Ruiru 11, Batian, SL-28, SL-34

AFRICA

MALAWI

It seems that coffee was introduced to Malawi in the late 1800s. One claim states that a single tree taken from the Edinburgh Botanical Gardens was brought to the country in 1878 by John Buchnan, a Scottish missionary. It first took root in southern Malawi, in the Blantyre region, and by 1900 annual coffee production was at 1,000 tonnes (1,100 tons).

Despite its auspicious start, coffee production collapsed not long after due to a combination of poorly maintained soils, pests and diseases, and the competition from the increasingly dominant production of Brazil.

For most of the first part of the 20th century there was little African ownership of the large coffee farms as the country was under British colonial rule. However, the cooperative movement started in 1946 and coffee production grew dramatically in the 1950s. While they looked like they might prove to be successful, all the cooperatives were dissolved in 1971 due to political interference. Coffee production in Malawi peaked in the 1990s at 7,000 tonnes (7,700 tons), and has since shrunk back to around 1,500 tonnes (1,650 tons) a year.

Despite the fact that it is landlocked, Malawi has built a strong agricultural export economy. In the case of coffee, some attribute its success to the lack of government interference in export, allowing direct relationships between sellers and buyers. However, for a long time quality was not of particular focus. Grading was a very simple system of Grade 1 and Grade 2, although in recent years there has been movement towards the AA-style grading system used throughout Africa.

The coffee varieties grown in Malawi certainly cover the extremes of the spectrum. There has been quite a lot of Geisha variety planted, the same variety that has generated so much interest in Central America. However, there is also quite a lot of Catimor throughout the country, a disease-resistant variety that is generally of much lower quality.

TRACEABILITY

Coffee in the south of Malawi is generally produced on large-scale, commercial estates and in the central and northern regions by smallholder farmers. Therefore it is possible to trace coffees back to a single farm, or to a large group of producers. Generally there should be excellent coffees available from both.

TASTE PROFILE

The coffees can be quite sweet and clean, though rarely as explosively fruity and complex as other coffees from East Africa.

Population: 16,363,000

Number of 60kg (132lb) bags in 2013:
30,000

Coffees from Malawi are rarely identified by their regions, and the regions themselves could be considered as defined pockets of coffee growing, rather than definable areas with distinct characteristics determined by the local terroir and microclimate.

CHITIPA DISTRICT

This area has a reputation of growing some of the best coffee in Malawi. It is close to the Songwe River, which provides a natural border between Malawi and Tanzania to the north. This area is home to the large Misuku Hills Cooperative.

Altitude: 1,700–2,000m (5,600–6,600ft)
Harvest: April–September
Varieties: Agaro, Geisha, Catimor, Mundo Novo, Caturra

RUMPHI DISTRICT

This area is located in the north of the country, close to Lake Malawi in the eastern part of the Nyika National Park. There are several areas here with clusters of producers, such as Chakak, Mphachi, Salawe, Junji and VunguVungu. The Phoka Hills and Viphya North cooperatives are located here.

Altitude: 1,200–2,500m (3,900–8,100ft)
Harvest: April–September
Varieties: Agaro, Geisha, Catimor, Mundo Novo, Caturra

NORTH VIPHYA

This region covers part of the North Viphya Plateau, which is separated from Nkhata Bay Highlands by the Lizunkhumi river valley.

Altitude: 1,200–1,500m (3,900–4,900ft)
Harvest: April–September
Varieties: Agaro, Geisha, Catimor, Mundo Novo, Caturra

SOUTHEAST MZIMBA

This region is named for the city of Mzimba, and there are several valley and river systems running through it.

Altitude: 1,200–1,700m (3,900–5,600ft)
Harvest: April–September
Varieties: Agaro, Geisha, Catimor, Mundo Novo, Caturra

NKHATA BAY HIGHLANDS

This region is just to the east of the regional capital city of Mzuzu.

Altitude: 1,000–2,000m (3,300–6,600ft)
Harvest: April–September
Varieties: Agaro, Geisha, Catimor, Mundo Novo, Caturra

Below: Coffee plantations in Malawi have a strong agricultural export economy and most coffee can be traced to a single farm.

Carrying 60kg (132lb) bags of freshly picked cherries, these Malawi women harvest coffee from one of the large-scale commercial estates that are common in northern and central regions of the country.

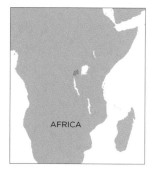

AFRICA

RWANDA

German missionaries first brought coffee to Rwanda in 1904, but the country did not produce enough to begin exports until 1917. After World War I, the League of Nations Mandate stripped Germany of its colonial rule over Rwanda, and handed it to the Belgians. This is why, historically, most of Rwanda's coffee has been exported to Belgium.

The first coffee trees were planted at the Mibirizi mission in Cyangugu province, and the place gives its name to the first Rwandan coffee variety, a natural mutation of Bourbon (see box on page 144). Gradually coffee cultivation spread into the Kivu region and ultimately the rest of Rwanda. In the 1930s, coffee became a compulsory crop for many producers around the country, mirroring the Belgian colonial approach in neighbouring Burundi.

The Belgians strictly controlled exports and enforced high taxes on the growers. This pushed Rwanda towards producing high volumes of low-quality coffee, which sold for low prices. However, the fact that Rwanda exported so little gave coffee an oversized impact and

a sense of importance for the farmers. There was little infrastructure to allow the production of quality coffee, not even a single washing station.

By the 1990s, coffee was Rwanda's most valuable export, but the events of the decade would decimate the coffee industry. In 1994, the widespread genocide in the country claimed nearly one million lives, and had a massive impact on the coffee industry. This was compounded by worldwide coffee prices falling to a very low level.

COFFEE'S ROLE IN RWANDA'S RECOVERY

Coffee was to become a symbol of positivity as Rwanda got back on its feet following the genocide. As foreign aid and interest streamed into the country, there was a strong focus on the coffee sector. Washing stations were built and there was a determined drive towards producing higher-quality coffee. The government took a more open approach to the coffee trade, and speciality coffee buyers from around the world have shown a strong interest in the country's coffees. Rwanda is the only African country to have hosted a Cup of Excellence competition, a project to find the very best lots and to bring them to market through an online auction system.

The first washing station was built in 2004 with assistance from the United States Agency for International Development (USAID). Many more followed and the number has grown dramatically in recent years with around three hundred in operation today. The PEARL project (Partnership for Enhancing Agriculture in Rwanda through Linkages) was successful in helping to spread knowledge and train young agronomists. It has since become the SPREAD

KEY

Coffee growing regions

UGANDA

DEMOCRATIC REPUBLIC OF THE CONGO

TANZANIA

NYAGATARE

Byumba

Gisenyi

GAKENKE

RWANDA

KAYONZA

RUTSIRO

KIGALI

Lake Kivu

KAMONY

Rwamagana

Kibuye

Gitarama

KARONGI

NGOMA

KIREHE

NYAMASHEKE

Nyanza

NYAMAGABE

HUYE

Cyangugu

Butare

0   miles   30

0   km   30

BURUNDI

Above: At a coffee washing station in Butare, a worker keeps the coffee cherries moving as the depulping machine separates the seeds from the fruit flesh.

project (Sustaining Partnerships to enhance Rural Enterprise and Agribusiness Development) and both projects have focused their efforts in the Butare region.

Rwanda is known as the 'land of a thousand hills' and certainly has the altitude and weather to grow great coffee. However, there is the problem of widespread soil depletion and transport still poses a challenge, often adding great expense to production costs.

When worldwide coffee prices increased around 2010, it was a challenge in Rwanda (and much of the rest of the world) to find suitable incentives to keep quality high. When the market pays high prices, there is little reason to spend money to increase quality, as even low-quality coffee is sufficiently profitable. However, recently the quality of Rwandan coffees has been excellent. Rwanda does grow and export a small amount of Robusta, but most of its output is fully washed Arabica.

THE POTATO DEFECT

This is a particular and unusual defect found only in coffees from Burundi and Rwanda. It is caused by an unknown bacteria entering the cherry's skin and producing an unpleasant toxin. It is not harmful to health, but when afflicted beans are roasted and ground they release an unmistakeable and pungent aroma that is eerily similar to the smell of peeling a raw potato. This defect affects only specific beans, so finding it in your coffee does not mean the whole bag is spoiled, unless it has all been ground.

Eradication is tricky. It is undetectable once post-harvest processing is finished, so a coffee roaster cannot do anything to detect it before roasting. Even after roasting it is difficult to discover until a bean with the defect is ground. It is possible to do some work during processing to identify the cherries that have had their skins broken and are likely to be tainted. Work is being done both on the ground and at research level to eradicate this particular defect.

TRACEABILITY

Coffees in Rwanda tend to be traceable back to washing stations and the numerous farmer groups and cooperatives that supply them. Each producer has on average just 183 trees, so it is not possible to find a coffee traceable to a single producer.

TASTE PROFILE

Amazing coffees from Rwanda often have a fruitiness and freshness reminiscent of red apples or red grapes. Berry fruit flavours and floral qualities are also fairly common.

LOCAL VARIETIES

MIBIRIZI

This is the name of the mission in Rwanda that received some Bourbon trees from Guatemala. Mibirizi is a natural variant of Bourbon, which appeared at the mission. It was initially grown in Rwanda and later spread to Burundi in the 1930s.

JACKSON

This is another Bourbon variant that was initially grown in Rwanda and has since spread to Burundi.

Population: 10,537,000

Number of 60kg (132lb) bags in 2013: 300,000

Coffee is grown across the whole of Rwanda, without specific geographic zones of constriction. Roasters may use the name of a district along with the name of the washing station or farmer group.

Above: Workers spread the coffee out on drying tables, where it will dry out for five days, in preparation for roasting or export.

SOUTHERN AND WESTERN REGION

Some stunning coffees come from this part of the country. Production seems particularly focused around the mountainous Huye region, the Nyamagabe region and the Nyamasheke region on the shores of Lake Kivu.

Altitude: 1,700–2,200m (5,600–7,200ft)
Harvest: March–June
Varieties: Bourbon, Mibirizi

EASTERN REGION

The altitude in the east of the country is not as high as in other regions, but great coffees are being produced in Ngoma and in Nyagatare in the extreme northeast.

Altitude: 1,300–1,900m (4,300–6,200ft)
Harvest: March–June
Varieties: Bourbon, Mibirizi

TANZANIA

AFRICA

Oral histories tell of coffee coming to Tanzania from Ethiopia in the 16th century. Brought by the Haya people and known as 'Haya Coffee' or *amwani*, this was probably a Robusta variety and has since become strongly entwined in Tanzanian culture. The ripe cherries would be boiled, then smoked for several days and chewed rather than brewed into a drink.

Coffee first became a cash crop for Tanzania (previously Tanganyika) under German colonial rule. In 1911, the colonists mandated the planting of Arabica coffee trees throughout the Bukoba region. Their methods were very different from the way the Haya people had traditionally dealt with coffee growing, and the Haya were reluctant to replace their food crops with coffee. However, the region did start to produce more and more coffee. Other parts of the country were less familiar with coffee, and so provided less resistance to growing it. The Chagga tribe, living around Mount Kilimanjaro, switched completely to coffee production when Germany put an end to the slave trade.

After World War I, control of the region fell to the British. They launched a campaign to plant over ten million seedlings in Bukoba but they, too, fell into conflict with the Haya, which often resulted in trees being uprooted. As a result, there was not a strong growth in production in the region, compared to that in the Chagga region. However, the first cooperative was formed in 1925, called the Kilimanjaro Native Planters' Association (KNPA). This was the first of several cooperatives, and the producers enjoyed their new-found ability to sell more directly to London and to achieve better prices.

After independence was granted in 1961, the Tanzanian government turned its attention to coffee, hoping to double production by 1970 – a goal they did not achieve. After struggling with low growth in industry, high levels of inflation and a declining economy, the government changed to a multiparty democracy.

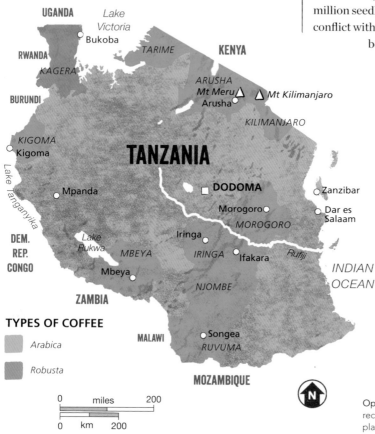

TYPES OF COFFEE

Arabica

Robusta

Opposite: Overlooked by Mount Kilimanjaro, these recently planted coffee trees form part of a new plantation in Mwika, Tanzania.

Above: A worker sorts through dried, harvested beans at a factory near the Ngorongoro Crater, Tanzania. The coffee produced in this country is almost entirely harvested from smallholder farms.

During the early and mid-1990s, reforms were implemented in the coffee industry to allow the more direct sale of coffee from producers to buyers, instead of driving everything through the State Coffee Marketing Board. The coffee industry suffered a serious setback in the late 1990s when coffee wilt disease spread through the country and caused significant losses of coffee trees in the north, close to the border with Uganda. Today

Tanzania's coffee production is about seventy per cent Arabica and thirty per cent Robusta.

TRACEABILITY

Around ninety per cent of coffee in Tanzania is produced by its 450,000 smallholder farmers. The remaining ten per cent comes from larger estates. It is possible to find coffees traceable back to a cooperative of growers and their washing station, or back to a single farm if it is an estate coffee. The better coffees I have tasted in recent years have come from the estates, and I would recommend seeking them out first.

GRADING

Tanzania uses what is sometimes called the British nomenclature of grading, similar to that in Kenya (see page 133). These grades include AA, A, B, PB, C, E, F, AF, TT, UG and TEX.

TASTE PROFILE

Complex, with bright and lively acidity and often with berry and fruity flavours, Tanzanian coffees can be juicy, interesting and delicious.

Population: 44,929,000

Number of 60kg (132lb) bags in 2013: 750,000

Tanzania produces a reasonable quantity of Robusta, although this production is focused in the northwest, near Lake Victoria. The other growing regions are, in some ways, defined by their high altitude.

KILIMANJARO

This is the oldest growing area in Tanzania for Arabica, so it is fair to say that it has had the most time to develop its recognition internationally and build its reputation. The long tradition of coffee production here means there is better infrastructure and facilities, although a lot of the trees are now very old and have comparatively low yields. Increasingly, coffee is facing competition from other crops.

Altitude: 1,050–2,500m (3,500–8,100ft)

Harvest: July–December

Varieties: Kent, Bourbon, Typica, Typica/Nyara

ARUSHA

Arusha borders the region around Mount Kilimanjaro, and in many ways is very similar. This region surrounds Mount Meru, an active volcano that has been quiet since 1910.

Altitude: 1,100–1,800m (3,600–5,900ft)

Harvest: July–December

Varieties: Kent, Bourbon, Typica, Typica/Nyara

RUVUMA

This region takes its name from the Ruvuma river and is in the extreme south of the country. The coffee tends to be centred around the Mbingo district, and is considered to have great potential for high quality, although in the past it has been held back by a lack of access to finance.

Altitude: 1,200–1,800m (3,900–5,900ft)

Harvest: June–October

Varieties: Kent, Bourbon, Bourbon derivatives such as N5 and N39

MBEYA

Centred around the city of Mbeya in the south of the country, this region is a key producer of high-value export crops including coffee, tea, cacao and spices. The area has recently seen increased interest from certification groups and non-government organizations looking to improve the quality of the coffee produced, which traditionally has not always been very high.

Altitude: 1,200–2,000m (3,900–6,600ft)

Harvest: June–October

Varieties: Kent, Bourbon, Typica

TARIME

This is a small region in the far north of the country, bordering Kenya, with a limited international profile. It is starting to produce some higher-quality coffees and has the opportunity to expand its production. It has a relatively low production and limited infrastructure for coffee processing, but the increased attention it has seen recently has led to coffee production being tripled in the last ten years.

Altitude: 1,500–1,800m (4,900–5,900ft)

Harvest: July–December

Varieties: Kent, Bourbon, Typica, Robustas

KIGOMA

This region is named for the regional capital city of Kigoma, and is situated on a plateau of gently rolling hills in the northeast of the country near the border with Burundi. The region has produced some stunning coffees, though the industry there is still in its infancy compared to the rest of the country.

Altitude: 1,100–1,700m (3,600–5,600ft)

Harvest: July–December

Varieties: Kent, Bourbon, Typica

AFRICA

ZAMBIA

Zambia has been, for quite some time, overlooked by much of the speciality coffee industry. One could argue that it is a chicken-and-egg situation, as historically little interest from speciality buyers has led to little investment in quality, and little investment in quality has led to little interest from speciality buyers.

Coffee was introduced to Zambia in the 1950s, by missionaries who brought Bourbon seed stock from Tanzania and Kenya. However, the industry did not gear up production until the late 1970s and early 1980s with the assistance of funding from the World Bank. Problems with pests and diseases led growers to adopt the Catimor hybrid, which is less delicious than Bourbon. This was, in some ways, a temporary switch and the government went back to recommending Bourbon, but there is still a fair amount of Catimor in the country.

Zambia's coffee exports peaked in 2005/2006 at around 6,500 tonnes (7,150 tons), but have dropped

Above and right: Once ripened, coffee cherries are picked by workers on Zambia's plantations, most of which are large, well-run estates that have good access to modern equipment.

dramatically since. Some attribute the drop to low prices and a crucial lack of long-term financing in the industry. In addition to this, the country's largest producer closed in 2008 after defaulting on its loans. The Northern Coffee Corp was producing one-third of the country's 6,000 tonnes (6,600 tons) at the time of closure. Total production dropped to just 300 tonnes (330 tons) in 2012, although it now seems to be recovering.

Most of Zambia's coffee comes from larger estates, although there has been some encouragement of smallholders too. The estates are generally well run, have good access to modern equipment (because coffee production started relatively late here), and may be owned by multinationals. Smallholder farming has struggled to take hold, access to fertilizers and equipment has been difficult and generally the quality has not been high. The lack of access to water and decent post-harvest

processing has further hindered the production of clean, sweet coffees.

TRACEABILITY

The best coffees in Zambia tend to come from single estates, although you may have to look hard for them. Not only is overall production small in Zambia, but high-quality coffees are not commonplace. Frustratingly, the country has the undeniable potential to produce stellar coffees, from its seed stock to its geography.

GROWING REGIONS

Population: 14,580,000
Number of 60kg (132lb) bags in 2013: 10,000

The regions in Zambia are not well defined, and are typically just referred to as Southern, Central, Copperbelt and Northern regions. Coffee is mainly grown in the Northern district of the Muchinga Mountains (an area that includes the regions of Isoka, Nakonde and Kasama) and around the capital city Lusaka.

Altitude: 900–2,000m (3,000–6,600ft)
Harvest: April–September
Varieties: Bourbon, Catimor

ASIA

Myth and history have shaped the inheritance of coffee cultivation in Asia. From Robusta beans smuggled into India by a pilgrim from Yemen to the lucrative export of Indonesian beans by the Dutch East India Company during the 16th century, Asia now supplies a significant percentage of commodity-grade coffee to the market. Yemen is perhaps the notable exception – its comparatively small export quantities of unique beans remain in strong demand globally.

ASIA

INDIA

The origins of coffee production in southern India are entwined with myth. The story goes that a pilgrim named Baba Budan passed through Yemen in 1670 while returning from Mecca and smuggled out seven coffee seeds, the export of which was strictly controlled. Because he took seven, a sacrosanct number in Islam, it was considered a religious act.

Baba Budan planted these first seeds in what is now known as the Chikmagalur district of the Karnataka region and there they thrived. The hills there now bear his name, Bababudangiri, and this is still an important coffee-growing area.

It wasn't until the middle of the 19th century, under British colonial rule, that coffee plantations in southern India began to flourish. This was short-lived, however, and coffee's popularity began to wane again. In the 1870s the industry suffered due to an increasing demand for tea, combined with an increasing incidence of leaf rust, which attacked the coffee plants. Many plantations switched to tea production, ironically the same plantations that had been successful exporting their coffee. Leaf rust did not drive coffee out of India, however, but instead encouraged research into rust-resistant varieties. This research was relatively successful and some new varieties were bred, although this was before the flavour of the coffee was deemed to be very important.

In 1942, the Coffee Board of India was created, by way of a government act that began the regulation of the industry. Some argue that by pooling coffees from many producers, the government reduced incentives for producers to improve the quality of their coffee. However, production certainly grew and in the 1990s India's output increased by an astonishing thirty per cent.

During the 1990s there was also a decrease in regulation governing how and where producers could sell their coffee. The domestic coffee market in India also grew rapidly. While India has a very low per capita consumption of coffee, tea being a far cheaper alternative, the population is so large that the total consumption is quite sizeable. The annual consumption per person is just 100g (3 1/2oz), but this results in a total consumption of two million bags of coffee per year. India produces just over five million bags in total, although the majority of this is Robusta.

Robusta is, in many ways, better suited to India than Arabica. The lower altitudes and climate make Robusta yields high. More care and attention is paid to the production of Robusta in India than in most other countries so it occupies the premium end of the market.

Left: Although tea is generally more popular in India, the country consumes two million of the five million bags of coffee it produces annually, most of which is the Robusta variety.

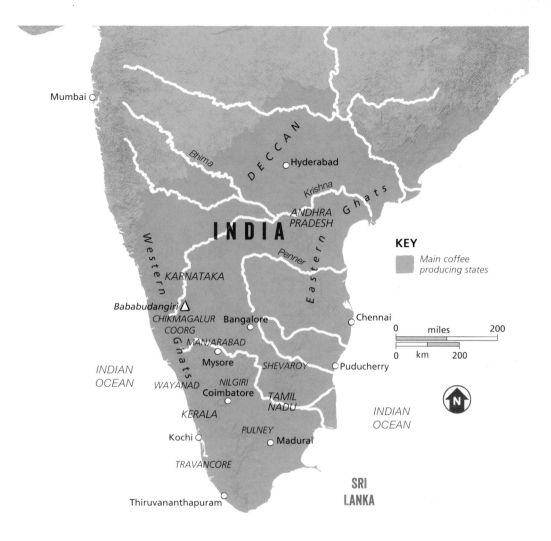

Even the best Robustas still carry the distinctive woody flavours of the species, but the relative lack of unclean flavours in Indian Robustas makes them popular with roasters who still like Robusta in their espresso blends.

MONSOONING

One of the better-known coffees from India is called Monsoon Malabar, and it is created by an unusual process called 'monsooning'. Monsooning is now a controlled process, but it began completely by accident. During its export from India to Europe at the time of the British Raj, coffee was transported in wooden boxes and was, therefore, subjected to the wet weather that came during the monsoon months. The raw coffee absorbed a great deal of moisture, which had a strong effect on the resulting cup of coffee.

As export practices improved, the demand for this unusual coffee still remained so the process was recreated in factories along the west coast. Monsooning is only done with naturally processed coffees; the raw coffee looks very pale afterwards and is somewhat brittle. Monsooned beans are difficult to roast evenly, and their brittle nature means that a bag of roasted coffee often contains lots of beans that have been damaged in the packing process. This is nothing to worry about, however, and is not the same thing as low-grade coffees that contain broken pieces in them and should be avoided.

During the monsooning process, coffee usually loses its acidity, but often gains pungent, wild flavours that make it somewhat divisive in the coffee industry. Some love the richness and intensity of the cup, while others believe the flavours are the result of defective processing and are very unpleasant.

TRACEABILITY

Because 98 per cent of India's 250,000 coffee producers are small growers, it is often difficult to find coffees traceable down to a single estate. However, these are often worth seeking out. Traceability may only be possible back to the point of processing or to a specific region.

TASTE PROFILE

The best coffees from India tend to be heavy, creamy and low in acidity, but rarely particularly complex.

GROWING REGIONS

Population: 1,210,193,000
Number of 60kg (132lb) bags in 2012: 5,303,000

Most of India's coffee is grown in four main states, each of which can be subdivided into a number of smaller geographic regions.

TAMIL NADU

Tamil Nadu (which translates simply as 'land of the Tamils') is the southernmost of India's 28 states. The capital city is Chennai (formerly Madras), and the region is famous for its monumental Hindu temples.

PULNEY

This is the largest area of coffee production in the state. There are a number of challenges here for the coffee growers, including a high incidence of leaf rust (which determines the choice of varieties to grow), labour shortages, absentee ownership, and a scarcity of water for post-harvest processing.

Altitude: 600–2,000m (2,000–6,600ft)
Harvest: October–February
Varieties: S795, Selection 5B, Selection 9, Selection 10, Cauvery

NILGIRI

Many growers in this mountainous region are tribal and have smallholdings with financial constraints. This region produces around twice as much Robusta as Arabica, and struggles with high rainfall and many different kinds of pests, including coffee berry borer. It is the westernmost of the growing regions, bordering Karnataka and Kerala.

Altitude: 900–1,400m (3,000–4,600ft)
Harvest: October–February
Varieties: S795, Kent, Cauvery, Robustas

SHEVAROY

This region produces almost exclusively Arabica. Most of the farmers in the region are smallholders, but the distribution of land is skewed in favour of larger farms. Only 5 per cent of the farms occupy around 75 per cent of the land under coffee. One of the problems with large farms in the area is the trend towards monocultures of trees used to shade the coffee, silver oak being extremely common here. Many consider that a diverse range of shade trees is important for biodiversity and sustainable production.

Altitude: 900–1,500m (3,000–4,900ft)
Harvest: October–February
Varieties: S795, Cauvery, Selection 9

KARNATAKA

This state produces the majority of the nation's coffee. It used to be known as Mysore, but was renamed Karnataka in 1973. The meaning of the name is not completely agreed, opinion divided between 'elevated lands' and 'the black region', the latter being a reference to the black cotton soil (vertisol) found in the area.

BABABUDANGIRI

This region is considered the home of Indian coffee, where Baba Budan first planted the seeds he smuggled from Yemen.

Altitude: 1000–1,500m (3,300–4,900ft)
Harvest: October–February
Varieties: S795, Selection 9, Cauvery

Left: Coffee berries dry in the sun at Coorg, part of the Tamil Nadu, one of India's four main coffee growing states.

CHIKMAGALUR

This is a larger region that encompasses Bababudangiri within it. It is centred around, and named for, the city of Chikmagalur. The region produces slightly more Robusta than it does Arabica.

Altitude: 700–1,200m (2,300–3,900ft)
Harvest: October–February
Varieties: S795, Selection 5B, Selection 9, Cauvery, Robustas

COORG

Many plantations in this region were started by the British in the 19th century, then sold to the locals when India gained independence in 1947. Nearly twice as much land here is used to grow Robusta as Arabica so, with its higher yield, nearly three times as much Robusta as Arabica is produced in the region.

Altitude: 750–1,100m (2,450–3,600ft)
Harvest: October–February
Varieties: S795, Selection 6, Selection 9, Robustas

MANJARABAD

This area is more focused on Arabica, although several of its estates have been recognized for the quality of their Robustas through competitions run by the Coffee Board of India.

Altitude: 900–1,100m (3,000–3,600ft)
Harvest: October–February
Varieties: S795, Selection 6, Selection 9, Cauvery

KERALA

This southwestern state produces just under one-third of the total Indian coffee production. It is home to the Malabar coast, and therefore the Monsooned Malabar coffees, and organic coffee production has had greater success in this region than any other. The export of spices began here in the 1500s, which brought the first Portuguese to the region and established a trade route that would pave the way for the European colonization of India.

TRAVANCORE

This region grows mostly Robusta, although some Arabicas are produced at higher altitudes.

Altitude: 400–1,600m (1,300–5,200ft)
Harvest: October–February
Varieties: S274, Robustas

WAYANAD

The low altitude in this part of India really only lends itself to Robusta production.

Altitude: 600–900m (2,000–3,000ft)
Harvest: October–February
Varieties: Robustas, S274

ANDHRA PRADESH

The Eastern Ghats mountain range runs along the east coast of India, providing the necessary altitude for coffee. Only a relatively small amount of coffee is produced in this region, though the majority is Arabica.

Altitude: 900–1,100m (3,000–3,600ft)
Harvest: October–February
Varieties: S795, Selection 4, Selection 5, Cauvery

A coffee plantation in a forest near the hill station of Madikeri. The region is part of an important coffee-growing area known as Chikamagalur, which is recognized as the birthplace of coffee in India.

ASIA

INDONESIA

The first attempt to grow coffee on the Indonesian archipelago was a failure. In 1696 the Governor of Jakarta (then Batavia) was sent a present of a few coffee seedlings by the Dutch Governor of Malabar in India. These plants were lost in a flood in Jakarta, so a second shipment was sent in 1699. These plants flourished.

Exports of coffee began in 1711, and were controlled by the Dutch East India Company, usually referred to by its Dutch initials VOC (Vereenigde Oostindische Compagniey). Coffee arriving in Amsterdam sold for high prices, 1kg (2lb) costing nearly one per cent of the average annual income. The price slowly came down during the 18th century, but coffee was undeniably very profitable for the VOC. However, as Java was under colonial rule at the time, it was not at all profitable for the farmers who grew it. In 1860 a Dutch colonial official wrote a novel entitled *Max Havelaar: Or the Coffee Auctions of the Dutch Trading Company,* which described the abuses of the colonial system. This book had a lasting impact on Dutch society, changing public opinion about the way coffee was traded and the colonial system in general. The name Max Havelaar is now used for an ethical certification within the coffee industry.

Initially Indonesia produced only Arabica, but coffee leaf rust wiped out much of the crop in 1876. There was some attempt to plant the Liberica species instead, but that also suffered at the hands of leaf rust, so production switched to the disease-resistant Robusta. Today Robusta still makes up a significant portion of the crop.

GILING BASAH

One of the unique aspects of coffee production in Indonesia, and the source of Indonesian coffee's deeply divisive taste, is the traditional post-harvest process of *giling basah*. This hybrid process combines elements of the washed and natural processes and is described on page 37. This semi-washed process has a dramatic effect on the cup quality. It significantly reduces the acidity of the coffee, and seems to increase its body too, creating a softer, rounder, heavier-bodied cup of coffee.

However, it also introduces a gamut of additional flavours, sometimes vegetal or herbal, sometimes woody or musty, sometimes earthy. This is not to say that all coffee processed this way is uniform in quality and has gone through some sort of flavour standardization. There are huge variations in the quality of these coffees.

The flavour of semi-washed coffees is particularly divisive within the coffee industry. If a coffee from Africa or Central America displayed the same flavours, regardless of how well the process was done, it would be considered defective and rejected immediately by any potential buyers. However, there are many people who find the intensity and heavy-bodied cups of coffee brewed from Indonesian semi-washed lots delicious, and so the industry continues to buy them.

In recent years, speciality buyers have encouraged producers throughout Indonesia to experiment more with the washed process (see page 33) to allow some appreciation of the taste of the variety and the land rather than the dominant flavours of the process. We shall see if demand for these coffees is strong enough to encourage widespread production of cleaner coffees, or if the industry will see continued demand for semi-washed lots and simply continue to meet it.

TASTE PROFILE

Semi-washed coffees tend to be very heavy bodied, earthy, woody and spicy with very little acidity.

Opposite: An Indonesian woman scales a large coffee tree to harvest the crop. Coffee has been exported from here since the 16th century, when the Dutch East India Company established a lucrative trade.

KOPI LUWAK

In Indonesia, Kopi Luwak refers to coffees that are produced by collecting the droppings of civet cats that have eaten coffee cherries. This semi-digested coffee is separated from the faecal matter and then processed and dried. In the last decade it has come to be seen as an amusing novelty, with unattributed claims of its excellent flavours, and it sells for spectacularly high prices. This has caused two main problems.

Firstly, the forgery of this coffee is quite commonplace. Several times more is sold than produced, and often low-grade Robusta is being passed off at high prices.

Secondly, it has encouraged unscrupulous operators on the islands to trap and cage civet cats, force-feed them with coffee cherries and keep them in terrible conditions.

I find Kopi Luwak abhorrent on just about every level. If you are interested in delicious coffee then it is a terrible waste of money. One-quarter of the money you might spend on a bag could instead buy you a stunning coffee from one of the very best producers in the world. I can only regard the practice as abusive and unethical and I believe people should avoid all animal-processed coffees, and not reward this despicable behaviour with their money.

TRACEABILITY

While it is possible to find coffees from individual farms on the islands, these are relatively rare. However, those that have been kept traceable, and have been fully washed (rather than semi-washed) are definitely worth trying.

Most coffee is produced by smallholders with just 1–2 hectares (2.2–4.4 acres) of land so usually a coffee is only traceable down to a specific washing station, or only a region. There is very wide variation in the quality of these regional coffees, and they can be something of a gamble.

Left: Large baskets of Robusta berries are raked out to dry in the sun in Tanggamus, Lampung Province, one of the largest coffee-producing regions in Indonesia.

GROWING REGIONS

Population: 237,424,000

Number of 60kg (132lb) bags in 2013: 11,667,000

From its origins in Java, coffee slowly spread around the other islands in the region, first to Sulawesi in 1750. It didn't reach Northern Sumatra until 1888, first being grown around Toba lake, and eventually appeared in the Tawar lake region in Gayo in 1924.

SUMATRA

The island of Sumatra has three main growing regions: the province of Aceh in the north, the Lake Toba region a little to the south and, more recently, coffee has been produced in the south of the island around Mangkuraja. It may be possible to trace coffees to smaller areas within these regions: Takengon or Bener Mariah in the Aceh region; and Lintong, Sidikalang, Dolok Sanggul or Seribu Dolok around Lake Toba. Traceability down to this level is relatively recent.

In the past it was common to see coffee sold under the name of 'Sumatra Mandheling'. There is no place called Mandheling, the name refers to an ethnic group from the island. Often Mandheling coffees were given a grade, either 1 or 2. The grading is apparently based on the cup quality rather than the green coffee, which is more usual, but I would be hesitant to recommend all grade 1's because the awarding can occasionally seem somewhat random.

It is unusual to separate different varieties into different lots, so most Sumatran coffee will probably be a mixture of unknown varieties. Coffees from Sumatra are shipped out of the port of Medan, but the hot, humid climate can have a negative effect on the coffee if it is left on the dockside too long before being shipped.

Altitude: Aceh 1,100–1,300m (3,600–4,300ft), Lake Toba 1,100–1,600m (3,600–5,200ft), Mangkuraja 1,100–1,300m (3,600–4,300ft)

Harvest: September–December

Varieties: Typica (including Bergandal, Sidikalang and Djember), TimTim, Ateng, Onan Ganjang

OLD BROWN JAVA

Some estates in Java choose to age their coffee before export, for anything up to five years. The raw coffee beans turn from the blue-green commonly associated with semi-washed coffee, through to a muddy shade of brown. Once roasted there is no acidity left in the coffee whatsoever, and there is an intense pungency and woodiness that some enjoy. However, if you like your coffee sweet, clean and lively, you may well hate it.

JAVA

It is more common to find large coffee estates here than anywhere else in Indonesia, due to the colonial history and practices of the Dutch. The four largest farms, previously government estates, cover over 4,000 hectares (8,800 acres) between them. For a long time the island enjoyed a stellar reputation for its coffee, although I am sure it was not long before other coffees came to substitute the real thing in the 'Mocha-Java' blend of a great many roasters. Javan coffees commanded huge premiums for a long time, although prices fell towards the end of the 20th century.

Much of the coffee is planted on the east side of Java, around the Ijen volcano, but there are producers on the west side of the island, too.

Altitude: 900–1,800m (3,000–5,900ft)

Harvest: July–September

Varieties: Typicas, Ateng, USDA

VARIETY NAMES

Variety names in Sumatra can be a little tricky. Most of the Arabica seed stock initially brought to the island would have been derived from the strain of Typica that was taken from Yemen. In Sumatra this is often called Djember Typica, but it should be noted that Djember also refers to a completely different variety (a less superior one) found in Sulawesi.

It is common to see varieties that have, at some point, been cross-bred with Robusta. The best-known hybrid is called the Hybrido de Timor, a parent of the more common Catimor variety. In Sumatra it is often called TimTim.

SULAWESI

Most of the coffee from Sulawesi is produced by smallholders, although there are seven large estates which make up about five per cent of the total production. Most of the Arabica on the island is grown high up around Tana Toraja. To the south is the city of Kalosi, which became a kind of brand name for coffees from the region. There are two other less well-known coffee-growing regions: Mamasa to the west, and Gowa south of Kalosi. Some of the most interesting coffees from the island are fully washed, and can be exceptionally enjoyable. I would recommend seeking them out if you get the opportunity. The semi-washed process is still common though, and the island also produces a good amount of Robusta. Coffee production can be somewhat disorganized throughout the region, as many smallholders grow coffee for supplemental income, concentrating their efforts on other crops.

Altitude: Tana Toraja 1,100–1,800m (3,600–5,900ft), Mamasa 1300–1700m (4,300–5,600ft), Gowa average of 850m (2,800ft)
Harvest: May–November
Varieties: S795, Typicas, Ateng

FLORES

Flores is a small island about 320km (200 miles) to the east of Bali, and among the Indonesian islands it was a latecomer to both growing coffee and developing a strong reputation for it. In the past it was not uncommon for a large portion of the coffee from Flores to be sold internally or blended into other coffees rather than being exported as 'Flores coffee'. The island has a mixture of active and dormant volcanoes, which have had a positive effect on the soils. One of the key growing regions is Bajawa. In terms of coffee processing, the semi-washed process is still extremely common in the area, although there is some fully-washed coffee being produced.

Altitude: 1,200–1,800m (3,900–5,900ft)
Harvest: May–September
Varieties: Ateng, Typicas, Robusta

BALI

Coffee came to Bali fairly late, and it was initially grown on the highland plateau of Kintamani. Coffee production in Bali suffered a significant setback in 1963 when the Gunung Agung volcano erupted, killing two thousand people and causing widespread devastation to the east of the island. By the late 1970s and early 1980s the government was doing more to promote coffee production, in part by handing out Arabica seedlings. One could argue that this had limited success, however, as today around eighty per cent of the island's production is Robusta.

While tourism provides the largest income for the island, agriculture is its biggest employer. In the past, Japan bought a substantial portion, if not all, of the coffee crop.

Altitude: 1,250–1,700m (4,100–5,600ft)
Harvest: May–October
Varieties: Typica and Typica derivatives, Robusta

Below: Raw coffee beans are dried at a plantation in Bali. Coffee production creates significant employment in the region and much of the coffee harvest is sold to Japan.

ASIA

PAPUA NEW GUINEA

Many people would associate Papua New Guinea's coffees with those from Indonesia, but it would be unfair to do so. Papua New Guinea rightly stands apart and the eastern half of New Guinea shares relatively little with neighbouring Papua when it comes to coffee.

The history of coffee production on the island is not long. While coffee was planted relatively early, in the 1890s, it was not treated as a commercial product at first. In 1926, however, 18 estates were established using seeds from Jamaica's Blue Mountain, and by 1928 coffee production had begun in earnest.

The industry began a more structured growth in the 1950s, with the creation of infrastructure to help facilitate the movement of coffee around the island.

Opposite: Plantations in Papua New Guinea's Eastern and Western Highlands are the most notable areas for coffee, most of which are owned by smallholders.

Further growth followed in the 1970s, perhaps spurred on by Brazil's drop back in production. The government sponsored a series of programmes to encourage small farms to be run by cooperatives. At that time the industry was more focused around managed estates, but since the 1980s the industry has begun to change and decentralize. This is probably due to the drop in coffee prices, which has left many estates in financial trouble. Smallholders aren't at such risk from market forces and so have been able to continue to produce coffee.

Today 95 per cent of producers are smallholders, often subsistence farmers. They produce around 90 per cent of the country's coffee, which is almost entirely Arabica. This means a very large proportion of the population is involved in the production of coffee, especially in the

PACIFIC OCEAN

Manus Island

Bismarck Archipelago

New Ireland

Wewak

Sepik

PAPUA NEW GUINEA

WESTERN HIGHLANDS

Madang

Kimbe

New Britain

Bougainville
Arawa

Mount Hagen

Mount Wilhelm

Goroka

CHIMBU

EASTERN HIGHLANDS

Lae

Solomon Sea

SOLOMON ISLANDS

INDONESIA

Fly

Gulf of Papua

PORT MORESBY

KEY

Coffee growing regions

0   miles   100

0   km   100

Above: Although coffee production in Papua New Guinea only took hold in the 20th century, it is now an established crop. Arabica forms the majority of exports and is mostly grown in highland regions.

highland regions. This has certainly presented challenges when it comes to producing large quantities of high-quality coffee, as many producers lack access to proper post-harvest facilities, and a lack of traceability in the product prevents clear rewards for higher-quality coffee.

TRACEABILITY

Several large estates still operate very successfully, so it is possible to find coffees from a single estate. There

GRADING

Exports are graded by quality, in descending order: AA, A, X, PSC and Y. The first three are awarded to estate coffees, while the last two are grades for smallholder coffees, PSC standing for Premium Smallholder Coffee.

is not a long history of traceability, and in the past some farms were acquiring coffee from other producers to pass off as their own. The idea of coffee being sold by region is also relatively new. However, the altitude and soils in the country offer great potential for quality, so there has been renewed interest from the speciality market in the last few years. Look out for coffees traceable to a specific estate or a group of producers.

TASTE PROFILE

Great coffees from Papua New Guinea often have a buttery quality, great sweetness and wonderful complexity.

Population: 7,060,000
Number of 60kg (132lb) bags in 2013:
1,000,000

Most of Papua New Guinea's coffee is produced in the Highlands regions, and the area shows great potential for producing some amazing coffees in the future. While some coffee is grown outside of these key regions, it is only a very small amount.

EASTERN HIGHLANDS

There is a single mountain chain that runs through the country, and the Eastern Highlands form part of it.

Altitude: 400–1,900m (1,300–6,200ft)
Harvest: April–September
Varieties: Bourbon, Typica, Arusha

WESTERN HIGHLANDS

This is the other key area of coffee production. Most of the coffee in this region grows around the regional capital of Mount Hagen, named for an old, inactive volcano. Coffee produced in this area is often milled in Goroka, so traceability of some coffees can be difficult. The combination of altitude and incredibly fertile soil makes the potential for quality in this region incredibly exciting.

Altitude: 1,000–1,800m (3,300–5,900ft)
Harvest: April–September
Varieties: Bourbon, Typica, Arusha

SIMBU PROVINCE

Simbu (officially spelled as Chimbu) is the third-largest producing region, but its output is substantially lower than either of the Highlands provinces. The name is derived from the local dialect and the word Sipuuuu, meaning 'thank you'. Most of the coffee here comes from the coffee gardens around the homes of smallholders. Nearly ninety per cent of the population is engaged in coffee production to some degree, and for many this is the only cash crop they grow.

Altitude: 1,300–1,900m (4,300–6,200ft)
Harvest: April–September
Varieties: Bourbon, Typica, Arusha

ASIA

VIETNAM

Vietnam could be considered an unusual inclusion in a book that focuses on high-quality speciality coffee, as it produces predominantly Robusta. However, Vietnam is different because of the impact it has had on every coffee-producing country in the world, and therefore merits inclusion to give some understanding.

Coffee was brought to Vietnam by the French in 1857, and was initially cultivated under the plantation model. However, this did not gain any momentum as a commercial venture until around 1910. Cultivation in the Buôn Ma Thuột region, in the Central Highland, was interrupted by the Vietnam war. After the war the coffee industry became increasingly collectivized, reducing yields and production. At this point around 20,000 hectares of land produced around 5,000–7,000 tonnes (5,500–7,700 tons) of coffee. Over the next 25 years, the amount of land under coffee would increase by a factor of 25 and the country's overall production by a factor of 100.

Much of the industry's growth was down to the Doi Moi reforms of 1986, which permitted privately owned enterprises in industries that produced commoditized crops. In the 1990s, a huge number of new companies were formed in Vietnam, many focusing on the large-scale production of coffee. At this time, specifically in between 1994 and 1998, prices for coffee were relatively high, which provided strong incentives to increase coffee production. Between 1996 and 2000, Vietnam's coffee production doubled and this would come to have a devastating effect on the global price of coffee.

Vietnam's massive increase in production, which made it the second-largest producer of coffee in the world, resulted in a state of global oversupply and this

TASTE PROFILE

Very little high-quality coffee is available in Vietnam, and so most tastes flat, woody, and lacks sweetness or much character.

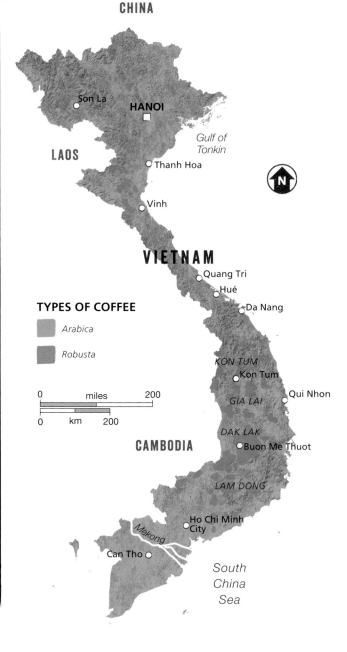

CHINA

Son La

HANOI

Gulf of Tonkin

LAOS

Thanh Hoa

Vinh

N

VIETNAM

Quang Tri

Hué

Da Nang

TYPES OF COFFEE

Arabica

Robusta

0   miles   200

0   km   200

KON TUM

Kon Tum

Qui Nhon

GIA LAI

DAK LAK

CAMBODIA

Buon Me Thuot

LAM DONG

Ho Chi Minh City

Mekong

Can Tho

South China Sea

caused a massive price crash. Despite the fact that Vietnam was producing Robusta rather than Arabica, it still affected the price of Arabica because many of the largest purchasers needed a commodity product rather than a quality one. Thus the oversupply of low-quality coffee worked in their favour.

From the high point of 900,000 tonnes (990,000 tons) of coffee in 2000, production declined sharply. However, as coffee prices recovered, so did Vietnam's production. The 2012/2013 crop was around 1.3 million tonnes (1.4 million tons) and it continues to have a large effect on the global industry. In recent years there has been a shift towards more Arabica, although the lack of altitude presents a challenge to achieving a high-quality product.

TRACEABILITY

There are several large estates in Vietnam, often controlled by multinational companies, so it is possible to see good levels of traceability. However, finding high-quality lots will prove extremely challenging.

Right: Vietnam is the second-largest producer of coffee in the world, and most coffee is harvested by hand. At a plantation in Buôn Ma Thuôt workers remove twigs and leaves from the fresh cherries.

GROWING REGIONS

Population: 89,709,000
Number of 60kg (132lb) bags in 2013: 27,500,000

Because there has been little demand for traceable coffee, there aren't strongly defined growing regions whose names are used by roasters.

CENTRAL HIGHLANDS

This region, a series of highland plateaus, contains the provinces of Dak Lak, Lam Dong, Gia Lai and Kon Tum and is primarily a producer of Robusta. The coffee industry is centred around Buôn Ma Thuôt, the capital of the province. Dak Lak and Lam Dong are the primary producers, growing about seventy per cent of the country's Robusta crop between them. Arabica has been grown in the Central

Highlands for about one hundred years, in the area around the city of Dalat in the Lam Dong region, but this makes up a very small part of the national production.

Altitude: 600–1,000m (2,000–3,300ft)
Harvest: November–March
Varieties: Robusta varieties, some Arabica (probably Bourbon)

SOUTH VIETNAM

There is some production northeast of Ho Chi Minh City, in the province of Dong Nai. This is primarily Robusta, and has attracted interest from large corporations such as Nestlé who are looking to improve their supply chain.

Altitude: 200–800m (650–2,600ft)
Harvest: November–March
Varieties: Robusta

NORTH VIETNAM

Arabica grows in the provinces of Son La, Thanh Hoa and Quang Tri in the north of the country, near the city of Hanoi. There is sufficient altitude for Arabica to grow well, but it is rare to see high-quality coffees produced here. Despite Arabica making up only three to five per cent of Vietnam's total production, this is now enough to make it the fifteenth-largest producer of Arabica in the world.

Altitude: 800–1,600m (2,600–5,200ft)
Harvest: November–March
Varieties: Bourbon, Sparrow (or Se), Catimor, Robusta

In the southern province of Binh Dong, a worker moves one bag among hundreds in a warehouse owned by communist exporters. Most of the beans grown in South Vietnam are of the Robusta variety.

YEMEN

Yemen has been producing coffee on a commercial basis for longer than any other country, and its coffee is distinctive, perhaps challenging, and certainly unusual. Despite a strong demand for Yemeni coffee over the centuries, its trade has never commoditized. Yemen is unique, from its coffee varieties and its terraced farming to its processing and its trade.

offee came to Yemen from Ethiopia, either through trade or those making pilgrimages from Ethiopia to Mecca, and was well established in the country in the 15th and 16th centuries. Export of its coffee introduced the world to the port of Mocha, and I think it is fair to say that 'mocha' is probably the most confusing word in all of coffee's lexicon (see box).

Agriculture in Yemen is somewhat unique, as only three per cent of the land is suitable for farming, water being the major limiting factor. Coffee is grown on terraced land at high altitudes and additional irrigation is required to keep the coffee trees healthy. Many farmers

depend on non-renewable sources of deep underground water, and there is some concern over depleting stocks. Fertilization of the soil is not particularly common, so there is an additional problem of depleting soil nutrients. All these factors, coupled with the sheer remoteness of the coffee-growing regions, go some way to explaining the huge number and variation of heirloom varieties of Arabica found in the country, most of them peculiar to their growing regions.

Yemen's coffee is picked by hand, with pickers visiting a tree several times in a season. Despite this, selective picking is not particularly commonplace, with underripe

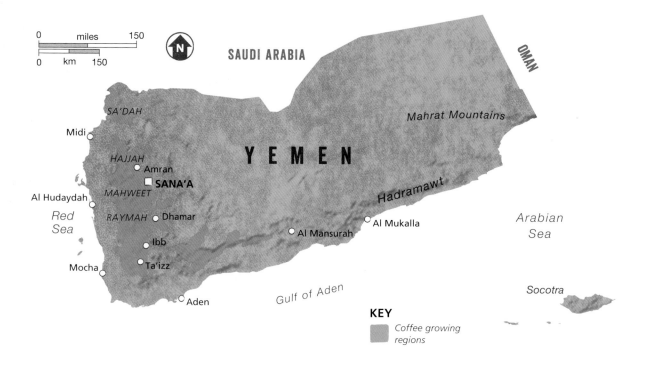

and overripe cherries often being harvested. Whole cherries are usually dried in the sun after harvesting, often on the roofs of the farmers' homes. Rarely do these roofs provide enough space, so the cherries are often piled too deep to dry correctly, resulting in defects such as uneven drying, fermentation and mould.

Each producer may only grow a very small amount of coffee. Data from the 2000 census shows that around 99,000 households produced coffee, and based on estimates of production the average household produced just 113kg (249lb) of raw coffee that year.

There remains a very strong global demand for Yemeni coffee, and about half of the exported coffee goes to Saudi Arabia. This strong demand, coupled with limited production and relatively high production costs, makes the coffees from Yemen sell for very high prices. This demand has not increased the traceability of Yemeni coffee at all, and it can travel through a network of middlemen from the farmer through to the exporter. Coffees can also sit for quite some time (often years) at the point of export, as some exporters sell their oldest stocks first, and warehouse their newer crops in caverns underground.

THE TERM 'MOCHA'

Originally, the word referred to the port in Yemen from where coffee was exported. This spelling soon changed to 'moka', and the term was used to describe the potent and pungent coffees produced in Yemen. Some naturally processed coffees from other countries are still described this way, such as Moka Harrar from Ethiopia.

The coffees from Yemen were often blended with coffees from Java, and the Mocha-Java blend was born. However, the name was not protected and thus became a kind of stylistic term used by many roasters to describe the flavour of a particular coffee blend they created, rather than to describe where the component coffees came from. The current use of the term 'mocha' to describe a mixture of hot chocolate and espresso only serves to further bewilder the consumer.

Right: In the old city of Al-Masnaah, northwest of Sana'a, a vendor makes coffee for his customers. The Yemeni coffee trade is several hundred years old and harvests continue to be highly sought after.

QESHER

Qesher, also Q'shr or Qishr, is a popular by-product of coffee production. It is the dried, but not roasted, husks removed from the coffee cherries during production. These husks are often brewed like tea and this is a reasonably popular way for Yemenis to consume a form of coffee. More recently, producers in Central America have been experimenting with the same product, there called cascara. This is usually just the dried fruit of the cherry, however, rather than both the fruit and the dried parchment seen in qesher.

TRACEABILITY

Trying to understand exactly where coffees come from in Yemen can be extremely confusing. Often the name of the coffee will include the term 'Mocha', indicating the port from which it was exported. Usually coffees are only traceable back to a particular region within Yemen, rather than to the farm where they were produced. It is also common to see the local names for different coffee varieties used to describe the coffee, such as Mattari.

Having better levels of traceability doesn't necessarily guarantee better quality. Often different coffees from different regions are blended together before export, and exported under the most valuable name. The high demand for Yemeni coffee is based on its unusual, wild and pungent flavours – and these come in part from defects in the process. If you want to try coffees from Yemen, it is advisable to source one from a supplier with whom you have already built some level of trust. Roasters will need to cup through a great many terrible samples to find a good one. Buying blindly as a consumer stacks the odds against you and you may end up with something that tastes dirty, rotten and unpleasant.

TASTE PROFILE

Wild, complex and pungent, a completely distinctive coffee experience, different from other coffees around the world. For some the wild, slightly fermented fruit quality is off-putting, while others prize it highly.

Opposite: Only three per cent of Yemen is suitable for agriculture owing to the scarcity of water. This terraced plantation in a traditional small fortress town is typical of Yemeni coffee farming methods.

GROWING REGIONS

Population: 25,235,000
Number of 60kg (132lb) bags in 2013: 200,000

Please note that westernized spellings of place names in Yemen can vary quite dramatically. Each region described in Yemen is a governorate, rather than a geographically defined region. Yemen has 21 governorates, but only 12 grow coffee and even fewer are key producers.

SANA'A

Many of the premium coffees exported from Yemen bear the names of the varieties grown in this region. Confusingly, Mattari can be used to describe a region (around Bani Matar), and the name of the variety is probably derived this way. The region is based around the city of Sana'a, one of the oldest continuously populated cities on earth, and at 2,200m (7,200ft) above sea level, also one of the highest. As a region, this is the largest producer of coffee in the country.

Altitude: 1,500–2,200m (4,900–7,200ft)
Harvest: October–December
Varieties: Heirloom varieties such as Mattari, Ismaili, Harazi, Dawairi, Dawarani, Sanani, Haimi

RAYMAH

This small governorate was established in 2004. It produces a reasonable amount of the country's coffee and has increasingly been the focus of water-management projects by non-government organizations to help increase coffee yields in the area.

Harvest: October–December
Altitude: average of 1,850m (6,050ft)
Varieties: Heirloom varieties such as Raymi, Dwairi, Bura'ae, Kubari, Tufahi, Udaini

MAHWEET

Located south of Sana'a, the city of At-Tawila rose to prominence between the 15th and 18th centuries as a hub for coffee-growing in the region. The city was a collection centre for coffee before it headed to ports for export.

Altitude: 1,500–2,100m (4,900–6,900ft)
Harvest: October–December
Varieties: Heirloom varieties such as Mahwaiti, Tufahi, Udaini, Kholani

SA'DAH

This governorate has unfortunately been plagued by civil war since 2004. Confusingly sada is an Arabic term for black coffee, and is popular throughout the Middle East, often served with the addition of spices.

Altitude: average of 1,800m (5,900ft)
Harvest: October–December
Varieties: Heirloom varieties such as Dawairi, Tufahi, Udaini, Kholani

HAJJAH

This is another small producing region, centred around the capital city of Hajjah.

Altitude: 1,600–1,800m (5,200–5,900ft)
Harvest: October–December
Varieties: Heirloom varieties such as Shani, Safi, Masrahi, Shami, Bazi, Mathani, Jua'ari

AMERICAS

The Americas supply the majority of the world's coffee beans, but the range and quality of bean exports varies hugely. Though Brazilian harvests provide one-third of the international coffee market, there is increasing interest in unusual varieties from smaller growers, such as the Geisha variety produced in Panama. Ecotourism and awareness of sustainable and cooperative farming methods are also changing the way plantations across the Americas harvest and grow crops.

SOUTH AMERICA

BOLIVIA

Bolivia has the potential to produce truly great coffees, and already does in very small quantities. The country's entire production is smaller than that of one of Brazil's larger coffee farms. Production is shrinking year on year, and coffee farms are disappearing at an alarming rate. We may soon see coffees from Bolivia (especially great ones) almost disappear.

Frustratingly there is little information available about the introduction of coffee and the history of coffee growing in Bolivia. There are reports of substantial coffee production in the country going back to the 1880s, but not a great deal more. The country is large, about the same size as Ethiopia or Colombia. It is landlocked, which has traditionally posed something of a challenge to the export of coffee, adding both time and cost.

Bolivia is relatively unpopulated, with just 10.5 million inhabitants. The population is often characterized as being incredibly poor, with around 25 per cent categorized as living in extreme poverty. The country's economy is reliant on minerals and natural gas as well as agriculture, although coffee has never really featured prominently. It is impossible to ignore the impact on the economy, and on agriculture, of coca grown for the drug trade. Farmers are increasingly switching from coffee to coca, because coca provides greater security for producers because the price is subject to less variance. In 2010 and 2011, while coffee prices were high, anti-drugs programmes funded by Bolivia and the US managed to encourage more farmers to switch to coffee production. However, the price of coffee has fallen again and many farmers have turned once more to coca.

The conditions for growing coffee in Bolivia are, in many ways, ideal. There is certainly the necessary altitude, and the climate has nicely defined wet and dry seasons. Most of the coffee grown here is old heirloom varieties, such as Typica and Caturra. Some excellent, clean and complex coffees have been coming out of Bolivia recently, although this wasn't always the case. In the past, producers picked and pulped the coffees they grew and then transported the pulp to a central processing station. There were two big problems: firstly,

changes in temperature on the journey to the processing station could result in the coffee freezing and, secondly, the pulp still contained enough moisture to keep fermenting. Often this resulted in a loss of quality or undesirable flavours creeping in. More and more, quality-conscious producers are doing the post-harvest work on their own farms. The US has funded the construction of a number of small coffee washing stations across the country as part of the anti-drugs programme. However, despite changes to help bolster quality, coffees from Bolivia still lack the reputation of those from neighbouring countries such as Colombia or Brazil.

Competitions such as The Cup of Excellence have helped shine a light on the best coffees in Bolivia. I would recommend seeking out and enjoying them while they are still around. Even though speciality coffee does yield a greater return, even quality-conscious farmers are still giving up coffee production.

TRACEABILITY

Coffees in Bolivia are typically traceable down to a single farm or cooperative. Due to land reforms, large-scale land ownership has reduced since 1991, and the 23,000

families that produce coffee in Bolivia do so from small farms, typically 1.2–8 hectares (3–20 acres). The export of Bolivia's output is handled by a small number, around thirty, of private exporting companies.

GROWING REGIONS

Population: 10,461,000
Number of 60kg (132lb) bags in 2013: 100,000

Coffee-growing regions in Bolivia have never been strongly defined and, as such, different roasters will use different naming conventions to describe which part of the country the coffee comes from.

YUNGAS

Approximately 95 per cent of Bolivia's coffee is produced in this region, and in the past it held a reputation for quality in Europe, though less so recently. It can be defined as the region of forest stretching down the east side of the Andes, and in fact crosses from Peru through Bolivia into Argentina. The region produces some of the highest-altitude coffee in the world and this is also where coffee has been grown the longest in Bolivia. In his 1935 book, *All About Coffee*, Ukers refers to coffee from here as 'Yunga'.

Yungas is to the west of La Paz so many coffee buyers have to travel along the famous Yungas Road, nicknamed the 'Road of Death', to reach the coffee producers there. The road is often a single lane, winding and dug into the sides of the mountains without any barrier to prevent vehicles dropping up to 600m (2,000ft) into the valleys below.

As the region is so large, many coffee roasters describe coffees as being from a more specific area, such as Caranavi, Inquisivi or Coroico, within the region.

Altitude: 800–2,300m (2,600–7,600ft)
Harvest: July–November

SANTA CRUZ

This is the most easterly of the departments in Bolivia, and generally it lacks the altitude for high-quality coffees. There is some coffee production around the Ichilo province, although coffee is far less important as a crop compared to rice or timber. This region is hugely important to the country's economy because most of the natural gas is found here.

Altitude: 410m (1340ft)
Harvest: July–November

BENI

This is a large and sparsely populated department in the northeast of the country. Technically, part of Beni falls within the geographical region of Yungas, but a small amount of coffee is grown in the department outside the Yungas region. Primarily this is a cattle ranching area, although many crops are grown here, from rice and cacao to tropical fruits.

Altitude: 155m (500ft)
Harvest: July–November

Left: Bolivia is ideal for coffee crops, but its topography means export and production are difficult – the old route from La Paz to Coroico seen here is known as the world's most dangerous road.

SOUTH AMERICA

BRAZIL

Brazil has been the world's largest producer of coffee for more than 150 years. Currently, Brazil grows around one-third of the world's coffee, although in the past its market share was as high as eighty per cent. Coffee was introduced to Brazil from French Guiana in 1727, while Brazil was still under Portuguese rule.

The first coffee in Brazil was planted by Francisco de Melo Palheta in the region of Para in the north of the country. According to myth, Palheta travelled to French Guiana on a diplomatic mission, seduced the wife of the governor there and was given the seeds hidden in a bouquet from her on his departure. The coffee he planted on his return home was probably used just for domestic consumption, and it remained a relatively unimportant crop until it began to work its way south, being passed from garden to garden as much as from farm to farm as a crop.

COMMERCIAL PRODUCTION BEGINS

The commercial production of coffee initially began around the Paraiba River, relatively close to Rio de Janeiro. This area suited coffee, not just because the land was ideal, but also because its proximity to Rio de Janeiro would facilitate export. In contrast to the smaller coffee farms that flourished in Central America, Brazil's first commercial farms were large, slave-driven plantations. This industrialized approach is still relatively uncommon in the rest of the world, and fairly unique to Brazilian coffee production. The approach to production was aggressive: the most powerful, or forceful, would win disputes over poorly defined property boundaries and a single slave looked after four to seven thousand plants. When the soil became depleted from the intensive farming, the farm would just move on to fresh land.

Coffee production boomed between 1820 and 1830, overtaking the demand of Brazilian coffee drinkers and beginning to feed the wider global market. Those who controlled coffee production became both incredibly wealthy and very powerful and were referred to as 'coffee barons'. Their needs would have a significant impact on the government's policies and its support of the coffee industry.

By 1830 Brazil produced thirty per cent of the world's coffee. This rose to forty per cent by 1840, although the massive increase in supply resulted in a drop in the global price for coffee. Up until the middle of the 19th century, Brazil's coffee industry was reliant on slave labour. More than 1.5 million slaves had been brought to Brazil to work on the coffee plantations. When the British put a stop to Brazil's slave trade with Africa in 1850, Brazil turned to migrant labour or its internal slave trade. There were great fears that the abolition of slavery in Brazil in 1888 would endanger the coffee industry, but the harvest continued successfully that year and onwards.

A SECOND BOOM

A second coffee boom ran from the 1880s through to the 1930s, a period named after the two most important products of the time. The huge influence of both coffee barons from Sao Paolo, and dairy producers in Minas Gerais, led to a political climate known as the *café com leite* period. This period also saw the Brazilian government start the practice of valorization, a protectionist practice designed to stabilize the price of coffee. The government would buy coffee from producers at an inflated price when the market was low and hold it until the market was high. This meant stable prices for coffee barons, and prevented oversupply from lower coffee prices.

By the 1920s Brazil was producing eighty per cent of the world's coffee, and coffee financed a huge amount of infrastructure in the country. This unabated production lead to a massive surplus of coffee that would only exacerbate the damage of the crash during the Great

TYPES OF COFFEE

Arabica

Conilon/Robusta

Depression in the 1930s. Brazil's government ended up burning around 78 million bags of stockpiled coffee in an effort to invigorate coffee prices, though it had little effect on them.

During World War II there was growing concern in the US that, with the European markets shut off, declining coffee prices could drive Central and South American countries towards Nazi or communist sympathy. In an attempt to stabilize the price of coffee, an international agreement was drawn up, based on a quota system. This agreement drove up the price of coffee until it stabilized in the mid 1950s and is considered a precursor to the much wider International Coffee Agreement (ICA) signed in 1962, which would come to encompass 42 producing countries. Quotas were fixed according to the indicator coffee price, determined by the International Coffee Organization (ICO). If prices dropped then quotas were reduced, and if prices climbed then quotas were increased.

This agreement lasted until 1989, when it broke down after Brazil refused to accept a reduction in its quota. Brazil believed that it was an extremely efficient producer, and could prosper outside of the agreement. The result of the breakdown of the ICA was an unregulated market, and prices dropped dramatically over the following five years, resulting in the coffee crisis that would inspire the Fair Trade movement within coffee production.

ON AND OFF YEARS

With Brazil being such a dominant supplier of the world's coffee, anything that affected production in Brazil had a knock-on effect on global pricing. One such factor was

ROBUSTA PRODUCTION

While not a focus of this book, it should be noted that Brazil is one of the world's primary producers of Robusta, along with Arabica. In Brazil Robusta is usually called conillon and is produced in regions such as Rondonia.

the alternating cycle of Brazil's annual crop. Over the years it became clear that Brazil's harvest would swing each year between a large and a small harvest. Some work has been done in recent years to try to mitigate this effect, creating less variation year to year and greater stability. The reason for this variation in crop is that a coffee tree will naturally have an alternating cycle of large and small crops, but this can be controlled by light pruning. Light pruning has not been a common practice in Brazil, with producers preferring to prune back hard so there is little crop the following year.

In the past there have been dramatic incidents such as the black frost of 1975, which reduced the following year's crop by nearly 75 per cent. As a result of the frost, the global price of coffee almost doubled immediately. In 2000 and 2001 there were two off years in a row, that resulted in a massive harvest in 2002, with a huge production of coffee. This coincided with another long period of low prices for coffee, caused by an excess of coffee on the global market.

MODERN COFFEE PRODUCTION

Brazil is undeniably the most advanced and industrialized coffee-producing country in the world. With a focus on yield and production, it has not retained a great reputation for producing coffees of the highest quality. Most large farms employ relatively crude picking techniques, such as strip picking, where the entire branch is stripped of its cherries in one go. If the plantations are large and flat (common in Brazil's larger coffee farms), they use harvesting machines to shake the cherries loose from the branches. Neither method takes ripeness into consideration, and as a result there can be a large number of unripe cherries in the harvested coffee.

For a long time Brazil also processed a great deal of its coffee by sun-drying the whole cherries on patios (see page 32). The introduction of the Pulped Natural

TASTE PROFILE

Better Brazilian coffees tend to be low in acidity, heavy in body and sweet, often with chocolate and nutty flavours.

Process in the early 1990s did help to improve quality, but for years Brazil's speciality coffee producers – who may pick by hand, who may wash their coffee, and who may grow interesting varieties at higher altitudes – have battled against the country's reputation for producing coffees with low acidity and increased body best suited to espresso blends.

However, while much of Brazil's coffee grows below the altitudes best suited to quality, it is still possible to find some very interesting and delicious coffees there. Equally, the country produces some very clean and sweet coffees without much acidity that many people (quite rightly) find delicious and very approachable.

DOMESTIC CONSUMPTION

Brazil has been actively trying to increase its internal coffee consumption, with increasing success. While giving children coffee at school from a young age may raise some eyebrows, the consumption in Brazil now rivals that of the United States. No raw coffee can be imported into Brazil, which means that a large percentage of the coffee grown in Brazil is consumed there, though generally the quality of coffee for domestic consumption is lower than that for export.

Coffee bars have appeared throughout the major cities, though the price of coffee in these places is similar to better coffee bars in the United States and Europe so they have become another symbol of the increasing divide between rich and poor in Brazil.

TRACEABILITY

High-quality Brazilian coffees are usually traceable down to a specific farm (*fazenda*), whereas the lower-quality coffees are bulk lots and not traceable. Coffees marked as 'Santos' have simply shipped from the port of Santos and the name has nothing to do with where the coffee was grown. Brazil probably breaks the rule of thumb, that traceability is linked to quality, as there are farms in Brazil producing more coffee than the whole of Bolivia. And while the coffee may be traceable due to the size of production, it will not necessarily be higher in quality as a result.

Opposite: A Brazilian worker opens the sluice of a washing tank, raking the clean beans on to a trailer.

GROWING REGIONS

Population: 201,033,000

Number of 60kg (132lb) bags in 2013:
47,544,000

There are many different coffee varieties grown across Brazil and many of them were developed in the country or evolved there, including Mundo Novo, Yellow Bourbon, Caturra and Catuai.

BAHIA

This large state in the east of Brazil is one of the northernmost coffee-growing areas in the country. In recent years there have been more and more interesting coffees from this region and many people sat up and took notice when, in the 2009 Cup of Excellence competition, five out of the top ten lots came from Bahia.

CHAPADA DIAMANTINA

This beautiful area of Brazil, known for its national park, is named after its geology: Chapada describes the steep cliffs in the region and Diamantina the diamonds found there in the 19th century. A notable number of farms in the region are producing coffee biodynamically, an organic method of production originally developed by Rudolph Steiner.

Altitude: 1,000–1,200m (3,300–3,900ft)
Harvest: June–September

Below: A farmer in Brazil uses a sieve to separate coffee cherries from the chaff, which is carried away by the wind.

CERRADO DE BAHIA/WEST BAHIA

This region lends itself to large-scale, industrialized and irrigated coffee production. In the late 1970s and early 1980s this region was part of a government project to encourage agriculture, which provided cheap credit and incentives to around six hundred farmers who moved here. By 2006, around 1.5 million hectares (3.7 million acres) of land were being cultivated, although coffee made up a relatively small part of this. A stable, warm and sunny climate lends itself to higher yields, so it is a little harder to find something truly astonishing from this part of Brazil.

Altitude: 700–1,000m (2,300–3,300ft)
Harvest: May–September

PLANALTO DE BAHIA

This coffee region has more of a focus on small-scale production, taking advantage of the cooler temperatures and higher altitudes to produce higher-quality coffees.

Altitude: 700–1,300m (2,300–4,300ft)
Harvest: May–September

MINAS GERAIS

In the southeast of the country, the state of Minas Gerais has some of the highest mountains in Brazil, providing good altitude for coffee.

CERRADO

Cerrado means tropical savannah but, although one could use this name to refer to the entire savannah that stretches through many states in Brazil, when it comes to coffee the name usually refers to the Cerrado region in the west of Minas Gerais. This area is relatively new to coffee production and perhaps this explains why it is dominated by large, mechanized farms. In fact, over ninety per cent of the farms in the region are larger than 10 hectares (24 acres).

Altitude: 850–1,250m (2,800–4,100ft)
Harvest: May–September

SUL DE MINAS

Historically this is home to a great deal of Brazil's coffee production, and there have been many generations of smallholder farmers here. Perhaps for this reason there are many more cooperatives in the region. Despite the prevalence of small farms it is still a well-industrialized area, with a lot of mechanical harvesting.

Certain areas within the region have attracted more attention recently, including Carmo de Minas. This particular municipality, around the village of Carmo, has a notable number of producers leveraging the soil and climate to grow better coffees.

Altitude: 700–1,350m (2,300–4,400ft)
Harvest: May–September

CHAPADA DE MINAS

This region is further north, away from the other coffee-growing areas clustered together to the south. Coffee growing took hold here in the late 1970s. It is a relatively small area of production, with some producers taking advantage of the flat land to mechanize their farms.

Altitude: 800–1,100m (2,600–3,600ft)
Harvest: May–September

MATAS DE MINAS

This is a region where coffee took root early, and one that became rich on the back of coffee and dairy between 1850 and 1930. While the area has diversified in recent years, around eighty per cent of its agricultural income still comes from coffee.

The uneven land here, with steep hillsides, means that harvesting is commonly done by hand. Even though there are many smallholders in the region (almost fifty per cent of the farms are smaller than 10 hectares/24 acres) there is not the established reputation for quality one might expect. However, this is changing for the better and there are plenty of farms producing great coffee here.

Altitude: 550–1,200m (1,800–3,900ft)
Harvest: May–September

SAO PAOLO

The state of São Paolo contains one of the better-known coffee-growing areas of Brazil, Mogiana. The region was named after the Mogiana Railroad Company, which built the 'coffee railroad' in 1883, leading to better transport and a great expansion of coffee production here.

Altitude: 800–1,200m (2,600–3,900ft)
Harvest: May–September

MATO GROSSO AND MATO GROSSO DO SUL

This area produces only a small amount of Brazil's annual harvest. Its large, flat highlands are better suited to the vast number of cattle raised here and the extensive soybean production.

Altitude: average of 600m (2000ft)
Harvest: May–September

ESPIRITO SANTO

While relatively small compared to other coffee-growing regions in Brazil, the second-largest chunk of the annual harvest is produced in Espirito Santo and the capital city, Vittoria, is a key port for export. However, nearly eighty per cent of the coffee it produces is conillon (Robusta). In the south of the region, the farmers tend towards Arabica production and there can be some more interesting coffees there.

Altitude: 900–1,200m (3,000–3,900ft)
Harvest: May–September

PARANÁ

Some argue that this state is the most southern coffee-growing region in the world, and it is an important agricultural area for Brazil. Despite having just 2.5 per cent of the country's land, it produces nearly 25 per cent of its agricultural output. Coffee was once the biggest crop here, but after the damage caused by frost in 1975, many producers diversified. While the region once produced 22 million bags of coffee, now it produces closer to 2 million. The first colonists here settled close to the coast, but coffee was the reason many moved inland. The lack of altitude prevents really high-quality coffees being grown here, but the cooler temperatures do help slow down the maturation of the fruit.

Altitude: up to 950m (3,100ft)
Harvest: May–September

COLOMBIA

SOUTH AMERICA

Coffee was probably first introduced to Colombia in 1723 by the Jesuits, though there are inevitably different accounts. It spread slowly as a commercial crop to various regions of the country, but its production did not become significant until the end of the 19th century. By 1912, coffee made up approximately fifty per cent of Colombia's total exports.

Colombia recognized the value of marketing and building its brand relatively early on. The creation in 1958 of Juan Valdez, the farmer who represents Colombian coffee, was perhaps their greatest success. Juan Valdez and his mule were created as the symbol of Colombian coffee and appeared on bags of coffee and also in various advertising campaigns, portrayed by three different actors over the years. Juan Valdez became a point of recognition, particularly in the US, and added value to Colombian coffee. The character built on the success of early marketing phrases such as 'Mountain Grown Coffee', and the constant promotion of '100% Colombian Coffee' meant that Colombia would stand apart in the minds of consumers across the world.

This marketing was, and continues to be, undertaken by the Federación Nacional de Cafeteros (FNC). This organization, created in 1927, is particularly unusual in the coffee-producing world. While many countries have organizations involved in the export and promotion of their coffee, few are quite as large and complex as the FNC. It was created as a private non-profit organization to defend the interests of coffee producers and is funded through a special tax on all coffee exported. As Colombia is one of the largest coffee producers in the world, the FNC is well funded and has become something of a monstrous, bureaucratic organization. This bureaucracy is perhaps inevitable as the FNC is now technically owned and controlled by its 500,000 coffee-producing members. While the FNC is involved in the more obvious roles of marketing, production and some financial matters, its reach goes deeper into coffee-growing communities and it has a hand in the creation of both social and physical infrastructure including rural roads, schools and health centres. It has also invested in other industries besides coffee to help spur on regional development and wellbeing.

KEY

Coffee growing regions

Caribbean Sea

Pico Cristóbal Colón

Barranquilla

Cartagena

SIERRA NEVADA

Valledupar

PANAMA

NORTH SANTANDER

Cauca

Magdalena

Cúcuta

VENEZUELA

ANTIOQUIA

Bucaramanga

Medellín

SANTANDER

PACIFIC OCEAN

CALDAS

RISARALDA

CUNDINAMARCA

Meta

Ibagué

QUINDIO

BOGOTÁ

VALLE

TOLIMA

Cali

DEL CAUCA

Guaviare

CAUCA

COLOMBIA

HUILA

NARIÑO

Apaporis

ECUADOR

Caquetá

BRAZIL

N

Putumayo

0   miles   200

0   km   200

PERU

THE FNC AND QUALITY

Recently there has been some friction between the FNC and the more quality-conscious section of the industry, as the FNC's perceived interests of the farmers may not always lead to the best possible quality in the coffee. The FNC has a research division called Cenicafé which breeds specific varieties and many believe the promotion of varieties like Castillo has favoured quantity of yield above cup quality. It is possible to see both sides of the argument, and as global climate change has an increasing impact on the stability of Colombia's production, it is increasingly difficult to argue against varieties that ensure livelihoods for producers, even at the expense of losing some great cups of coffee.

TRACEABILITY

As part of the promotion of Colombian coffee, the FNC created the terms 'Supremo' and 'Excelso'. These terms relate only to the size of the bean, and it is important to understand that they have no relation to quality. Unfortunately this classification obscures any

Above: Colombia is one of the largest producers of coffee in the world, and export is controlled by a national federation. The country's well-defined growing regions produce a varied range of crops.

traceability as coffee marketed this way may come from many, many farms and be blended before being sieved mechanically to the necessary sizing grade. Essentially this is generic coffee, and its naming offers no help when trying to buy quality. The speciality coffee section of the industry has been working to maintain traceability, so when looking for something incredibly enjoyable, make sure the beans come from a distinct place, rather than just being a certain size.

TASTE PROFILE

Colombian coffees have a huge range of flavours, from the heavier, chocolatier coffees through to jammy, sweet, fruity lots. A huge spectrum of flavours exists across the regions.

Plantations in the mountainous territory of Risaralda, one of Colombia's western-central departments, produce some of the country's best-known coffee.

GROWING REGIONS

Population: 47,073,000

Number of 60kg (132lb) bags in 2013: 10,900,000

Colombia has well-defined growing regions, and they produce an impressive variety of coffees. Whether you want rounder, heavier coffees or something vibrant and fruity (or something in between) there is probably a coffee in Colombia that fits the bill. The regions are geographically defined, rather than politically, so it is not unusual to find that there are common traits to the coffees produced in each region. If you enjoy one coffee from a region, you will probably enjoy many of the others.

The coffee trees in Colombia yield two harvests each year, the main harvest and the second harvest, known locally as the *mitaca* harvest.

CAUCA

Among others, this area is best known for its coffees grown around Inza and the city of Popayán. The Meseta de Popayán is a high plateau with attractive growing conditions provided by the altitude, its proximity to the equator and the surrounding mountains, which protect the coffee against the humidity of the Pacific and the trade winds from the south. The result is a very stable climate year round, and the region has notable volcanic soil too. Historically there has been a predictable, single rainy season each year in October to December.

Altitude: 1,700–2,100m (5,600–6,900ft)

Harvest: March–June (main crop) November–December (mitaca crop)

Varieties: 21% Typica, 64% Caturra, 15% Castillo

VALLE DEL CAUCA

The valley of Cauca is one of the most fertile parts of the country, with the Cauca river running down between two large Andean mountain ranges. The area was one of the epicentres of the Colombian armed conflict. Typical of Colombia, most farms are pretty small and the area has around 75,800 hectares (187,300 acres) under coffee production, split between 26,000 farms owned by 23,000 families.

Altitude: 1,450–2,000m (4,750–6,600ft)

Harvest: September–December (main crop) March–June (mitaca crop)

Varieties: 16% Typica, 62% Caturra, 22% Castillo

TOLIMA

Tolima is among the last strongholds of Colombia's notorious rebel group FARC, which had maintained control of the area until relatively recently. Tolima has suffered in recent years from the fighting, which has made access difficult. Quality coffees from this area tend to come from small farmers in very small micro-lots via cooperatives.

Altitude: 1,200–1,900m (3,900–6,200ft)

Harvest: March–June (main crop) October–December (mitaca crop)

Varieties: 9% Typica, 74% Caturra, 17% Castillo

HUILA

The department of Huila has a combination of great soil and great geography for growing coffee, and some of the most complex, fruit-driven Colombian coffees I have tasted have come from here. The region has more than seventy thousand coffee growers, covering more than 16,000 hectares (39,500 acres) of land.

Altitude: 1,250–2,000m (4,100–6,600ft)

Harvest: September–December (main crop) April–May (mitaca crop)

Varieties: 11% Typica, 75% Caturra, 14% Castillo

QUINDIO

Quindio is a small region in the centre of the country, just to the west of Bogotá. Coffee is an incredibly important part of the economy here, as the region suffers high levels of unemployment. However, the risks involved in growing coffee, due to the effects of climate change and the increased incidences of diseases affecting coffee plants, has led many farmers to grow citrus fruits and macadamia nuts instead.

Quindio is home to the National Coffee Park, a theme park based around coffee and coffee production. At the end of June each year, the municipality of Calarcá has, since 1960, hosted the National Coffee Party. This is a day of celebration around coffee, including a national beauty contest of coffee.

Altitude: 1,400–2,000m (4,600–6,600ft)

Harvest: September–December (main crop) April–May (mitaca crop)

Varieties: 14% Typica, 54% Caturra, 32% Castillo

RISARALDA

This is another well-established coffee-producing region and here a large number of farmers belong to cooperatives. As a result, there has been some interest from ethical labelling organizations. Coffee plays an important social and economic role in the area, providing jobs and employment to many. While many people moved to the region in the 1920s, often to grow coffee, the recession at the turn of the millennium saw some wide-scale emigration back to other regions and other countries. The capital city is also a transport hub for the regions of Caldas and Quindio, and the interdepartmental road network is known as the Autopista del Café (Coffee Highway).

Altitude: 1,300–1,650m (4,300–5,400ft)

Harvest: September–December (main crop) April–May (mitaca crop)

Varieties: 6% Typica, 59% Caturra, 35% Castillo

NARIÑO

Some of the highest coffees in Colombia are grown in Nariño, and they can also be some of the most stunning and complex. It is challenging to grow coffee at these high altitudes in many areas, as the plants suffer from 'die back'. However, Nariño is close enough to the equator that the climate is sufficiently suitable for coffee plants. The vast majority of Nariño's forty thousand producers are smallholders with less than 2 hectares (4.4 acres) each. Many have formed groups and institutions to provide each other with support and to interact with the FNC. In fact, the average farm size is less than 1 hectare (2.2 acres), and only 37 producers in the region own more than 5 hectares (11 acres) of land.

Altitude: 1,500–2,300m (4,900–7,500ft)
Harvest: April–June
Varieties: 54% Typica, 29% Caturra, 17% Castillo

CALDAS

Along with Quindio and Riseralda, the state of Caldas is part of the Colombian Coffee-Growing Axis, or Coffee Triangle. Between them they grow a large portion of the nation's coffee. Historically this was considered some of the best coffee in Colombia, but now other regions are more competitive on that front.

The region is also home to Cenicafé, the National Coffee Research Centre run by the FNC. It is considered to be one of the world's leading institutions for research into all aspects of coffee production, and it is here that a number of varieties unique to Colombia (such as the disease-resistant Colombia and Castillo varieties) have been created.

Altitude: 1,300–1,800m (4,300–5,900ft)
Harvest: September–December (main crop) April–May (mitaca crop)
Varieties: 8% Typica, 57% Caturra, 35% Castillo

ANTIOQUIA

This department is the birthplace of both coffee in Colombia and the FNC. This is a key growing region with around 128,000 hectares (316,000 acres) of coffee, the most of any region. The coffee is produced by a mixture of large estates and cooperatives of small producers.

Altitude: 1,300–2,200m (4,300–7,200ft)
Harvest: September–December (main crop) April–May (mitaca crop)
Varieties: 6% Typica, 59% Caturra, 35% Castillo

CUNDINAMARCA

This department surrounds the capital city of Bogotá, one of the highest capital cities in the world at 2,625m (8,612ft) above sea level, higher than coffee would grow. This was the second region in Colombia to produce coffee for export, with its production peaking just before World War II. At that time it produced about ten per cent of the nation's coffee, but the percentage has since declined. In the past this region had some very large estates, some with over one million coffee trees.

Altitude: 1,400–1,800m (4,600–5,900ft)
Harvest: March–June (main crop) October–December (mitaca crop)
Varieties: 35% Typica, 34% Caturra, 31% Castillo

SANTANDER

This was one of the first regions in Colombia to produce coffee for export. The region has a little less altitude than some of the others, and this can often be detected in the coffees as they veer more towards round and sweet, rather than juicy and complex. A great deal of coffee from this region is certified by the Rainforest Alliance, and the biodiversity of the region is considered very important.

Altitude: 1,200–1,700m (3,900–5,600ft)
Harvest: September–December
Varieties: 15% Typica, 32% Caturra, 53% Castillo

NORTH SANTANDER

In the north of the country, bordering Venezuela, this region was producing coffee very early on, and may have been the first area in Colombia to grow coffee.

Altitude: 1,300–1,800m (4,300–5,900ft)
Harvest: September–December
Varieties: 33% Typica, 34% Caturra, 33% Castillo

SIERRA NEVADA

This is another region at lower altitudes, and again the coffees here tend to be heavier and rounder, rather than more elegant and lively. Coffee is grown on the Andean mountains in this area and the incredibly steep hillsides (ranging from fifty to eighty degrees) offer a particular challenge to the farmers. The name, a common one in many Spanish-speaking countries, translates as 'snow-topped mountains'.

Altitude: 900–1,600m (3,000–5,200ft)
Harvest: September–December
Varieties: 6% Typica, 58% Caturra, 36% Castillo

CENTRAL AMERICA

SOUTH AMERICA

COSTA RICA

Coffee has been grown in Costa Rica since the early 19th century. When the country's independence from Spain was declared in 1821, the municipal government gave away free coffee seeds to encourage production and records show there were around seventeen thousand trees in Costa Rica at that point.

I n 1825 the government continued its promotion of coffee by exempting it from certain taxes, and in 1831 the government decreed that if anyone grew coffee on fallow land for five years, they could claim ownership of it.

While a small amount of coffee had been exported to Panama in 1820, the first real exports began in 1832. Although this coffee was ultimately bound for England, it first passed through Chile where it was rebagged and renamed as 'Café Chileno de Valparaíso'.

Direct export to England followed in 1843, not long after the English became increasingly invested in Costa Rica. This ultimately led to the establishment of the Anglo-Costa Rican Bank in 1863, which provided finance to allow the industry to grow.

For nearly fifty years, between 1846 and 1890, coffee was the sole export of the country. Coffee drove

Below: The Doka Coffee plantation in San Isidro de Alajuela is typical of Costa Rica's organized coffee production. Wet mills widely adopted in the 19th century are one of its export trade's many advantages.

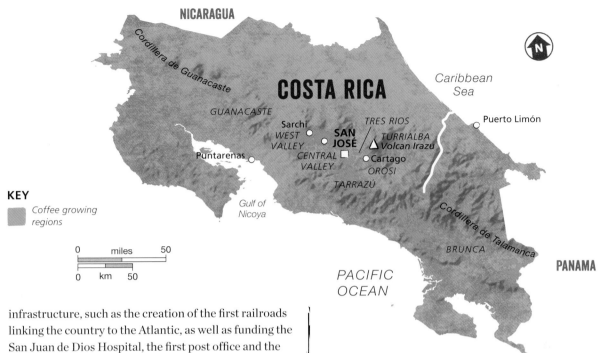

COSTA RICA

KEY

Coffee growing regions

Cordillera de Guanacaste

GUANACASTE

Sarchí
WEST
VALLEY

SAN
JOSÉ

TRES RIOS

TURRIALBA
△ Volcan Irazu

Puerto Limón

Puntarenas

CENTRAL
VALLEY

Cartago
OROSI

Gulf of
Nicoya

TARRAZÚ

Cordillera de Talamanca

BRUNCA

PACIFIC
OCEAN

PANAMA

NICARAGUA

Caribbean
Sea

0 miles 50

0 km 50

infrastructure, such as the creation of the first railroads linking the country to the Atlantic, as well as funding the San Juan de Dios Hospital, the first post office and the first government printing office. It would have an impact on culture too, as the National Theater is a product of the early coffee economy, along with the first libraries and the Santo Tomás University.

Costa Rica's coffee infrastructure had long given it an advantage when it came to fetching a better price on the international market. The wet process had been introduced in 1830, and by 1905 there were two hundred wet mills in the country. Washed coffees achieved higher prices, and at this time processing coffee in this way added to its perceived quality.

The coffee industry continued to grow until it began to reach its geographical limits. The population was still spreading from San José to the rest of the country, and farmers were looking for new land upon which to grow crops. However, not all of the land in the country was suitable for growing coffee, something that still checks the growth of the industry to date.

It is undeniable that Costa Rican coffee held a good reputation and achieved good prices for its coffees for a very long time, even though the coffees it was producing were typically clean and pleasant rather than interesting or unusual. There was a drive in the later part of the 20th century to move away from heirloom varieties, towards high-yielding varieties. While higher yields make economic sense, many in the speciality coffee industry felt that the cup quality decreased and became even less interesting. However, there have been recent changes

that have brought a great deal of interest back to the higher-quality coffees produced in the country.

THE GOVERNMENT'S ROLE

Right from the start, coffee production was strongly encouraged in Costa Rica, with land being given away to those who wished to grow the crop on it. In 1933 the government, under pressure from the coffee-growing community, created the rather bombastically titled Institute for the Defence of Coffee. Initially the institute was to play a role in trying to prevent small coffee growers from being exploited by those who bought their coffee cherry cheaply, processed it and sold it for a much greater profit. They did this by setting a limit on the profits that could be made by larger processors.

In 1948 the government body for coffee became the Oficina del Café, though some of the responsibilities for coffee went to the Department of Agriculture. This organization became the Instuto del Café de Costa Rica (ICAFE), which still exists today. ICAFE has a wide-ranging involvement in the coffee industry, running experimental research farms and promoting the quality of Costa Rican coffee worldwide. It is funded by a 1.5 per cent tax on all exports of coffee from Costa Rica.

Left: Costa Rica's rapidly growing tourist trade has encouraged tours of coffee farms thoughout the country, some of which are adopting organic farming methods.

Opposite: Queues of pickers at Carrizal de Alajuela wait to measure their freshly harvested crop. The plantation specializes in growing and selling high-quality coffee for export.

they were able to increase control over their coffee and the diversity of styles and coffees from all regions of Costa Rica dramatically increased. In the past, a unique and unusual coffee would have been blended in with coffees of neighbouring farms, but not any longer.

This makes Costa Rican coffees exciting to explore, as it is now easier than ever to taste several different coffees from a particular area side by side, and begin to see the effect geography can have on taste.

COFFEE AND TOURISM

Costa Rica is the most developed, and is considered the safest, of the Central American countries. This makes it an incredibly popular tourist destination, especially with North Americans. Tourism has come not only to displace coffee as the primary source of income from abroad, but has also collided and combined with it. Ecotourism is particularly popular in Costa Rica, and it is possible to visit and take tours of many coffee farms in the country. Typically those offering tours are the larger farms, with less focus on absolute quality, but it is nonetheless interesting to have the opportunity to see how coffee farming works up close.

TRACEABILITY

Currently land ownership is extremely common in Costa Rica, with ninety per cent of coffee producers there owning small- to medium-sized farms. As such it is possible to find coffees traceable to an individual farm or a particular cooperative.

THE MICRO MILL REVOLUTION

Costa Rican coffee had a long-standing reputation for good quality, and as such fetched a premium price in the commodity marketplace. What it lacked, as the speciality coffee market developed, was much in the way of traceable coffee. Typically coffees exported from Costa Rica around the turn of the millennium carried marks that were essentially brands created by the large mills or *beneficios*. These brands obscured exactly where the coffee had been grown and the unique terroir or qualities that it may possess. There was little in the processing chain to keep the individual lots distinct.

In the mid to late 2000s, however, there was a dramatic increase in micro mills. Farmers were investing in small-scale post-harvest equipment of their own and doing more of the processing themselves. This meant

TASTE PROFILE

Costa Rican coffees are typically very clean and sweet, though often very light bodied. However, recently micro mills are producing a wider range of flavours and styles.

GROWING REGIONS

Population: 4,586,000

Number of 60kg (132lb) bags in 2012: 1,396,000

Costa Rica has been successful in the past in marketing its coffees under the names of the regions that produce them. However, there is a wide diversity of flavours within each region, so it is well worth exploring each of the different regions to see what they can produce.

CENTRAL VALLEY

With the capital city of San José located here, this is the most heavily populated region in Costa Rica, and the one that has been growing coffee for the longest. It is typically divided into the sub-regions of San José, Heredia and Alajuela. There are three key volcanoes in the area – Irazu, Barva and Poas – which affect the topography and the soil.

Altitude: 900–1,600m (3,000–5,200ft)

Harvest: November–March

WEST VALLEY

The first farmers settled in the West Valley region during the 19th century and brought coffee with them. The region is divided into six sub-regions, centred around the cities of San Ramón, Palmares, Naranjo, Grecia, Sarchi and Atenas. The city of Sarchi lends its name to a specific coffee variety called Villa Sarchi (see page 25). The highest altitudes in the region are found around Naranjo, and some stunning coffees can be found throughout this area.

Altitude: 700–1,600m (2,300–5,200ft)

Harvest: October–February

TARRAZÚ

The region of Tarrazú has a long-standing reputation for quality, and for years the coffee from here could almost have been considered a high-quality grade. That coffee was probably just a mill grade collected from different farms and blended together to create a large lot. However, the brand of Tarrazú gained sufficient strength over the years that coffee from outside the region was being marketed as Tarrazú to increase its value. The highest coffee farms in the country are in this region and, like many of the other regions, it benefits from a distinct dry season during harvest.

Altitude: 1,200–1,900m (3,900–6,200ft)

Harvest: November–March

Above: Baskets of freshly picked cherries at the Doka Coffee plantation. Workers receive greater profits according to the percentage and size of ripe fruit picked.

TRES RIOS

A small region just to the east of San José, Tres Rios also benefits from the effects of the Irazu volcano. This area was considered relatively remote until recently, but now the greatest challenge to the coffee-growing industry is no longer gaining access to power or infrastructure, but the threat from urban development. More land is required for housing, and Tres Rios is producing less and less coffee each year, as land is sold for property development.

Altitude: 1,200–1,650m (3,900–5,400ft)
Harvest: November–March

OROSI

Another small region but further east from San José, Orosi has over a century of coffee production in its history. The region is essentially a long valley, compromising the three sub-regions of Orosi, Cachí and Paraíso.

Altitude: 1,000–1,400m (3,300–4,600ft)
Harvest: August–February

BRUNCA

The region of Brunca is split into two cantons: Coto Brus, which borders Panama, and Pérez Zeledón. Of the two, Coto Brus depends more on coffee as an integral part of its economy. Italian settlers arrived here after World War II and, with Costa Ricans, started coffee farms in the area.

Pérez Zeledón's coffee was first planted and produced by settlers from the Central Valley region of the country, towards the end of the 19th century. A lot of the coffee grown in this region is either Caturra or Catuai.

Altitude: 600–1,700m (2,000–5,600ft)
Harvest: August–February

TURRIALBA

The harvest in this region is earlier than most, due to the weather and particularly the rainfall in the area. With less defined wet and dry seasons, it isn't unusual to see multiple flowerings on coffee trees here. The weather may present something of a challenge for coffee production, as coffees of very high quality are relatively scarce.

Altitude: 500–1,400m (1,600–4,600ft)
Harvest: July–March

GUANACASTE

This western region is large but there are only relatively small areas of it under coffee. The area is more dependent on beef ranching and rice than on coffee. There is still a sizeable production, though much of it is grown at lower altitudes making stunning coffees less common here.

Altitude: 600–1,300m (2,000–4,300ft)
Harvest: July–February

SOUTH AMERICA

CUBA

Coffee came to Cuba from the island of Hispaniola in 1748, but there was little coffee industry to speak of until the influx of French settlers in 1791, fleeing the Haitian revolution. By 1827 there were around two thousand coffee farms on the island and coffee became a major export, generating more money than sugar.

Castro's revolution, from 1953 to 1961, brought with it the nationalization of coffee farms and production dropped almost immediately. Those who volunteered to farm coffee had no experience and those who had previously worked the land had fled the country in the wake of the revolution. Coffee production struggled on the island, and little in the way of incentives or encouragement from the government did much to bolster the industry, though production did peak in the 1970s at around 30,000 tonnes (30,000 tons) of coffee. As Cuba's coffee industry was faltering, many Central American countries continued to enjoy greater exports and success in international markets.

The breakdown of the Soviet Union left Cuba increasingly isolated, and the trade embargo placed on Cuba by the United States removed a major potential market. Japan has been the major importer of Cuban coffee, though Europe remains a strong market. The best coffees are typically exported, usually around one-fifth of the total production, leaving the rest for domestic consumption. Cuba's own production does not cover domestic demand and in 2013 the country spent nearly $40 million on imported coffee. The coffee being imported into Cuba is not of the highest quality so it is relatively cheap, but high market prices have led to the reappearance of the habit of mixing in roasted peas to bulk out the coffee.

Right now Cuban coffee production remains low at around 6,000–7,000 tonnes (6,600–7,700 tons) a year. Much of the equipment used is old, and many producers are still reliant on mules. Roads are often badly damaged by alternating rain and drought and are poorly maintained. Coffee is usually dried in the sun, though some mechanical drying takes place, and most of the coffees grown for export are washed. Cuba's climate and topography are well suited to coffee growing and its scarcity may add much to its value, but there are many challenges facing those producers wishing to create high-quality coffees.

TRACEABILITY

Cuban coffees are unlikely to be traceable down to a single farm, and are often only traceable down to a particular region or sub-region of the country.

'CUBAN COFFEE'

A number of Cuban coffee preparations have spread around the world, including Cortadito, Café con Leche and Café Cubano. The latter refers to an espresso that is sweetened as it is brewed, by adding sugar to the ground coffee.

In the United States especially, and in other places, it is not uncommon to see 'Cuban Coffee' advertised. True Cuban coffee is illegal in the United States due to the trade embargo, but this term is often used to describe a Café Cubano. Coffees, often from Brazil, are selected to represent the flavours one might expect from Cuba but there are, of course, concerns about confusion among customers and mislabelling of goods.

TASTE PROFILE

Cuban coffees have a typical island coffee profile: relatively low in acidity with a heavier body.

Population: 11,167,000

Number of 60kg (132lb) bags in 2013: 150,000

Cuba is the largest island in the Caribbean. Much of it is relatively low-lying plains but there are some mountainous areas suitable for coffee.

SIERRA MAESTRA

This mountainous region runs the length of the southern coast and has a long history of guerrilla warfare, from the 1500s to the revolution in the 1950s. Most of the coffee production on the island is located here.

Altitude: 1,000–1,200m (3,300–3,900ft)

Harvest: July–December

Varieties: Mostly Typica, some Bourbon, Caturra, Catuai, Catimor

SIERRA DEL ESCAMBRAY

A small amount of Cuba's coffee is grown in this mountain range in the middle of the island.

Altitude: 350–900m (1,100–3,000ft)

Harvest: July–December

Varieties: Mostly Typica, some Bourbon, Caturra, Catuai, Catimor

SIERRA DEL ROSARIO

Coffee farms have existed in this region since 1790, though relatively little of Cuba's coffee is grown here now. Instead the mountains are home to Cuba's first Biosphere Reserve, and this is a protected area.

Altitude: 300–550m (1,000–1,800ft)

Harvest: July–December

Varieties: Mostly Typica, some Bourbon, Caturra, Catuai, Catimor

Above: Though the climate and topography suit the crop, Cuba's coffee industry suffers from poor infrastructure and equipment.

DOMINICAN REPUBLIC

SOUTH AMERICA

Coffee came to the Spanish-controlled portion of the island of Hispaniola, what is now the Dominican Republic, in 1735. The first plantings were probably on a hill in Bahoruco Panzo, near Neyba. By the end of the 18th century, coffee had become the second most important crop after sugar, though both relied heavily on slavery until the revolution of 1791.

Coffee production really took root between 1822 and 1844, particularly in the region of Valdesia in the southern mountains. This region contains several coffee-growing areas and became the primary production area in the country by 1880.

By 1956 the country had started to export coffees from specific regions, predominantly Bani, Ocoa and Valdesia. In the 1960s the farmers in these regions became more organized, and a mill was opened in 1967 with 155 members.

As in many coffee-producing countries, the turmoil and unpredictability of prices at the end of the 20th century have lead to a decreased dependence on coffee as an export product. Many producers diversified into beans or avocados, though a good number of them have retained a small amount of coffee in case prices recover.

Although Valdesia is not one of the main government-designated growing regions, they have sought to protect its origin name with the launch, in 2010, of the Café de Valdesia brand.

EXPORT VS DOMESTIC CONSUMPTION

Interestingly it seems that since the late 1970s the quantity of coffee produced in the Dominican Republic has varied little, but exports have dropped dramatically. Currently only about twenty per cent of the coffee harvested is sold for export. This is because domestic coffee consumption is relatively high at approximately 3kg (6¹/₂lb) per person per year, more than the United Kingdom. In 2007, around half of exports were shipped via Puerto Rico, though this acts as a gateway to the United States. The rest of the coffee was destined for Europe and Japan.

Since 2001, more and more of the coffee destined for export has been organically grown and certified, adding value and revenue to the industry. But while organic production is overall a good thing, it should be reiterated that it does not necessarily make a better cup of coffee.

TASTE PROFILE

Typical of coffees grown on islands, the better lots tend to be quite mild, low to middling in acidity and relatively clean.

Some argue that the high domestic consumption of coffee in the Dominican Republic has resulted in lower quality overall, as the coffee is not competing with other exporting countries for this particular market. Nonetheless, there are still great coffees to be found in the Dominican Republic.

TRACEABILITY

While it is possible to get some extremely traceable coffees, usually down to a particular farm, much of what is exported is not particularly traceable past the growing region. These coffees are often graded by bean size, with designations such as 'Supremo', which may carry a premium but not one that is based on cup quality.

GROWING REGIONS

Population: 9,445,000

Number of 60kg (132lb) bags in 2013: 450,000

The climate in the Dominican Republic is a little different to many other coffee-producing countries. It doesn't have clear seasons, neither in terms of temperature nor in terms of rainfall. This means that coffee production is often taking place, to some extent, throughout the year, though the main harvest tends to be from November to May.

BARAHONA

This region is on the southwest side of the island and the coffee here is grown in the Bahoruco mountain range. The area has established a reputation for high quality, compared to the island's other regions. Agriculture is the main industry here, and coffee the main product.

Altitude: 600–1,300m (2,000–4,300ft)
Harvest: October–February
Varieties: 80% Typica, 20% Caturra

CIBAO

Coffee is an important product in this region, along with rice and cacao. Cibao is on the north side of the island, and its name means 'place where rocks abound'. The name refers specifically to the valley between the Central and Septentrional mountain ranges.

Altitude: 400–800m (1,300–2,600ft)
Harvest: September–December
Varieties: 90% Typica, 10% Caturra

CIBAO ALTURA

This region is defined as being the higher-altitude areas within the Cibao region.

Altitude: 600–1,500m (2,000–4,900ft)
Harvest: October–May
Varieties: 30% Typica, 70% Caturra

Left: Crops from the mountainous Barahona region in the Dominican Republic are of especially high quality.

CENTRAL MOUNTAINS (CORDILLERA CENTRAL)

This mountain range is the highest in the Dominican Republic, and is also known as the 'Dominican Alps'. The geology of the region is notably different from the surrounding areas so the coffee here is the only coffee on the island that is grown on granite substrate, rather than calcium.

Altitude: 600–1,500m (2,000–4,900ft)
Harvest: November–May
Varieties: 30% Typica, 65% Caturra, 5% Catuai

NEYBA

This region (also spelled Neiba) is named after its capital city, and is in the southwest of the island. The region is quite flat and low and is primarily used for grapes, plantain and sugar, but coffee does grow higher up in the Sierra del Neyba mountains.

Altitude: 700–1,400m (2,300–4,600ft)
Harvest: November–February
Varieties: 50% Typica, 50% Caturra

VALDESIA

This is probably the best known of the growing regions on the island, and has been award a Denomination of Origin to protect the value of its exports. As it is well defined and protected, it has gained a good reputation, and a small premium associated with it.

Altitude: 500–1,100m (1,600–3,600ft)
Harvest: October–February
Varieties: 40% Typica, 60% Caturra

Plantations, such the Dom Jiminez Estate near San José, are increasingly recognizing the benefit of providing sustainable practices, including housing and social programmes for workers.

SOUTH AMERICA

ECUADOR

Coffee came relatively late to Ecuador, arriving in around 1860 in the province of Manabí. Coffee production spread throughout the country and by around 1905 exports to Europe began from the port of Manta. Ecuador is one of the relatively few countries to grow both Arabica and Robusta coffee.

After disease ravaged much of the cocoa crop in 1920s, many farmers began to focus on coffee. Exports began to grow from 1935, and what was 220,000 bags then became around 1.8 million bags by 1985. The world coffee crisis of the 1990s caused an inevitable drop in production, but by 2011 production was back to around one million bags per year. Until the 1970s coffee had been Ecuador's main export crop, but it was later replaced by oil, shrimps and bananas.

Ecuadorians consume more soluble coffee than they do fresh and, interestingly, the cost of coffee production in Ecuador is high enough that soluble coffee manufacturers there import coffee from Vietnam instead of buying it in Ecuador.

Ecuador does not hold a great reputation for quality coffee. In part this is because forty per cent of its production is Robusta but still most of Ecuador's exported coffee is relatively low quality. To keep production costs down, much of the crop is dried either on the tree before picking, or on patios, and the term to describe this natural process locally is *café en bola*. This coffee generally ends up in soluble coffee, and around 83 per cent of the country's export has been naturally processed. Colombia is one of the main importers because manufacturers of soluble coffee there will pay a better price than local ones. This is because Colombian coffee is expensive due to the strength of the national brand in foreign markets.

While coffee has been produced in Ecuador for a long time, there are those who feel that it is only now worth considering coffee from this country as a hidden gem full of potential. There is certainly the geography and climate to produce extraordinary coffees, and it will be interesting to see if investment from the speciality coffee industry results in some great new coffees hailing from Ecuador in the future.

TRACEABILITY

It is rare to find coffee traceable down to a single estate. It is more common to see a lot from a group of producers, or sometimes a lot can be put together by an exporter. Lots like this can come from a large numbers of farmers, but may still be excellent.

TASTE PROFILE

Coffees from Ecuador are beginning to live up to their potential for quality, with sweeter and more complex coffees becoming available. They are made more interesting by a pleasant acidity.

Population: 15,224,000

Number of 60kg (132lb) bags in 2013: 676,000

Ecuadorean coffees are coming to increasing prominence within the speciality coffee industry, and while lower-lying regions are less likely to produce great coffees, the higher altitude areas hold great potential.

MANABI

Nearly fifty per cent of the Arabica in Ecuador is produced here. But with almost all of the coffee in this region growing below 700m (2,300ft), this area does not have the necessary altitude to produce excellent coffees.

Altitude: 500–700m (1,600–2,300ft)
Harvest: April–October
Varieties: Typica, Caturra, Robusta

Opposite and below: Ecuadorian coffee crops are not recognized for their quality, as much of the harvest is processed naturally – a method known locally as *cafe en bola*.

LOJA

Around twenty per cent of the Arabica in the country comes from this mountainous region in the south, and from a geographical perspective this region has the greatest potential for quality. Most of the focus from the speciality coffee sector is here. However, the area is susceptible to difficult weather which can, as happened in 2010, result in an increase in damage from coffee berry borer (see page 16).

Altitude: up to 2,100m (6,900ft)
Harvest: June–September
Varieties: Caturra, Bourbon, Typica

EL ORO

This coastal region in the southwest of the country includes part of the Andes mountain chain and produces less than ten per cent of Ecuador's annual coffee production. The main focus on coffee is around the town of Zaruma (not to be confused with the region of Zamora).

Altitude: 1,200m (3,900ft)
Harvest: May–August
Varieties: Typica, Caturra, Bourbon

ZAMORA CHINCHIPE

This province is just to the east of Loja and has sufficient altitude to produce great coffee, although only four per cent of the country's Arabica is produced here. Organic production is relatively common in this area.

Altitude: up to 1,900m (6,200ft)
Harvest: May–August
Varieties: Typica, Caturra, Bourbon

GALAPAGOS

A small amount of coffee is produced on the Galapagos islands, and its proponents claim that the climate there mimics a much higher altitude, allowing higher-quality coffee to be grown. Coffees like this can be extremely expensive, and rarely does the quality in the cup match the price.

Altitude: 350m (1,100ft)
Harvest: June–September and December–February
Varieties: Bourbon

SOUTH AMERICA

EL SALVADOR

Coffee was first produced commercially in El Salvador in the 1850s. It soon became a favoured crop, with tax breaks for producers. Coffee production became an important part of the economy and the country's main export, and by 1880 El Salvador was the fourth-largest producer of coffee in the world, producing more than twice as much as it does today.

The growth of the coffee industry came about in part because El Salvador was moving away from its previous dominant crop, indigo, after the invention of chemical dyes in the mid-19th century. The land used to grow indigo had been controlled by a relatively small landed elite. Coffee production required a different type of land, so these landed families used their influence in government to pass laws to push the poor from their land so that it could be absorbed into the new coffee plantations. Compensation to those indigenous people was all but nonexistent, sometimes they were simply offered the chance to work seasonally on the newly established coffee plantations.

By the early 20th century, El Salvador would become one of the most progressive of the Central American nations, the first with paved highways and investment in ports, railroads and lavish public buildings. Coffee helped fund infrastructure and integrate indigenous communities into the national economy, but it also served as a mechanism for the landed elite to maintain political and economic control over the country.

The aristocracy of the time exerted their power through the support of military rule from the 1930s, and this became a period of relative stability. The growth of the coffee industry in the decades that followed helped support the development of a cotton industry and light manufacturing. Up until the civil war of the 1980s,

KEY

Coffee growing regions

El Salvador had a reputation for quality and efficiency in its coffee production, with well-established relationships with importing countries. The civil war, however, would have a dramatic impact on this, as production fell and foreign markets looked elsewhere for their coffee.

HEIRLOOM VARIETIES

Despite the drop in production and exports, the civil war had an unexpected benefit for the coffee industry. Throughout much of Central America at the time, coffee producers were replacing their heirloom varieties with newly developed high-yield varieties. The cup quality of these new varieties did not match that of the heirloom varieties, but yield was favoured over quality. El Salvador, however, never went through this process. The country still has an unusually high percentage of heirloom Bourbon trees, in total producing about 68 per cent of its coffee. Combined with its well-drained, but mineral-rich

Above: El Salvador's unusually high percentage of heirloom coffee varieties and agriculturally rich farmland mean exports for its sweet flavoured coffees have increasing potential.

THE PACAS VARIETY

In 1949 a mutation of the Bourbon variety was discovered by Don Alberto Pacas on one of his farms. It was named after him, and was later crossed with Maragogype, a variety of coffee with very large beans, to create the Pacamara variety. Both desirable varieties remain in production in the region and in neighbouring countries. For more information on varieties see pages 22–25.

volcanic soils, the country has the potential to produce some stunningly sweet coffees.

This has been the focus of much of El Salvador's

In a sea of ripe coffee cherries at El Paste near Santa Ana, this worker shovels the harvest ready for processing. The Apaneca-Ilamatpec region is the biggest producer of coffee in El Salvador.

recent coffee marketing and it has worked hard to regain its standing among the coffee-producing countries and re-establish old relationships with consuming nations. Large estates still exist in El Salvador, but there are also a lot of small farms. It is a great country to explore, as there are many stunning coffees, full of sweetness and complexity.

TRACEABILITY

The infrastructure in place means that it is relatively easy to retain the traceability on high-quality coffees right back to farm level, and many farms are able to create micro-lots based around process and variety.

TASTE PROFILE

The Bourbon variety coffees from El Salvador are famously sweet and well balanced, with a pleasing soft acidity to give balance in the cup.

GROWING REGIONS

Population: 6,134,000

Number of 60kg (132lb) bags in 2013: 844,000

Most coffee roasters do not use the region names when describing coffees. While they are distinct, well-defined regions, some would argue that El Salvador itself is so small that it could be classified as a single region, with clearly defined pockets of coffee growing within it.

APANECA-ILAMATEPEC MOUNTAIN RANGE

With a reputation for great quality, this area produces many competition-winning coffees, despite the volcanic activity here. The Santa Ana volcano erupted as recently as 2005, having a massive impact on production for a couple of years. This is the largest-producing region of the country and it was probably here that coffee was first cultivated in El Salvador.

Altitude: 500–2,300m (1,600–7,500ft)

Harvest: October–March

Varieties: 64% Bourbon, 26% Pacas, 10% others

ALOTEPEC-METAPAN MOUNTAIN RANGE

This mountain range is one of the wetter regions of El Salvador, with over one-third more rainfall than average. The region borders both Guatemala and Honduras, yet despite its proximity to those countries the coffees here remain distinct and different.

Altitude: 1,000–2,000m (3,300–6,600ft)

Harvest: October–March

Varieties: 30% Bourbon, 50% Pacas, 15% Pacamara, 5% others

EL BÁLSAMO-QUEZALTEPEC MOUNTAIN RANGE

Some of the coffee farms in this region overlook the capital city of San Salvador, from high up on the sides of the Quetzaltepec volcano. This region was home to the pre-Hispanic Quetzalcotitán civilization, who worshipped the feathered serpent god Quetzalcoat, still a common symbol in Salvadorian culture today. The mountain range also takes its name from the Peruvian Balsam produced there, an aromatic resin used in perfumes, cosmetics and medicines.

Altitude: 500–1,950m (1,600–6,400ft)

Harvest: October–March

Varieties: 52% Bourbon, 22% Bourbon, 26% mixed & others

ALTITUDE CLASSIFICATIONS

El Salvador still sometimes classifies coffee based on the altitude at which it was grown. These classifications have no relation to either quality or traceability.

Strictly High Grown (SHG): grown above 1,200m (3,900ft)

High Grown (HG): grown above 900m (3,000ft)

Central Standard: grown above 600m (2,000ft)

CHICHONTEPEC VOLCANO

Coffee was late coming to this region in the centre of the country, with barely fifty bags of coffee being produced here in 1880. However, the volcanic land is extremely fertile, and today the area is home to many coffee farms. The traditional practice of planting alternating rows of coffee and orange trees for shade is still common: some believe this imparts an orange blossom quality to the coffee, though others attribute this soft citrus element to the Bourbon variety that is grown here.

Altitude: 500–1,000m (1,600–3,300ft)
Harvest: October–February
Varieties: 71% Bourbon, 8% Pacas, 21% mixed & others

TEPECA-CHINAMECA MOUNTAIN RANGE

This region is the third-largest producer of coffee in the country. Here they serve coffee with corn tortillas called tustacas, made with salt and dusted with sugar or made with a little panela (cane sugar).

Altitude: 500–2,150m (1,600–7,100ft)
Harvest: October–March
Varieties: 70% Bourbon, 22% Pacas, 8% mixed & others

CACAHUATIQUE MOUNTAIN RANGE

Captain General Gerardo Barrios was the first Salvadorian president who saw the potential economic value of coffee and it is rumoured that he was one of the first to cultivate coffee in El Salvador, on his property in this region, close to Villa de Cacahuatique, now called Ciudad Barrios. This mountain range is known for its abundance of clay, used to make pots, platters and decorative items. Farmers here often have to dig large holes in the clay-like earth and fill them with rich soil, in which to plant their young trees.

Altitude: 500–1,650m (1,600–5,400ft)
Harvest: October–March
Varieties: 65% Bourbon, 20% Pacas, 15% mixed & others

The powdery remains of coffee shells at La Majada estate in El Salvador are recylced for use as compost. Minerals and trace elements in the waste help nourish soil for the plants.

GUATEMALA

CENTRAL AMERICA

SOUTH AMERICA

Many believe that coffee was first introduced to Guatemala by the Jesuits around 1750, though there are accounts of it being grown and served in the country in 1747. As in El Salvador, coffee only became an important crop in Guatemala after 1856, when the invention of chemical dyes reduced demand for indigo, which was at that time the main cash crop.

The government had already made some attempts to diversify away from indigo. In 1845 it formed the Commission for Coffee Cultivation and Promotion, which produced educational materials for coffee producers and also helped establish a price and levels of quality. In 1868 the government distributed around one million coffee seeds, in an effort to further stimulate the industry.

When Justo Rufino Barrios came to power in 1871 he made coffee the backbone of the economy. Unfortunately, his reforms resulted in the indigenous people of Guatemala being further deprived of their land, as they led to the sale of around 400,000 hectares (990,000 acres) of what was considered public land. These became large coffee plantations. The efforts to stimulate coffee production certainly worked, however, and by 1880 coffee made up around ninety per cent of Guatemala's exports.

Coffee would again be involved in the country's politics following the global depression in 1930. Jorge Ubico had come to power and worked to lower the price of coffee to help stimulate export. He built extensive infrastructure, but gave more power and land to the United Fruit Company (UFC), an American corporation that grew to be extremely powerful. Ubico ultimately resigned due to a general strike and protests against him.

There followed a period of democratic free speech, and President Arbenz proposed a land reform act in 1953 to expropriate land (largely that controlled by the UFC) to redistribute it for agricultural purposes. Both large coffee plantation owners and the UFC (supported by

Opposite: Washing coffee beans at Finca Vista Hermosa Coffee Plantation, Agua Dulce, Guatemala.

KEY

Coffee growing regions

the US State Department) fought against the reforms. In 1954 a CIA coup overthrew the Arbenz government and the proposed land reforms never took place. This set the country down a path towards a civil war that lasted from 1960 to 1996. Many of the issues that provoked the war – poverty, land distribution, hunger, and racism towards indigenous people – are still issues today.

TASTE PROFILE

A wide range of flavours are present in Guatemala's coffees, from lighter, very sweet, fruity and complex coffees through to the heavier, richer and more chocolatey cups.

Guatemala's coffee production peaked at the turn of the millennium, as many producers moved away from coffee into macadamia nuts and avocados after the coffee crisis in 2001. Coffee leaf rust has also been an increasing problem for producers throughout the country, damaging a large portion of their production.

TRACEABILITY

Guatemalan coffees should be traceable down to farm level, or down to a cooperative or producer group. While some regions in Guatemala are now protected denominations of origin, the country has a long history of traceability and estates producing high-quality coffee because many farmers have their own wet mills and process their own coffee.

GROWING REGIONS

Population: 15,438,000
Number of 60kg (132lb) bags in 2013: 3,143,000

Guatemala has been more successful than most countries at defining its key regions, and marketing the coffees from these regions as being quite different from each other. In my experience, there are some flavour characteristics more common in certain regions, but there are no hard and fast rules for this.

SAN MARCOS

San Marcos is both the warmest and the rainiest of the coffee-growing regions in Guatemala. The rains come earlier to the mountain slopes facing the Pacific, so flowering is generally earlier too. The rainfall can provide challenges to post-harvest drying, so some farms rely on a mixture of sun drying and mechanical drying. Agriculture is a large part of the economy in this department, which produces grain, fruit, meat and wool.

Altitude: 1,300–1,800m (4,300–5,900ft)
Harvest: December–March
Varieties: Bourbon, Caturra, Catuai

ACATENANGO

Coffee production in this region is centred around the Acatenango valley, which is named after the volcano there. In the past, many producers here sold their coffee to 'coyotes' who would ship the cherries over to the Antigua region and process it there. Antigua had a better reputation for coffee, and so it commanded a higher price. This practice is now less common, as coffees from Acatenango can be excellent and are becoming more widely recognized so it is more profitable to keep them properly traceable.

Altitude: 1,300–2,000m (4,300–6,600ft)
Harvest: December–March
Varieties: Bourbon, Caturra, Catuai

ATITLÁN

The coffee farms here are located around lake Atitlán. Sitting at around 1,500m (4,900ft) above sea level, the lake has captured the minds of writers and travellers over many years because of its stunning beauty. In the late morning and early afternoon, strong winds are common here and are known locally as *xocomil*, 'the winds that carry away sin'.

There are a number of private nature reserves here, set up to preserve the biodiversity of the area and help prevent deforestation. Coffee production is under pressure due to increased labour costs and competition for the labour force. Urban sprawl is also increasing pressure on land use and some farmers are finding it is more profitable to sell their land than continue to grow coffee.

Altitude: 1,500–1,700m (4,900–5,600ft)
Harvest: December–March
Varieties: Bourbon, Typica, Caturra, Catuai

COBÁN

This region is named after the town of Cobán, which grew and thrived due to the German coffee producers who held a great deal of power here until the end of World War II. The lush rainforest comes with a very wet climate, which proves something of a challenge to coffee drying. The region is also somewhat remote, making transport more difficult and expensive but there are, nonetheless, stunning coffees coming from here.

Altitude: 1,300–1,500m (4,300–4,900ft)

Harvest: December–March

Varieties: Bourbon, Maragogype, Catuai, Caturra, Pache

NUEVO ORIENTE

Unsurprisingly for a region whose name means 'New East', Nuevo Oriente is located in the east of the country by the border with Honduras. The climate is dryer here and most of the coffee is produced by smallholders. Coffee production arrived here quite late, beginning in the 1950s.

Altitude: 1,300–1,700m (4,300–5,600ft)

Harvest: December–March

Varieties: Bourbon, Catuai, Caturra, Pache

HUEHUETENANGO

This is one of the better-known regions of Guatemala, and the most enjoyable to pronounce. The name translates from the Nahautl as 'place of the ancients' or 'place of the ancestors'. This area has the highest non-volcanic mountains in Central America and they are well suited to coffee growing. This region is probably the most dependent on coffee as an export and there are some truly astonishing coffees produced here.

Altitude: 1,500–2,000m (4,900–6,600ft)

Harvest: January–April

Varieties: Bourbon, Catuai, Caturra

FRAIJANES

This coffee-growing plateau surrounds the capital of Guatemala City. There is fairly regular volcanic activity in the area, which benefits the soil, but occasionally also endangers life and causes problems with infrastructure. Unfortunately the amount of land under coffee continues to decrease as the city grows and land use changes.

Altitude: 1,400–1,800m (4,600–5,900ft)

Harvest: December–February

Varieties: Bourbon, Caturra, Catuai, Pache

ANTIGUA

Antigua is probably the best-known coffee-producing region in Guatemala, and one of the best-known in the world. The region is named after the city of Antigua, famous for its Spanish architecture and a UNESCO World Heritage Site. The region attained a Denomination of Origin in 2000 under the name 'Genuine Antigua Coffee', after the market had become devalued by coffee fraudulently labelled as Antigua. This has prevented coffee from other origins being sold as Antigua, but it has not stopped the fraudulent practice of bringing cherries in from other regions to be processed there. Nonetheless, it is possible to find clearly traceable coffees from Antigua and while some are overpriced, others are of excellent quality and are worth seeking out.

Altitude: 1,500–1,700m (4,900–5,600ft)

Harvest: January–March

Varieties: Bourbon, Caturra, Catuai

Above: Many Guatemalan farmers have their own wet mills and coffee production facilities, which aids traceability of beans.

Though changing land use and varying temperatures influence the amount of coffee produced and the way it is processed in Guatemala, much of the coffee is treated in the traditional way and dried by sun.

UNITED STATES: HAWAII

Hawaii is the only coffee-producing region in a First-World country. This changes the economics, as well as the marketing, of the coffee. The producers here have been successful at engaging consumers directly – often entwining the coffee with a visit to the islands – but many coffee professionals feel that the quality of the coffee may not merit its price.

Coffee was first brought to Hawaii in 1817, although these initial plantings were unsuccessful. In 1825 the governor of Oahu, Chief Boki, was en voyage from Europe and stopped off in Brazil where he picked up some coffee plants. These plants did thrive and coffee production was soon widespread across the islands. The Bourbon variety was probably brought to the Big Island in 1828, and the first commercial plantation in Kauai began operation in 1836. However, plantations in the Hanalei Valley area of Kauai were destroyed by the coffee blight insect in 1858. The only region that continued to produce coffee from these initial plantings is the Kona region on the Big Island.

In the late 1800s, the industry attracted immigrants from China and then Japan, who came to work on the plantations. In the 1920s, many Filipinos arrived to work on the coffee farms during harvest time and the sugar cane plantations in the spring.

However, coffee did not become hugely important to the island economy until the 1980s, when sugar production ceased to be sufficiently profitable. The event triggered a renewed interest in coffee right across the state.

KONA

The best-known growing region in Hawaii, and one of the best-known in the world, is the Kona region on the

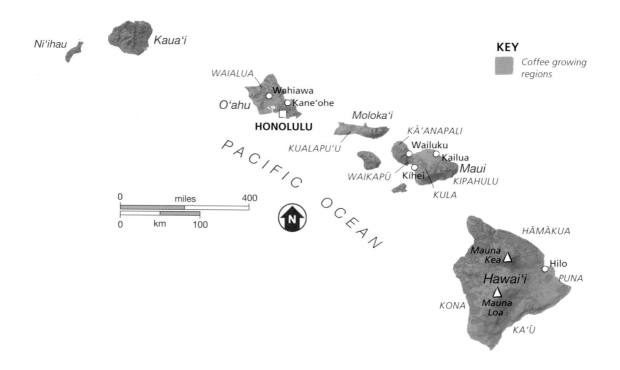

KEY

Coffee growing regions

Big Island. A long history of coffee production has helped cement the reputation of the region, although its success has lead to its exploitation through the mislabelling of coffee. Legislation on the island now means that any Kona blend must state the quantity of coffee from Kona on it, and the use of the '100% Kona' trademark is carefully controlled. A farm called Kona Kai in California had previously fought the awarding of any trademark or

Above: At the Dole Food Company on Waialua's coffee and cocoa farm, beans are spread out to be dried by sun. Waialua is the largest estate on Oahu Island and grows Typica berries.

protection for the name, but in 1996 its executive was found guilty of filling his 'Kona Coffee' bags with beans from Costa Rica.

More recently, the region has been challenged by the problem of coffee berry borer (see page 16). The island has introduced a number of measures to combat the blight, with some success, although there were fears that a reduction in yield would drive the already high price of Kona coffee even higher.

TRACEABILITY

It will come as no surprise that in a developed country the expectations of traceability should be high. Coffees are usually traceable down to a specific farm. In many cases, the farms roast their own coffees to sell direct to consumers and tourists. Many also export some of their crop, predominantly to the mainland United States.

KONA GRADING

Kona has its own grading system, mostly based on the size of the beans, but also divided into Type 1 and Type 2. Type 1 are the standard coffee beans, with two beans per cherry, while Type 2 coffees are exclusively peaberries (see page 21).

Within Type 1, Kona Extra Fancy are the largest beans, then they decrease in size through the following grades: Kona Fancy, Kona Number 1, Kona Select and Kona Prime.

Within Type 2 there are only two grades: Kona Number 1 Peaberry and the smaller Kona Peaberry Prime.

There are requirements for a maximum level of defects in most of the grades, but these are quite generous and not themselves a reliable indicator of quality.

TASTE PROFILE

Typically lower in acidity, with a little more body. Approachable but rarely complex and fruited.

GROWING REGIONS

Population: 1,404,000

Number of 60kg (132lb) bags in 2012: 43,181

Hawaii's reputation is dominated by a single region: Kona. The other islands are also worth exploring, however, if you like a typical island coffee with relatively low acidity, a little more body and less fruitiness in the cup.

KAUAI ISLAND

This growing region is dominated by a single company running 1,250 hectares (3,100 acres) of coffee production. The Kauai Coffee Company started growing coffee to diversify away from sugarcane in the late 1980s. Due to its size, it is a heavily mechanized farm.

Altitude: 30–180m (100–600ft)

Harvest: October–December

Varieties: Yellow Catuai, Red Catuai, Typica, Blue Mountain, Mundo Novo

OAHU ISLAND

This is another island that is dominated by the Waialua Estate, which is around 60 hectares (155 acres) in size. This farm, which started production in the early 1990s, is fully mechanized in its production and also grows cacao.

Altitude: 180–210m (600–700ft)

Harvest: September–February

Varieties: Typica

MAUI ISLAND

Maui has one large commercial coffee farm, Ka'anapali, which has the unusual addition of a selection of small plots of land with houses and coffee plantations for sale. Although the plots are owned by different people, the coffee production is done centrally. This large estate was a sugar plantation from 1860 to 1988, when production was turned over to coffee.

Altitude: 100–550m (350–1,800ft)

Harvest: September–January

Varieties: Red Catuai, Yellow Caturra, Typica, Mokka

KULA, MAUI ISLAND

This small region takes advantage of the slopes of the Haleakala volcano to achieve some decent elevation for coffee growing. Coffee is relatively new to the area.

Altitude: 450–1,050m (1,500–3,500ft)

Harvest: September–January

Varieties: Typica, Red Catuai

WAIKAPU, MAUI ISLAND

This is the newest region of coffee production in Hawaii. A single farm operates here, held by a company based in the neighbouring island of Molokai, called Coffees of Hawaii.

Altitude: 500–750m (1,600–2,450ft)

Harvest: September–January

Varieties: Typica, Catuai

KIPAHULU, MAUI ISLAND

This is a very low region on the southeast coast of Maui. Coffee is often grown on organic farms as part of a diverse set of crops.

Altitude: 90–180m (300–600ft)

Harvest: September–January

Varieties: Typica, Catuai

KAULAPUU, MOLOKAI ISLAND

This region is also dominated by a single coffee company, Coffees of Hawaii. The large farm is mechanized, often a requirement to reduce operational costs in an environment where labour is extremely expensive.

Altitude: 250m (800ft)

Harvest: September–January

Varieties: Red Catuai

KONA, BIG ISLAND

Unlike many other growing regions in Hawaii, there is a more diverse industry here with over 630 farms producing coffee. Typically run by individual families, these farms are usually less than 2 hectares (5 acres). Yields here may well be the highest per area of anywhere in the world and as the farms are so much smaller than elsewhere in Hawaii, it is common to see manual harvesting of the trees.

Altitude: 150–900m (500–3,000ft)

Harvest: August–January

Varieties: Typica

KAU, BIG ISLAND

Coffee production started in this region relatively recently, after the closure of the sugar mill in 1996. Until 2010, the farmers and cooperatives in the area had to travel to the neighbouring regions of Puna or Kona to have the coffee processed after harvest. However, a mill has now been constructed to alleviate the problem.

Altitude: 500–650m (1,600–2,150ft)

Harvest: August–January

Varieties: Typica

PUNA, BIG ISLAND

This region had around 2,400 hectares (6,000 acres) of land under coffee production at the end of the 19th century, but production ceased as sugar rose to prominence. However, the sugar mill closed in 1984 and some farmers are starting to grow coffee here again. Most farms in this area are relatively small – around 1.2 hectares (3 acres).

Altitude: 300–750m (1,000–2,450ft)

Harvest: August–January

Varieties: Red Catuai, Typica

HAMAKUA, BIG ISLAND

Coffee arrived here in 1852, and eight plantations were initially established. Like elsewhere in Hawaii, sugar soon became the favoured crop so coffee production declined. However, since the mid 1990s, some farms have started going back to coffee.

Altitude: 100–600m (350–2,000ft)

Harvest: August–January

Varieties: Typica

Opposite: Kalalau Valley on Kauai Island, typifies the landscape of Hawaii's plantations.

HONDURAS

SOUTH AMERICA

Since it is now the largest producer of coffee in Central America, it is surprising how little is known about the introduction of coffee to Honduras. What is probably the earliest record, dated to 1804, discusses the quality of the coffee produced there. This dates the arrival of coffee to before 1799, as the plants would take a few years to produce a crop.

It has only really been since 2001 that Honduras' production of coffee has increased dramatically. While the coffee industry drove the growth and development of infrastructure in much of Central America during the 1800s, due to Honduras' late blossoming the infrastructure simply was not there. This has provided a challenge for quality and has meant that much of the coffee produced under this new expansion was destined for the commodity market. Only more recently have we begun to see excellent coffees coming out of Honduras.

Opposite: Coffee crops are well suited to the soil in Honduras but the country's high rainfall can make it difficult for farmers to dry beans.

The national coffee institute, the Instituto Hondureño del Café (IHCAFE), was established in 1970 and is working to improve quality: in each of the six regions it has defined, there is a coffee-tasting laboratory to assist local producers.

Honduras was producing just under six million bags of coffee a year by 2011, more than Costa Rica and Guatemala combined. Around 110,000 families are involved in the production of coffee across the country. As for its future, there are concerns about the impact of leaf rust (see page 16). A state of national emergency was declared after harvests were badly damaged in 2012/2013 and the effects of leaf rust usually last a few years.

KEY
Coffee growing regions

CLASSIFICATION OF COFFEE

Honduras uses a similar system to El Salvador and Guatemala, which describes and categorizes coffees by the altitude at which they were grown. Above 1,200m (3,900ft) a coffee can be described as Strictly High Grown (SHG), and above 1,000m (3,300ft) as High Grown (HG). While there is some correlation between altitude and quality, it is most common to see less traceable lots marketed this way, though more traceable coffees often carry the initials, too.

TASTE PROFILE

A range of different flavours are found in Honduran coffees, but the best often have a complex fruity quality, and a lively, juicy acidity.

THE PROBLEM OF CLIMATE

While the land is well suited to growing great coffee, the weather poses a challenge. The high rainfall often makes it difficult to dry the beans after processing, so some producers use a combination of sun drying and mechanical drying. This has landed Honduras with a reputation for producing great coffees that can fade quite quickly, but much work is being done to address this problem. Much of the coffee is warehoused before shipping in extremely hot conditions near Puerto Cortez, which can further degrade it. There are obviously always exceptions to the rule, however, and the very best coffees from Honduras generally hold up better over time.

TRACEABILITY

It is possible to get high levels of traceability in Honduras, down to estate level or down to a specific cooperative or producer group.

Population: 8,250,000

Number of 60kg (132lb) bags in 2013:
4,200,000

Although it is not described by IHCAFE as a coffee-growing region, many roasters label coffee as being from the Santa Barbara region of Honduras. Several coffee regions cross into the Santa Barbara department (a governmental division of the country). Some would argue that it requires its own description, but it seemed more appropriate to stay within the official guidelines and use the growing regions listed below. There are some excellent Pacas variety lots coming from the Santa Barbara area. They have a distinctive and quite intense fruity quality when well produced, and are definitely worth seeking out.

Left: Many Honduran farmers grow beans of Bourbon, Caturra, Typica and Catuai varieties but leaf rust across all regions has recently devastated crops.

COPÁN

Copán is a department in the west of Honduras, named after the city of Copán, famous for its Mayan ruins. The region borders Guatemala, and areas like this remind me of the importance of focusing on exactly where a coffee is from rather than simply its country of origin. Geopolitical borders can be somewhat arbitrary, and consumer expectations of a coffee from Honduras and one from Guatemala are (unfortunately) quite a long way apart. Contained within Copán is the northern part of the Santa Barbara coffee region.

Altitude: 1,000–1,500m (3,300–4,900ft)
Harvest: November–March
Varieties: Bourbon, Caturra, Catuai

MONTECILLOS

This region contains within it several sub-regions of note. The most notable are Marcala, now a protected name, and La Paz. Marcala is a municipality inside the department of La Paz. Roasters are more likely to use these names in order to be more accurate, instead of marking their coffee with the wider region name of Montecillos.

Altitude: 1,200–1,600m (3,900–5,200ft)
Harvest: December–April
Varieties: Bourbon, Caturra, Catuai, Pacas

AGALTA

This region stretches right across the north of Honduras. Much of it is protected forest, so ecotourism plays a significant role in the local economy.

Altitude: 1,000–1,400m (3,300–4,600ft)
Harvest: December–March
Varieties: Bourbon, Caturra, Typica

OPALACA

Opalaca contains within it the southern part of the coffee-producing areas of Santa Barbara, as well as Intibucá and Lempira. It is named after the Opalaca mountain range, which stretches through the region.

Altitude: 1,100–1,500m (3,600–4,900ft)
Harvest: November–February
Varieties: Bourbon, Catuai, Typica

COMAYAGUA

This region, in western central Honduras, is dense with tropical rainforest. The city of Comayagua in the region was once the capital city of Honduras.

Altitude: 1,100–1,500m (3,600–4,900ft)
Harvest: December–March
Varieties: Bourbon, Caturra, Typica

EL PARAISO

This is one of the oldest and also the largest growing region in Honduras, in the east of the country near the border with Nicaragua. Recently the region has suffered badly with coffee leaf rust.

Altitude: 1,000–1,400m (3,300–4,600ft)
Harvest: December–March
Varieties: Catuai, Caturra

JAMAICA

The story of coffee on the island begins in 1728, when the Governor, Sir Nicholas Lawes, received a coffee plant from the Governor of Martinique. Lawes had already experimented with several crops, and he planted the coffee in the St Andrew area. Initially its production was relatively limited; in 1752 Jamaica exported only 27 tonnes (30 tons) of coffee.

The real boom started in the second half of the 18th century, with coffee spreading from the St Andrew area up to the Blue Mountains. In 1800, 686 coffee plantations were in operation, and by 1814 Jamaica's annual production was around 15,000 tonnes (16,500 tons) (although some estimates are considerably higher).

After this boom, the industry started to see a slow decline. The primary reason was probably the lack of labour, although other factors also played a role. The slave trade had been abolished in 1807, but the emancipation of slaves on the island did not happen until 1838. While there had been some efforts to recruit formers slaves as private labourers, coffee struggled to compete with other industries. And when combined with both poor soil management and the loss of the favourable trade conditions that Britain had previously extended

its colonies, it resulted in a steep decline for coffee. By 1850 there were only around 180 plantations left, and production had dropped to 1,500 tonnes (1,650 tons).

At the end of the 19th century, Jamaica was producing around 4,500 tonnes (5,000 tons) of coffee but serious issues with quality were starting to appear. In 1891, legislation had been passed to try to spread knowledge about coffee production in an effort to increase quality, and infrastructure was put in place for the centralized processing and grading of coffee. This programme had limited success, although a Central Coffee Clearing House was constructed in 1944 for all coffee to pass through before export, and in 1950 the Jamaican Coffee Board was formed.

From this point onwards coffees from the Blue Mountain region made slow and steady gains in reputation until they came to be considered among finest coffees in the world. At that time, however, few well-processed coffees were available and today Jamaica's coffees cannot really compete against the very best coffees from Central and South America, or East Africa. Jamaican coffees tend to be clean, sweet and very mild. They lack the complexity or distinct characteristics that one may expect from speciality grade coffees. However, they were consistently producing, and cleverly marketing, clean and sweet coffees long before other producers were, and this gave their coffees a distinct advantage for some time.

Below: Since the early 20th century, Jamaican coffee has become known for its clean, sweet and mild flavours.

TASTE PROFILE

Clean, sweet coffees though rarely complex or juicy and fruity.

Population: 2,711,000

Number of 60kg (132lb) bags in 2013: 18,000

There is really only one growing region of note in Jamaica, and it is probably one of the most famous growing regions in the world.

BLUE MOUNTAIN

The subject of one of the most successful pieces of marketing in coffee's history, this particular region of Jamaica is clearly defined and well protected. Only coffees grown between 900 and 1,500m (3,000 and 4,900ft) in the parishes of Saint Andrew, Saint Thomas, Portland and Saint Mary can be referred to as 'Jamaica Blue Mountain'. Coffees grown between 450 and 900m (1,500 and 3,000ft) can be called 'Jamaica High Mountain', and anything below this may be called 'Jamaica Supreme' or 'Jamaica Low Mountain'.

The traceability of Blue Mountain coffees can be somewhat confusing, as most of the coffees are sold under the name of the mill in which they are processed. These mills may occasionally keep a large estate's coffee separate, but usually they buy from the myriad of smallholders who grow coffee in the region.

For a long time, the majority of Jamaica's Blue Mountain production was sold to Japan. It was exported in small wooden barrels rather than in jute bags. Also worth noting is that, due to its ability to achieve very high prices, there is usually a fair amount of coffee fraudulently mislabelled as Blue Mountain on the market.

Altitude: 900–1,500m (3,000–4,900ft)

Harvest: June–July

Varieties: Jamaica Blue Mountain (a Typica derivative), Typica

Left: The provenance of Blue Mountain coffee is tightly controlled, based on the altitude of crops. Distinctive wooden barrels further emphasize the brand.

MEXICO

The first coffee plants were probably brought to Mexico around 1785, most likely from Cuba or what is now the Dominican Republic. There are reports of plantations in the region of Veracruz in 1790. However, due to the wealth earned from Mexico's rich mineral deposits, for many years there was little drive behind energizing and creating a coffee industry.

The first widespread land registration in Mexico was prompted by border disputes with neighbouring Guatemala. This allowed a small number of rich Europeans to purchase large tracts of land and have the security necessary to begin investing in the infrastructure required for coffee plantations. The displaced indigenous people were often forced up into the mountains, and then over time tempted back to work on the plantations.

Only after the Mexican revolution ended in 1920 did coffee growing spread to small farms. In 1914 there had been a redistribution of land back to indigenous people and to labourers and many of those trapped working on coffee plantations were freed and were able to return to their communities, taking their coffee-growing skills with them. This redistribution of land broke up many of the larger haciendas, and this was the beginning of smallholder production in Mexico.

In 1973 the government formed the Mexican Coffee Institute (Instituto Mexicano del Café) referred to as INMECAFE. They were tasked with providing technical assistance and financial credit to producers, and work within the International Coffee Agreement to meet and stay within the agreed production quotas. This investment in the industry lead to a rapid expansion in both production and the amount of land dedicated to coffee. In some rural areas, production increased by almost nine hundred per cent.

Below: Since the late 1980s, many Mexican coffee producers have successfully formed collectives to purchase and run coffee plantations. Fair Trade and organic exports are increasingly common.

KEY

Coffee growing regions

However, the 1980s saw the Mexican government change its policy towards coffee, in part due to its heavy borrowing and the drop in the price of oil that lead to it defaulting on its loans. Support of the industry slowly began to decline and, in 1989, INMECAFE collapsed completely and the government sold off its state-owned coffee processing facilities. The effect on the industry was devastating. Credit had dried up, and many farmers struggled to find places to sell their coffee. This lead to an increase in predatory coffee brokers, known as coyotes, who would buy coffee from farmers very cheaply to resell at a profit.

The loss of INMECAFE, combined with the coffee price crisis caused by the breakdown of the 1989 International Coffee Agreement, had a strong effect on the quality of coffee being produced, too. With less income, huge numbers of producers ceased using fertilizers, stopped investing in pest protection and spent less time and resources on weeding and farm management. In some cases farmers simply stopped harvesting their coffee.

Interestingly, some producers (particularly in the states of Oaxaca, Chiapas and Veracruz) responded by forming collectives to take over many of the responsibilities previously held by INMECAFE, including the collective purchasing and running of coffee mills, technical assistance, political lobbying and even assistance in developing direct relationships with buyers.

Coffee producers in Mexico seem to have embraced coffee certifications; Fair Trade and organic in particular are quite common. Mexico sells a great deal of its coffee to the United States, so it is relatively rare to find excellent examples of Mexican coffee elsewhere in the world.

TRACEABILITY

Most coffee in Mexico is produced by smallholders, rather than large estates. Traceability should be possible down to a producer group, cooperative or occasionally down to a farm.

TASTE PROFILE

Mexico produces quite a range of coffees across its regions, from lighter-bodied, delicate coffees through to sweeter coffees with caramel, toffee or chocolate flavours in the cup.

GROWING REGIONS

Population: 118,395,000
Number of 60kg (132lb) bags in 2013:
3,900,000

Coffee is also grown outside of the key growing regions listed below, and should not be ignored if offered by a roaster or retailer you trust. Production from these regions is very small compared to the major areas.

CHIAPAS

This region borders Guatemala. The Sierra Madre mountain range offers both the necessary altitude, as well as the beneficial volcanic soils, for good coffee production.

Altitude: 1,000–1,750m (3,300–5,750ft)
Harvest: November–March
Varieties: Bourbon, Typica, Caturra, Maragogype

OAXACA

Most farmers in this region own less than 2 hectares (4.4 acres) of land and there are several large cooperatives operating here. There are also a few larger estates, although some are starting to diversify into tourism.

Altitude: 900–1,700m (3,000–5,600ft)
Harvest: December–March
Varieties: Bourbon, Typica, Caturra, Maragogype

VERACRUZ

This is a large state in the east of the country along the coast of the Gulf of Mexico. This area contains some of the lowest coffee production in Mexico, but also some very high-altitude plantations around Coatepec, that produce better coffee.

Altitude: 800–1,700m (2,600–5,600ft)
Harvest: December–March
Varieties: Bourbon, Typica, Caturra, Maragogype

Right: A farmer turns over the coffee beans he has spread out to dry on his porch on a small cooperative near Tapachula, Mexico.

NICARAGUA

Coffee was first brought to Nicaragua by Catholic Missionaries in 1790 and initially it was grown as something of a curiosity. It was not until around 1840 that it gained economic significance in response to an increasing global demand for coffee. The first commercial plantations appeared around Managua.

The hundred-year period between 1840 and 1940 is often referred to as the 'Coffee Boom' years in Nicaragua, and during this time coffee had a dramatic effect on the economy. As coffee gained importance and value, so it required the input of more and more resources and labour. By 1870, coffee was Nicaragua's principal export crop and the government strove to make it easier for foreign companies to invest in the industry and to acquire land. Previously public land was sold to private individuals, and the government encouraged the creation of large farms with the Subsidy Laws passed in 1879 and 1889, which paid planters $0.05 for every tree they planted over five thousand trees.

By the end of the 19th century, Nicaragua came to resemble something of a banana republic, with most of the profit from coffee either leaving the country or going to a small number of local landowners.

The first growers' cooperative was formed in the early 20th century, and the idea of cooperatives was promoted again from time to time during the Somoza family dictatorship between 1936 and 1979. However, the overthrow of the Somoza family by the Sandinistas, and the ushering in of communism in 1979 was the beginning of a difficult time for coffee industry. The Contras, rebel groups backed by the US and the CIA, formed to oppose the new government, targeted the coffee industry as part of their campaign, attacking vehicles transporting coffee farm workers, as well as sabotaging coffee mills.

Despite these setbacks, in 1992 coffee was still Nicaragua's primary export. However, the crash in coffee prices between 1999 and 2003 massively damaged the coffee sector again. Three of the largest six banks in the country collapsed due to their level of exposure to coffee production. The effect of low prices was perhaps multiplied further after the devastation of Hurricane Mitch in 1998, and the drought at the turn of the millennium.

Things are now, however, looking up for Nicaraguan coffee and more farmers are focusing on quality. In the past, the traceability of coffee was poor, and most was sold as a mill brand or as being from a particular region. Now the levels of traceability are very high.

TRACEABILITY

You should be able to find coffees traceable down to single estates, or to producer groups or cooperatives.

TASTE PROFILE

A range of flavours are found in Nicaraguan coffees. They are typically quite complex and capable of pleasing fruit-like flavours and clean acidity.

Population: 6,071,000

Number of 60kg (132lb) bags in 2013: 1,500,000

Nicaragua has a number of smaller growing regions, including Madriz, Managua, Boaca and Carazo, which are not listed below but that do produce some excellent coffees.

JINOTEGA

The name of the region, and its capital city, is derived from the Nahuatl word *xinotencatl*, but there is disagreement as to what this actually means. It is either 'city of old men' or 'neighbours of the Jiñocuabos', the latter probably being the accurate one. The region's economy has long been dependent on coffee, and it is still the primary producing region in Nicaragua.

Altitude: 1,100–1,700m (3,600–5,600ft)
Harvest: December–March
Varieties: Caturra, Bourbon

MATAGALPA

Another region named after its capital city, a city with a museum dedicated to coffee. Coffee from this region is produced by a mixture of estates and cooperatives.

Altitude: 1,000–1,400m (3,300–4,600ft)
Harvest: December–February
Varieties: Caturra, Bourbon

NUEVA SEGOVIA

This region is on Nicaragua's northern border, and in recent years it has begun to distinguish itself for producing some of the very best coffees in the country, with a great deal of success in the country's Cup of Excellence competition.

Altitude: 1,100–1,650m (3,600–5,400ft)
Harvest: December–March
Varieties: Caturra, Bourbon

Left and opposite: Coffee is one of Nicaragua's most important exports and the trade has survived political upheaval and natural disasters.

PANAMA

Coffee plants probably arrived in Panama with the first European settlers in the early 19th century. In the past, Panama did not have a very good reputation for its coffees, and its production was about one-tenth of that of its neighbour Costa Rica, but now there is increasing interest from the speciality coffee community in the high-quality coffees it can produce.

Panama's geography is such that there are a number of distinct microclimates in its coffee-growing regions, and there are some incredibly skilled and dedicated producers currently growing coffee. This means that there are some stellar coffees being produced, though these often come with relatively high asking prices.

These high prices are partly determined by the other major factor influencing the industry there: real estate. There is a high demand for land from North Americans wishing to buy a home in a stable, beautiful and relatively cheap country. Many farms that once produced coffee have now been sold as homes for ex-pats. Panama also has a higher standard of labour laws, so coffee pickers

tend to be paid a higher wage here, a cost that is passed on to the consumer.

HACIENDA LA ESMERALDA

When it comes to discussing the price of coffee, one particular farm in Panama merits a mention and it is hard to think of another single estate that has had such a strong influence on the coffee industry in Central America. That farm is Hacienda La Esmeralda, owned and operated by the Peterson family.

Right: The distinctive Geisha variety is commonly associated with crops from Panama. Its floral, citrusy flavour and efforts by local farmers to maintain high quality has created a growing demand.

KEY

Coffee growing regions

PACIFIC OCEAN

At a time when the commodity price of coffee was relatively low, the Specialty Coffee Association of Panama organized a competition called the Best of Panama: the best lots of coffee from different farms in Panama were ranked and then put up for an online auction. Hacienda La Esmeralda had been growing a distinct variety called Geisha (see page 24) for some years, but this competition brought their coffee to a wider audience. They won the competition for four successive years from 2004 to 2007, and then again in 2009, 2010 and a category of the 2013 competition. From the outset this coffee broke records when it achieved a price of $21/lb in 2004, which incrementally crept up to $170/lb in 2010. A small lot of its naturally processed coffee sold for $350.25/lb in 2013, leaving no one in doubt that this was the most expensive single-estate coffee in the world.

Unlike some other very high-priced coffees (such as the appalling novelty-driven Kopi Luwak, or some of the Jamaica Blue Mountain coffees), this farm achieved its prices due to the genuinely high quality of its coffee, although high demand and great marketing undoubtedly played a role. This record-breaking coffee tastes quite unusual: extremely floral and citrusy though quite light and tea-like in body. These characteristics are attributed to the Geisha variety.

The impact of this farm can be seen in the number of farms in Panama, and in Central America, who have started planting Geisha. For many producers this variety seemed like a promise of higher prices, and to some extent this has proven to be true, as Geisha lots are usually sold for higher prices than other varieties.

TRACEABILITY

One should expect high levels of traceability from Panama. Coffees are often traceable down to a single estate and it is not unusual to see distinct lots from one particular estate, such as a coffee produced by a distinctive post-harvest process or one from a specific variety of the coffee plant.

TASTE PROFILE

The better coffees tend to be citrusy and floral, light bodied, delicate and complex.

Population: 3,406,000

Number of 60kg (132lb) bags in 2013: 100,000

Panama's regions have been defined more by how coffee has been sold than by geography. Previously, when coffee was more widespread, the regions listed below could have been grouped as one entity, as they are small and closely clustered together.

BOQUETE

This is the best-known of Panama's producing regions. Its mountainous topography produces various distinct microclimates. The fairly cool weather and frequent mists help slow the maturation of the coffee cherries and some argue this mimics the effects of higher altitude.

Altitude: 400–1,900m (1,300–6,200ft)
Harvest: December–March
Varieties: Typica, Caturra, Catuai, Bourbon, Geisha, San Ramon

VOLCAN-CANDELA

This region produces much of Panama's food, and some stunning coffees. Named after the Volcan Baru volcano and Piedra Candela city, the region borders Costa Rica.

Altitude: 1,200–1,600m (3,900–5,200ft)
Harvest: December–March
Varieties: Typica, Caturra, Catuai, Bourbon, Geisha, San Ramon

RENACIMIENTO

Another district within the Chiriquí province, on the border with Costa Rica. The district itself is relatively small, so it is not a primary producer of Panama's speciality coffees.

Altitude: 1,100–1,500m (3,600–4,900ft)
Harvest: December–March
Varieties: Typica, Caturra, Catuai, Bourbon, Geisha, San Ramon

Left: A plantation in Volcan is one of many in this region producing stunning coffees.

SOUTH AMERICA

PERU

Coffee was first brought to Peru between 1740 and 1760, at a time when the Viceroyalty of Peru covered a larger area than the country does today. Although the climate was well suited to large-scale coffee production, all coffee grown in the first hundred years or so was consumed locally. The first exports of coffee, to Germany and England, did not begin until 1887.

In the 1900s, the Peruvian government defaulted on a loan from the British government and ended up giving them two million hectares (five million acres) of land in Central Peru as repayment. One-quarter of this land was turned over to plantations, growing crops, which included coffee. Migrant workers from the highlands came to work on these farms and some ended up owning some land themselves. Others would later buy land from the British when they left Peru.

Unfortunately for the coffee industry, Juan Velasco's government brought in laws in the 1970s that would cripple growth. The International Coffee Agreement had guaranteed sales and prices, so there had been little incentive to create proper infrastructure. When state support was withdrawn, the coffee industry sunk into disarray. The quality of the coffee and Peru's market position further suffered at the hands of the communist party, The Shining Path, whose guerrilla activity destroyed crops and drove farmers from their land.

The vacuum left in Peru's coffee industry has recently been filled by non-government organizations such as Fair Trade, and now a large quantity of coffee from Peru is FT certified. More and more land is also being devoted to coffee: in 1980 there were 62,000 hectares (154,000 acres), today there are 95,00 hectares (235,000 acres). Peru is now one of the largest producers of coffee in the world.

The infrastructure within Peru still stands in the way of the country producing extremely high-quality lots. Few mills are situated close to farms, which means that the coffee is often travelling longer than is desirable after harvest before processing starts. Some coffees end up being bought and blended with other coffees, then resold en route to the coast for export. Interestingly, around one-quarter of the hundred thousand small producers in the country are now members of cooperatives, although it is important to remember that Fair Trade certification can only apply to

KEY

Coffee growing regions

ECUADOR

COLOMBIA

Napo

AMAZON BASIN

Amazon

AMAZONAS

Marañon

Chachapoyas

Moyobamba

CAJAMARCA

SAN MARTÍN

Cajarmarca

Huallaga

Ucayali

BRAZIL

Trujillo

Marañon

Nevado Huascarán

PERU

PACIFIC OCEAN

Urubamba

JUNÍN

LIMA

Huancayo

CUSCO

Apurímac

Cusco

Nasca

PUNO

BOLIVIA

Puno

Lake Titicaca

Arequipa

Altiplano

0 miles 200

0 km 200

CHILE

coffee produced by a cooperative. There is also a strong culture of organic production in Peru, though this rarely yields higher cup quality. In fact, the organic coffees produced in Peru are often so cheap that they end up bringing down prices paid to other farmers, regardless of them producing higher-quality coffee.

Perhaps because of this, and also because of the widespread cultivation of the Typica variety, leaf rust is increasingly a problem for Peruvian producers. While the 2013 crop was good, there have been severe outbreaks of leaf rust, which may well reduce overall production in the near future.

TASTE PROFILE

Typically Peruvian coffees have been clean, but a little soft and flat. They are sweet and relatively heavy bodied but not very complex. Increasingly there are distinctive and juicier coffees becoming available.

GROWING REGIONS

Population: 30,475,000
Number of 60kg (132lb) bags in 2013: 4,200,000

Some coffee is grown outside of the main regions listed below, but not in the same quantities and without the same level of recognition. Some might argue that Peru is well placed to deal with the increased temperatures that may come with climate change, as it has plenty of land at higher altitudes that may become suitable for growing coffee in the future.

CAJAMARCA

Cajamarca is a state in the north of the country named for its capital city, and covers the northern end of the Peruvian Andes. The region benefits from an equatorial climate and soils suitable for coffee. Most producers in the region are smallholders, although they are often well organized and belong to producers' organizations, which supply technical help, training, loans, community development and other support. One of these organizations in the region, CENFROCAFE, works with 1,900 families to promote coffee roasting and runs a local café to help the farmers diversify.

Altitude: 900–2,050m (3,000–6,750ft)
Harvest: March–September
Varieties: Bourbon, Typica, Caturra, Pache, Mondo Novo, Catuai, Catimor

JUNIN

This region produces 20–25 per cent of Peru's coffee and here the coffee grows in amongst the rainforest. The area did suffer in the 1980s and 1990s as a result of guerrilla activity, and the neglect of the trees during this period allowed plant diseases to spread. The coffee industry had to be restarted from almost nothing in the late 1990s.

Altitude: 1,400–1,900m (4,600–6,200ft)
Harvest: March–September
Varieties: Bourbon, Typica, Caturra, Pache, Mondo Novo, Catuai, Catimor

CUSCO

Cusco is a region in the south of the country where coffee, in some ways, is the legal alternative to the other popular crop in this area: coca. Most of the coffee is grown by smallholders, rather than larger estates. The area thrives on tourism, and many visitors travel through the city of Cusco on their way to see Machu Picchu.

Altitude: 1,200–1,900m (3,900–6,200ft)
Harvest: March–September
Varieties: Bourbon, Typica, Caturra, Pache, Mondo Novo, Catuai, Catimor

SAN MARTIN

This region is on the eastern side of the Andes, and many farmers produce coffee on plots 5–10 hectares (10–24 acres) in size. In the past this was the main area of coca production in Peru, although cooperatives in the region now promote the idea of diversification by growing other crops alongside coffee, such as cacao and honey. In recent years the level of poverty in the region has dropped dramatically, from 70 per cent down to 31 per cent of the population.

Altitude: 1,100–2,000m (3,600–6,600ft)
Harvest: March–September
Varieties: Bourbon, Typica, Caturra, Pache, Mondo Novo, Catuai, Catimor

Peru's limited infrastructure stands in the way of the country producing coffee of outstanding quality. The delivery and processing of fresh harvests are often delayed and few mills are located near plantations.

VENEZUELA

SOUTH AMERICA

The introduction of coffee to Venezuela is generally credited to a Jesuit priest named José Gumilla in around 1730. Venezuela came to be known for its plantations of tobacco and cacao run on slave labour, and from around 1793 there is evidence of large coffee plantations too.

From around 1800, coffee took an increasingly important role in the economy. During the Venezuelan War of Independence, from 1811 to 1823, cacao production began to drop but coffee production surged. The first boom in the country's coffee industry took place between 1830 and 1855, when Venezuela produced around one-third of the world's coffee. Coffee continued to grow in production, peaking in 1919 with a total export of 1.37 million bags. Together, coffee and cacao accounted for 75 per cent of the country's entire export revenue. Most of the coffee went to the United States.

Below: Though Venezuelan coffee production was strong in the early-20th century, crops are increasingly rare and have suffered from political resistance and poor remuneration for farmers.

In the 1920s, Venezuela's economy became increasingly dependent on petroleum, although coffee remained a good source of revenue. Much of the revenue was spent on national infrastructure, until the prices dropped in the 1930s and the production and processing infrastructure suffered as a consequence. This period also saw a shift towards privatization in the coffee industry, stripping peasants of much of their power to grow their own coffee on public land.

Since this period, the nation has been fundamentally dependent on petroleum products and other mineral exports. Coffee production and exports had remained relatively high, with Venezuela nearly matching the production of Colombia, but that changed under the government of Hugo Chávez. In 2003, the government introduced strict regulations on coffee production, which meant the country increasingly had to rely on imports for domestic consumption, mostly from Nicaragua and Brazil. Venezuela exported 479,000 bags of coffee in 1992/1993 and this dropped again to 19,000 in 2009/2010. Government-fixed sales prices have been considerably below the cost of production, which has inevitably damaged the industry. Few can predict how the situation will change in the wake of Chávez's death.

TRACEABILITY

As so little coffee is exported from the country, coming across Venezuelan coffees of quality is rare. While some should be traceable down to single estates, it is more common to see coffees described by their region names. Generally speaking, the low altitude and lack of focus on cup quality means I would recommend trying Venezuelan coffees only if they are being provided by a roaster whose coffees you generally enjoy and who you trust.

TASTE PROFILE

The better coffees from Venezuela are quite sweet, a little low in acidity and relatively rich in terms of mouthfeel and texture.

GROWING REGIONS

Population: 28,946,000

Number of 60kg (132lb) bags in 2013: 900,000

Coffees from Venezuela are currently quite rare. There are hopes that this may change in the future but it seems unlikely in the short term.

WESTERN REGION

This region produces a large percentage of the country's coffee. It is easier to find export grades marked with the name of the state in which they were produced, such as Táchira, Mérida or Zulia, rather than the region. Some people make comparisons between coffees from this region and those from neighbouring Colombia.

Altitude: 1,000–1,200m (3,300–3,900ft)

Harvest: September–March

Varieties: Typica, Bourbon, Mundo Novo, Caturra

WEST CENTRAL REGION

This region contains the states of Portuguesa and Lara, some of the primary coffee-producing regions in the country, as well as Falcón and Yaracuy. The best coffees are considered to come from this region, relatively close to the Colombian border. These coffees are commonly referred to as Maracaibos, named for the port from which they are exported.

Altitude: 1,000–1,200m (3,300–3,900ft)

Harvest: September–March

Varieties: Typica, Bourbon, Mundo Novo, Caturra

NORTH CENTRAL REGION

A small amount of Venezuela's production comes from the states of Aragua, Carabobo, the Federal Dependencies, Miranda, Cojedes and Guárico in this region.

Altitude: 1,000–1,200m (3,300–3,900ft)

Harvest: September–March

Varieties: Typica, Bourbon, Mundo Novo, Caturra

EASTERN REGION

This region is home to the states of Sucre, Monagas, Anzoátegui and Bolívar. It is sometimes possible to find a type of coffee called Caracas produced in this region.

Altitude: 1,000–1,200m (3,300–3,900ft)

Harvest: September–March

Varieties: Typica, Bourbon, Mundo Novo, Caturra

GLOSSARY

ARABICA Short for *coffea arabica*, the most widely grown species of the coffee plant. It is considered superior to robusta, the other species commonly grown.

AROMATIC COMPOUND A chemical compound within coffee that contributes to the aroma of the coffee when ground or brewed.

BLOOM Pouring a small amount of water on to the coffee at the start of a pour-over brew in order to start the extraction process is called the 'bloom' because of the way the coffee swells when it gets wet.

BREW RATIO The relationship between the amount of ground coffee used and the amount of water used to brew it.

BREW TIME The total amount of time water is in contact with coffee when it is being brewed.

BURR GRINDER A coffee grinder that has two sharp cutting discs, usually metal, that can be adjusted to grind coffee to the desired grind size.

C-PRICE The price of commodity coffee traded on the stock market. This price is considered the base price for coffee trading.

CHERRY The fruit of the coffee tree is often called a cherry, or berry. The two seeds inside the cherry are the coffee beans.

COFFEE BERRY BORER A pest that afflicts the coffee crop, burrowing into the fruit and consuming the beans inside.

COMMODITY COFFEE Coffee that has no value linked to its quality, and whose traceability is neither important nor often available.

COOPERATIVE A group of farmers working together for their mutual benefit.

CREMA The layer of brown foam that appears on top of an espresso, caused by the drink being brewed under high pressure.

CUP OF EXCELLENCE COMPETITION A programme established to find, evaluate and rank fine-quality coffee from a particular country, and then sell the winning coffees through an international online auction system.

CUP QUALITY The combination of the positive taste and flavour attributes of a particular coffee.

CUPPING The process of brewing, smelling and tasting coffee used by professional tasters in the coffee industry.

DARK ROAST Coffee roasted for a longer time, until the bean is a very dark brown, with an oily surface.

DEFECT A flaw in the coffee bean that contributes an unpleasant taste.

DIALLING IN The process of adjusting an espresso grinder until the resulting coffee tastes good and is properly extracted.

DRY MILL A facility that will hull, sort and grade parchment coffee, ready for export.

DRY PROCESS A post-harvest process in which the whole coffee cherry is dried before being hulled to extract the green coffee inside.

EXTRACTION The process of brewing coffee in which a percentage of the ground coffee is dissolved in the water.

FAIR TRADE MOVEMENT A group of organizations looking to certify and reward cooperatives of coffee producers, with a guaranteed premium and minimum price for their coffee.

FAST ROAST The commercial technique of roasting coffee very quickly, often in less than five minutes, as part of the process of making instant/soluble coffee.

FULLY WASHED A post-harvest process in which the coffee beans are squeezed from the fruit, fermented and washed clean before being dried.

GILING BASAH A post-harvest process common in Indonesia, in which the coffee is hulled from its parchment layer while still at high moisture levels and then dried. This contributes a particular earthy quality to the coffee's flavour. *See also* semi-washed process.

GREEN COFFEE The coffee industry term for raw, unfrosted coffee. This is the state in which coffee is traded internationally.

GRIND SIZE The size of the particles of ground coffee. The finer and smaller the pieces, the easier it is to extract flavour from the coffee.

HEIRLOOM VARIETIES A term used for varieties of coffee that have been traditionally grown for some time.

HONEY PROCESS A post-harvest process, similar to the pulped natural process, in which the coffee bean is squeezed from the fruit but a variable amount of fruit flesh is left on during the drying phase.

IN REPOSO Also known as 'resting', this describes the period of time when raw coffee is stored in parchment before it is hulled, graded and exported. This process is considered important in stabilizing the moisture content within the bean.

INTERNATIONAL COFFEE AGREEMENT First signed in 1962, this is a quota system in place between many coffee-producing countries and some importing countries in order to prevent supply and demand swings on the global market and stabilize pricing.

LATTE ART The patterns created by carefully pouring foamed milk into espresso coffee.

LEAF RUST An orange/brown fungus that attacks the leaves on a coffee tree, eventually causing the tree to die.

LIGHT ROAST A coffee roasted in such a way as to preserve its acidity and fruitier flavours. The term refers to the coffee bean being a lighter shade of brown.

LOT A distinct quantity of coffee, which has gone through some sort of selection process.

MICROFOAM The tiny bubbles of foam created when milk is steamed properly.

MICRO-LOT Typically ten bags (each weighing 60 or 69kg/132 or 152lb) or fewer of a particular selection from a farm or producer group.

MIEL PROCESS *see* honey process

MONSOONING Along India's Malabar Coast, harvested coffee beans are exposed to the monsoon rain for three or four months, causing them to lose their acidity.

MOUTHFEEL A term used to describe the texture and tactile attributes of the coffee when drinking it, ranging from very light and tea-like through to rich and creamy.

NATURAL PROCESS A post-harvest process in which the coffee beans are picked and then carefully dried in the sun until the entire cherry is dry.

OVEREXTRACTION This refers to extracting more of the soluble material than desired when brewing coffee, resulting in the cup that tastes bitter, harsh and unpleasant.

PARCHMENT The protective papery layer surrounding the coffee bean, which is removed before the coffee is exported.

PARCHMENT COFFEE Coffee that has been harvested and processed, but still has its papery layer surrounding the bean. This protective layer prevents a decrease in quality before the coffee is exported.

PEABERRY Term used to describe a single bean forming inside a coffee cherry instead of two.

POTATO DEFECT A defect common in parts of East Africa, as a result of which a single bean will smell strongly of potato skins when ground and brewed.

PULPED NATURAL PROCESS A post-harvest process in which the coffee beans are squeezed mechanically from the fruit before being dried on patios or raised beds.

RATIO (BREW), *see* Brew ratio

ROBUSTA One of the two main commercially produced species of coffee, robusta is considered lower in quality than arabica, but is easier to grow at lower altitudes and more resistant to pests and disease.

RUST-RESISTANT VARIETIES Varieties of arabica and robusta that are resistant to a fungus called leaf rust or roya, which consumes the leaves on the tree, ultimately killing the plant.

SCREEN SIZE Coffee beans are sorted by size using large screens with varying size holes in them. This is part of the grading process before a coffee is exported.

SEMI-WASHED PROCESS *see* pulped natural process

SILVERSKIN A very fine, papery layer that clings to the coffee bean. It comes loose during roasting, and is then referred to as 'chaff'.

SLOW ROAST A slower, gentler roasting process, typically used by those looking to roast a coffee in such a way that it tastes as good as possible. Depending on the roasting machine and technique, the process can take between 10 and 20 minutes per roast.

SMALLHOLDER A producer who owns a small amount of land on which to grow coffee.

SPECIALITY MARKET The market for coffee traded on the basis of its quality and flavour. This term covers every aspect of the industry, including producers, exporters/importers, roasters, cafés and consumers.

STRENGTH OF COFFEE A term to describe how much dissolved coffee a cup of coffee contains: typically a cup of brewed coffee is 1.3–1.5 per cent dissolved coffee and the rest is water. With espresso, the ratio may be closer to 8–12 per cent dissolved coffee.

STRIP PICKING A harvesting technique that involves pickers running their hands down a branch to remove all the cherries in one motion. While quick, this technique means unripe cherries are harvested along with ripe ones, and the cherries will need to be sorted later in the process.

TAMPING When making espresso, this is the process of pushing the ground coffee down so that it forms an even, flat bed before it is brewed under very high pressure. This helps ensure the coffee brews evenly.

TERROIR The combined effect of geography and climate on the way a coffee tastes.

TRACEABILITY The transparency of the supply chain in coffee, and its preservation, so one can know exactly who produced a particular lot of coffee.

TYPICA The oldest variety of arabica that has been used in commercial coffee production.

UNDEREXTRACTION In the process of brewing coffee this happens when we fail to dissolve all of the desired solubles in ground coffee leaving us with a sour, often astringent cup of coffee.

WASHED PROCESS A post harvest process where the coffee cherries are squeezed, forcing the beans out. These beans are then fermented to break down the sticky fruit flesh that is clinging to them. This is then washed off and the coffee is then dried carefully and slowly.

WASHING STATION A facility that receives coffee cherries, and processes them until they are dry, parchment coffee using a variety of post harvest processes.

WET PROCESS *see* washed process

WET-HULLED PROCESS *see* semi-washed process

WET MILL *see* washing station

INDEX

Page references in **bold** are major references; those in *italics* are illustrations

PICTURE ACKNOWLEDGEMENTS

Alamy Carol Lee 140–41; F. Jack Jackson 176; hemis/Franck Guiziou 92–93; Image Source 60–61; imageBROKER/Michael Runkel 166; Jan Butchofsky 168–69; Joshua Roper 196; mediacolor's 228–29; Phil Borges/Danita Delimont 206; Philip Scalia 214–15; Stefano Paterna 212–13; Vespasian 23; WorldFoto 132.

Blacksmith Coffee Roastery (www.BlacksmithCoffee.com) 24 left.

Corbis 2/Philippe Colombi/Ocean 237; Arne Hodalic 100; Bettmann 8–9; David Evans/National Geographic Society 185, 186; Eduardo Munoz/Reuters 204–05; Frederic Soltan/Sygma 102; Gideon Mendel 32–33 below; Ian Cumming/Design Pics 230; Jack Kurtz/ZUMA Press 234–35; James Sparshatt/Design Pics 158–59; Jane Sweeney/JAI 18–19; Janet Jarman 236; Juan Carlos Ulate/Reuters 194, 197, 198–99; KHAM/Reuters 172–73; Kicka Witte/Design Pics 225; Michael Hanson/National Geographic Society 128–29; Mohamed Al-Sayaghi/Reuters 175; Monty Rakusen/cultura 46–47; NOOR KHAMIS/Reuters 136; Pablo Corral V 246; Reuters/Henry Romero 32–33 above; Rick D'Elia 143; Stringer/Mexico/Reuters 232; Swim Ink 2, LLC 114; Yuriko Nakao/Reuters 223.

Enrico Maltoni 95, 96.

Getty Images Alex Dellow 58–59; B. Anthony Stewart/National Geographic 108; Bloomberg via Getty Images 26-27, 156–57; Brian Doben 240–41; Bruce Block 148; Dimas Ardian/Bloomberg via Getty Images 162–63; Frederic Coubet 130–31; Gamma-Keystone via Getty Images 42–43; Glow Images, Inc. 29 above; Ian Sanderson 6; Jane Sweeney 20; John Coletti 29 below; Jon Spaull 202–03; Juan Carlos/Bloomberg via Getty Images 209, 210–11; Kelley Miller 16 below; Kurt Hutton 104–05; Livia Corona 189; Luis Acosta/AFP 190–91; Mac99 244–45; MCT via Getty Images 38–39; Melissa Tse 165; Michael Boyny 180–81; Michael Mahovlich 30, 216, 219; Mint Images RF 64, 66; National Geographic/Sam Abell 161; Philippe Bourseiller 134–35; Philippe Lissac/GODONG 127; Polly Thomas 231; Ryan Lane 51; SambaPhoto/Ricardo de Vicq 16 above; SSPL via Getty Images 13; Stephen Shaver/Bloomberg via Getty Images 171; STR/AFP 201; WIN-Initiative 226.

Gilberto Baraona 25 right.

James Hoffmann 36.

Lineair Fotoarchief Ron Giling 123.

Mary Evans Picture Library INTERFOTO/Bildarchiv Hansmann 54.

Nature Picture Library Gary John Norman 150–51 centre.

Panos Sven Torfinn 144–45; Thierry Bresillon/Godong 124–25 above.

Robert Harding Picture Library Arjen Van De Merwe/Still Pictures 138–39.

Shutterstock Alfredo Maiquez 239; Anawat Sudchanham 207; Athirati 28; ntdanai 17; Stasis Photo 16 centre; trappy76 14-15.

SuperStock imagebroker.net 147.

Sweet Maria's (www.sweetmarias.com) 220–21.

Thinkstock OllieChanter 70-71; Paul Marshman 150 left.

AUTHOR'S ACKNOWLEDGEMENTS

Researcher: Ben Szobody

Research assistance, translation and motivation: Alethea Rudd

I'd like to thank Ric Rhinehart and Peter Giuliano for their astonishing generosity of time and wisdom. I'm extremely grateful to everyone in the Square Mile Coffee Roasters team, past and present, for being constantly inspiring and supportive.

Dedicated to my mother and to Keith for all they've done for me.